Ascent of the Thunder Dragon

Ascent of the Thunder Dragon

The Surprising Spiritual Life and Legacy of Bhutan's Founder

The Story of Zhabdrung Ngawang Namgyal

SASHA WAKEFIELD

with a foreword by His Eminence Samten Dorji Rinpoche

SHAMBHALA

Shambhala Publications, Inc.
2129 13th Street
Boulder, Colorado 80302
www.shambhala.com

Excerpt from H. P. Blavatsky, *Collected Writings*, volume 6, © 1954, was reproduced by permission of Quest Books, the imprint of The Theosophical Publishing House (www.questbooks.net).

Cover art: "Bhutan, Bumthang Valley, Gaytsa Village large painted dragon house wall painting," Neil McAllister/Alamy
Cover design: Daniel Urban-Brown

9 8 7 6 5 4 3 2 1

First Edition
Printed in the United States of America

Shambhala Publications makes every effort to print on acid-free, recycled paper.
Shambhala Publications is distributed worldwide by Penguin Random House, Inc., and its subsidiaries.

LIBRARY OF CONGRESS CATALOGING-IN-PUBLICATION DATA
Names: Wakefield, Sasha author
Title: Ascent of the Thunder Dragon: The surprising spiritual life and
    legacy of Bhutan's founder, the story of Zhabdrung Ngawang Namgyal
Description: Boulder, Colorado: Shambhala Publications, [2026] |
    Includes bibliographical references and index. |
Identifiers: LCCN 2025003634 | ISBN 9781645474326 trade paperback
Subjects: LCSH: Ngag-dbang-rnam-rgyal, Zhabs-drung I, 1594-1651 |
    'Brug-paLamas—Bhutan—Biography | 'Brug-pa lamas—Tibet Region—
    Biography |LCGFT: Biographies
Classification: LCC BQ974.G355 W35 2026
LC record available at https://lccn.loc.gov/2025003634

The authorized representative in the EU for product safety and compliance is eucomply OÜ, Pärnu mnt 139b-14, 11317 Tallinn, Estonia, hello@eucompliancepartner.com.

Dedicated to
My teacher

Contents

དཔལ་ལྡན་འབྲུག་པའི་ཆོས་སྡེ།
གཞུང་གྲྭ་ཚང་སྐྱེ་བ།
འབྲུག་ཐིམ་ཕུག།

Central Monastic Body
THIMPHU, BHUTAN

It is with great delight and amazement that I express my appreciation to Ms. Sasha—endowed with excellent wisdom—for always showing immense respect for the religion and cultural flourishing in Bhutan but, most importantly, for writing a biography of Chabgon Ngawang Namgyal based on her reverence and understanding. This book, in general, will help people from all over the world, and particularly those of all ages within Bhutan, to understand the life and legacy of this great bodhisattva.

With prayers that the blessings of Chabgon Lama enter the minds of all who come across this book.

His Eminence Samten Dorji Rinpoche
Former Tsugla Lopen of the Central Monastic Body (Zhung Dratshang)
February 10, 2025

Preface

Deep within the heart of the eastern Himalayas lies a mystical Buddhist kingdom: Bhutan. Embraced by pristine blue pine forests and roaring icy rivers, it has remained cloaked in intrigue for centuries. Wedged between China and India, it has, over the past fifty years, cautiously unlatched its door to the outside world. In 1974 it saw the beginnings of tourism, with television arriving on the scene much later in 1999. Democracy soon followed. The nation has been lauded by some as one of the happiest countries. It has also earned the title of being the first carbon-negative country in the world.

Preserving Bhutan's ancient Buddhist culture and environment is, however, not a recent development. It was high on the priority list of Jigme Singye Wangchuck, the fourth king of Bhutan, way back in the 1970s, well before well-being was in vogue or climate change a major global concern. In fact, its constitution impressively mandates that 60 percent of its landmass be maintained as forest cover.

Bhutan is now a democratic constitutional monarchy. The process of democratization from an absolute monarchy began in the late 1990s and was accelerated by the abdication of the fourth king in December 2006. His responsibilities were handed over to his eldest son, Jigme Khesar Namgyel Wangchuck who became the fifth Druk Gyalpo (Dragon King), assuming the role of head of state. The first democratic parliamentary election took place in March 2008.

But the history of Bhutan as a nation-state began centuries earlier when Zhabdrung Ngawang Namgyal[1] (1594-1651), a dignified lama,[2] arrived on its doorstep in 1616. To understand Bhutan, we must therefore understand this Buddhist monk. His story is as profoundly moving as he is inspirational, and it is this amazing life and legacy that will be explored within the pages of this book.

Writing this book was no simple task. Should I write a monotonous who-when-where account of Zhabdrung Ngawang Namgyal, or should I attempt to craft a book that brings Bhutan's founding father to life—a story that resonates with today's readers? I chose the latter because it better reflects my spiritual journey and the unique perspective on Zhabdrung that I have had the privilege of capturing as an "outsider," one who has called Bhutan their second home since first setting foot there as a tourist more than a decade and a half ago.

To understand how I came to write a book on this legendary Buddhist saint, however, one must understand a bit about my spiritual journey.

A great Buddhist master from Bhutan and my teacher once said to me, "Just relax...no doubt, no ego, no expectation," during one of our initial meetings in the capital city of Thimphu while instructing me on a particular meditation practice. The seriousness with which he delivered this message, accompanied by his piercing gaze, stopped me in my tracks, time freezing for what seemed like an eternity. I felt like a naughty schoolgirl being brought back into line. It was in that moment, back in 2014, that I realized I had been given a valuable clue to enhance my spiritual practice, though I didn't fully grasp its significance at the time. But a clue was enough to propel me further down the spiritual path and momentarily quench my thirst for knowledge, a thirst that had developed when I was just a ten-year-old schoolgirl in Australia.

At that time in my childhood, I recall repeatedly asking my mother, "When am I going to meet my teacher?" Her response was always, "What do you mean? You have many teachers at school."

I was born into a loving atheist family where religion was viewed as a tool for controlling the masses. This view was shaped, no doubt, by my parents' childhood experiences. Yet I wasn't seeking "religion"; I was searching for something beyond what I could express.

I wanted to know what life was all about, and I intuitively felt that this required a spiritual teacher or guide. From a young age, I wanted my life to have meaning and purpose. I so desperately wanted to find my North Star, but I didn't know where to begin.

Shortly thereafter, one evening during dinner, I spontaneously blurted out, "I have to go to Bhutan; I have to find my teacher." This moment remains etched in my memory as vividly as if it happened yesterday. It felt like an out-of-body experience, leaving both my parents in a state of bewilderment. Neither they nor I had any idea if such a place even existed.

My constant pestering led my parents to reach for the atlas and begin searching for this mysterious place, which they spelled as "Bootan." Unable to find the location, they eventually dismissed my spontaneous outburst, attributing it to my overactive imagination. I recall my mother exclaiming, "It's probably somewhere in Africa." "Bootan" remained forgotten for decades until the moment I set foot on its soil, preparing to acclimate to the Himalayan altitude before my upcoming trek to Everest Base Camp in Nepal.

During my early adult years, while reading a wide variety of spiritual books—including works by luminaries such as Dilgo Khyentse Rinpoche, Chögyam Trungpa Rinpoche, the Fourteenth Dalai Lama, Helena Petrovna Blavatsky, and Paramahansa Yogananda—the phrase "when the student is ready, the teacher appears" kept recurring. Patience wasn't a forte of mine, but encountering these words provided a glimmer of hope. I began to ease up on my incessant questioning, holding on to the belief that perhaps one day I'd be fortunate enough to meet a genuine spiritual master—someone in whom I could place unwavering trust.

I refused to entrust my mind to just any guru. Despite my stubborn nature, I had the sensibility to be cautious about whom I trusted for spiritual guidance. By then, I had a strange inkling that finding a spiritual teacher held the key to my quest for meaning. Until I finally met my "teacher," I relied on my gut instinct and books to expand upon and access the inner knowingness of all things spiritual.

Ever since I met this Buddhist master, the phrase "no doubt, no ego, no expectation" would echo through my mind like a broken record. These thoughts would arise in the most unexpected places—the gym, while driving, watching TV, or even scaling a cliff to reach a remote monastery during a hike in the Kingdom of Bhutan. Perhaps my mind was processing what these words truly meant. I soon noticed that these words of wisdom would appear when I was alone and in the "zone"—a state where my mind wasn't preoccupied with intellectualizing or sporadic thoughts.

But it wasn't until my teacher, who spoke only a little English, assigned me the challenging exercise of writing a book about Zhabdrung Ngawang Namgyal that I truly understood the significance of these words.

The responsibility fell upon me via a monk chosen to translate. My teacher's request was crystal clear: he wanted a book that portrayed Zhabdrung in a modern and relatable way, appealing to a wide readership. Furthermore, he encouraged me to infuse the book with my own perspective, offering readers a glimpse into my unique take on this notable individual. As the monk conveyed the message, I noticed his taut facial expression, hinting at the daunting task that lay ahead. What an immense honor, but also a huge undertaking at the same time! My mind went into a tailspin: *Where do I even begin? This is uncharted territory for me—*doubt. *What if I stuff up? People will surely criticize me—*ego. *I want the book to be perfect. I don't want there to be any mistakes or inaccuracies—*expectation.

I couldn't refuse the request. He was my Rinpoche (precious one) after all, a spiritual teacher I had longed for most of my life, who knew me better than I knew myself, and to whom I held unflinching devotion.[3] I decided then and there to carry out the task to the best of my abilities.

On my first visit to Bhutan in 2006, I caught a glimpse of Zhabdrung Ngawang Namgyal's uniqueness. Paintings and statues of this distinguished lama, with his characteristically long beard, greeted me at every temple I visited. With each subsequent visit I began to understand how special he was to the Bhutanese. His image adorned the walls of every household, alongside photos of the great kings and the seventieth Je Khenpo, the supreme head of the Drukpa Kargyu order in Bhutan. His statue was always placed alongside the buddhas in their intricately adorned altar rooms. The mere mention of Zhabdrung Ngawang Namgyal seemed to fill the people with great reverence and was always met with a gentle smile. It is safe to say that for the people of Bhutan, Zhabdrung remains in their hearts and minds a figure without whom the course of this wonderful nation could have been vastly different.

This book has been an evolving work in progress over countless months and late nights, bearing witness to numerous obstacles. It was as much a spiritual journey for me of letting go of doubt, ego, and expectation as it was a project to document the many aspects of this great Buddhist master. As the book progressed, I peeled away layers of my own doubt, ego, and expectation until I reached a point where I rested in the present moment and let the book take its own form, for better or worse.

My hope is that you, the reader, will gain even a fraction of what I have learned in writing this book and will develop a deeper awareness and reverence for this great being's service to humanity. Achieving this fulfills my purpose.

Sasha Wakefield
Thimphu, Bhutan

Maps

Notes and Disclaimer

The maps in this book aim to depict the boundaries as accurately as possible during the time of Zhabdrung Ngawang Namgyal, based on the limited information available from that period. For familiarity, however, the southern boundary of Bhutan is shown as demarcated in 1865.

Dates provided are approximations based on historical records and research. While every effort has been made to ensure accuracy, some dates remain open to interpretation.

Explanations of concepts are presented from the perspective of Mahayana Buddhism.

During the era of the Tsang Desis (secular rulers of the Tsang region of Tibet) and earlier, Tibet was not a unified state but a collection of regional rulerships governed by competing powers. Tibet's history as a distinct cultural and political entity dates back to the seventh century, during the reign of King Songtsen Gampo, who unified much of the Tibetan Plateau and established the Tibetan Empire. References to Tibet in this book should be understood within this historical context of regional fragmentation and evolving political unity.

The name Bhutan likely emerged in the latter half of the eighteenth century, influenced by British usage. In this book, the name Bhutan refers to the unified state as it existed during Zhabdrung's time.

The views expressed in this book are solely those of the author.

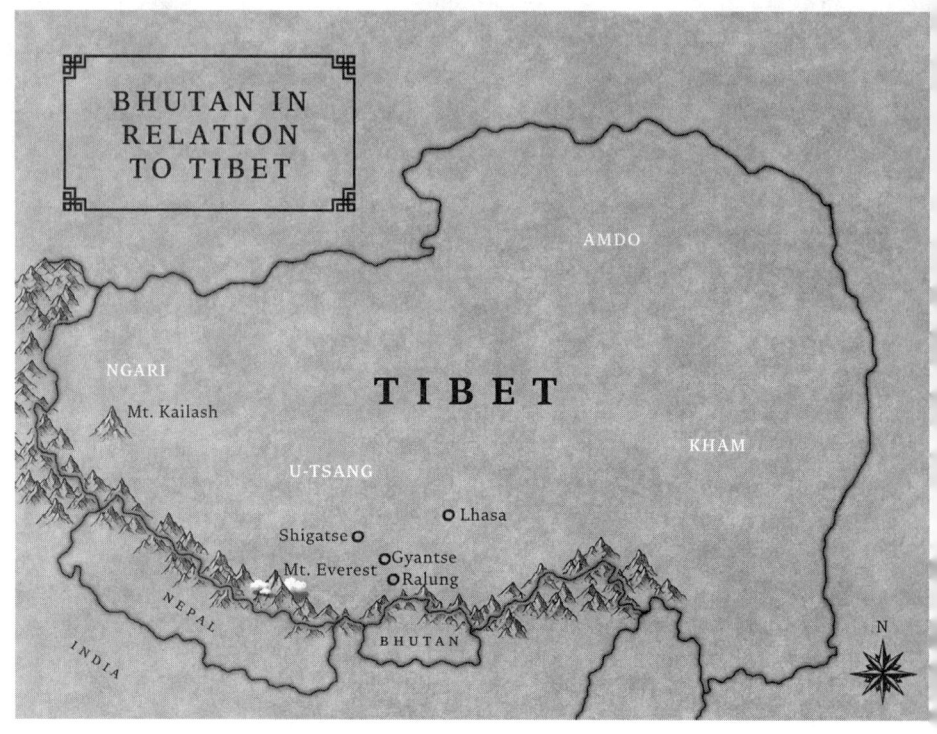

Map showing the U-Tsang, Kham, Ngari, and Amdo regions of Tibet, along with the location of Ralung Monastery in relation to Bhutan (Map design © 2024 Dawa Penjor)

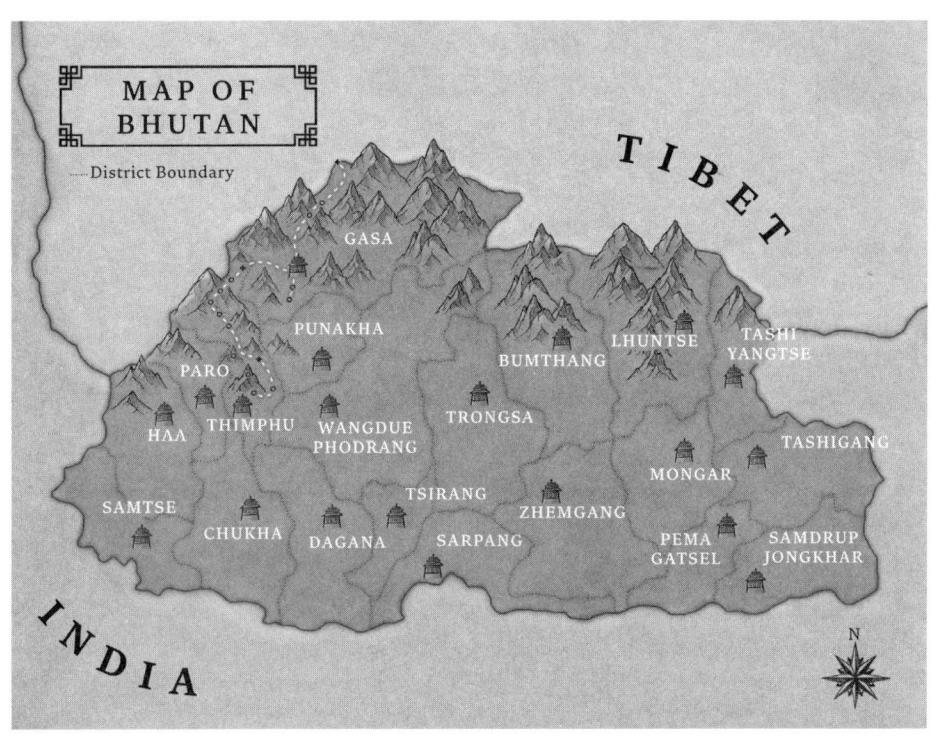

Map of Bhutan showing its twenty districts (Map design © 2024 Dawa Penjor)

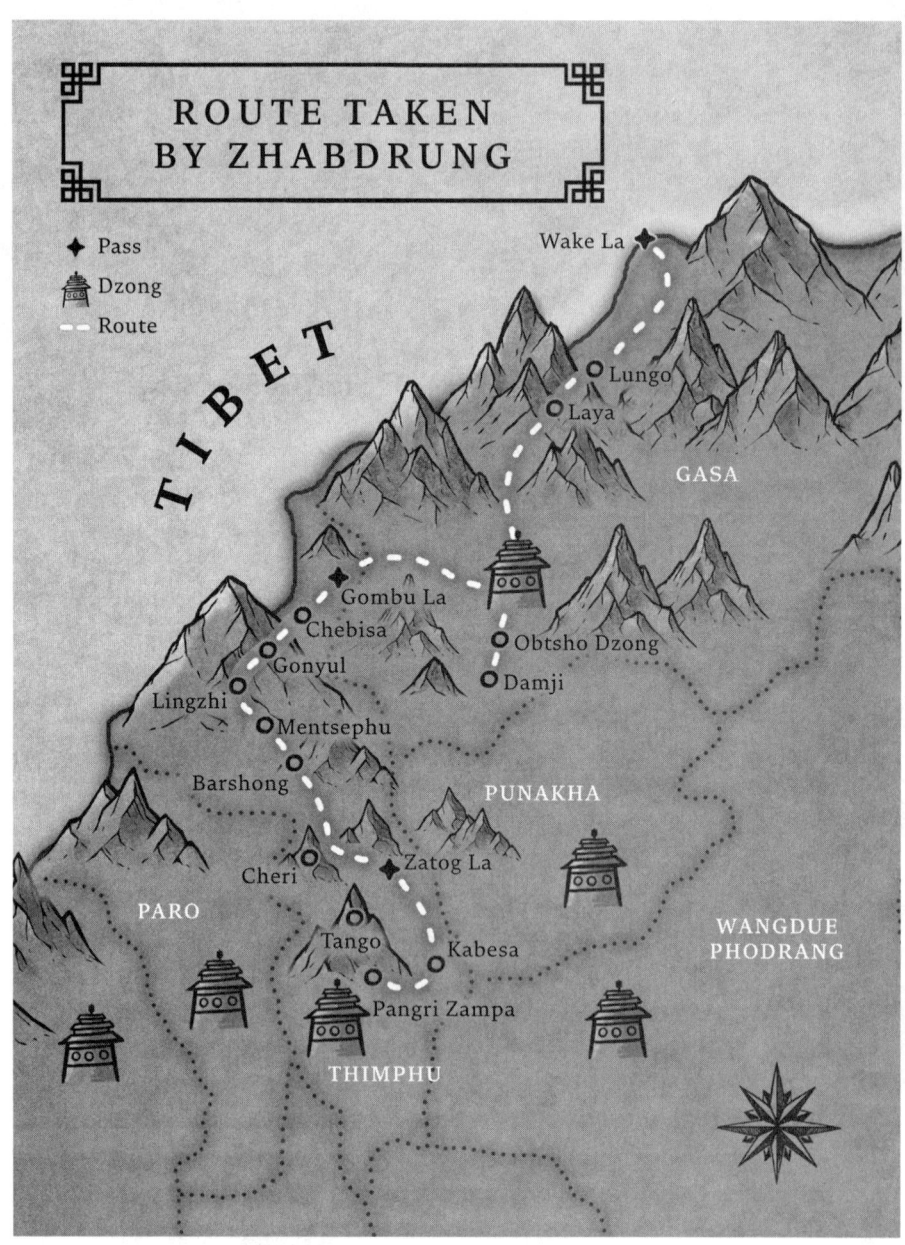

Map illustrating Zhabdrung's route to Bhutan based on oral and textual accounts
(Map design © 2024 Dawa Penjor)

PART ONE

The Background

Zhabdrung Ngawang Namgyal as a young man inspired by an original mural
(Artwork © 2024 Karma Tshering Wangchuk)

Introduction

Writing about a historic and inspirational spiritual figure such as Zhabdrung, and tackling such a complex subject, requires a comprehensive understanding of both the historical context and the spiritual principles that underpin his story. To truly appreciate his prophesied destiny in Bhutan and the intricate layers of his being, the scene must be set, and key concepts and prophecies unpacked. Only then can justice be given to this remarkable man and his achievements. Stick with these explanations—I promise they will make Zhabdrung's story not just more understandable but truly fascinating.

Uncovering his true story, however, demanded that I use reliable texts—accounts authored by individuals who had personally known him, and respected scholars who had dedicated themselves to the study of this legendary figure. Complicating matters further, these invaluable sources were written in Chokey, the classical Tibetan writing system, adding another challenging layer to the project. It was also crucial to explore the enduring legacy that Zhabdrung left behind and how this legacy has been perpetuated through the ages. Only by piecing together these elements could I offer an informed perspective as an outsider.

And a spiritual topic that I found so compelling in relation to Zhabdrung were the numerous prophecies made about him— prophecies that were made centuries before he was born, predicting his great deeds and connection to Bhutan. So much so that I have dedicated an entire chapter to these prophecies. These prophecies are as astounding to our conventional understanding of the nature of reality as they are significant, providing a clear indication of Zhabdrung's importance, particularly for Bhutan.

I also share personal experiences from my spiritual journey where they relate to Zhabdrung's story, illustrating that such phenomena are not mere tales from a distant past but continue to manifest in the twenty-first century. I recount events such as petals falling from the sky, creatures appearing under impossible circumstances, seeing jewels that have arisen from cremated remains, and witnessing omniscience. These experiences have taught me the importance of keeping an open mind.

Arriving in Bhutan as a non-Buddhist Australian, I never could have foreseen the transformative path that awaited me. Through these narratives I aim to highlight the spiritual dimensions often overlooked and even dismissed, showing that anything is possible if you are willing to take risks and follow your intuition. My journey into Bhutan, filled with unexpected twists and turns, has certainly enriched my life in more ways than one.

Why This Book?

The aim of this book is to foster a shared understanding of this great Buddhist luminary with a wider audience. It aspires to present a balanced, reader-friendly account of Zhabdrung's life purpose and the multifaceted legacy that he left behind after his entrance into permanent retreat[4] in 1651, widely regarded as his year of death.

While much has been written about Zhabdrung's secular contributions to Bhutan, I found a significant gap in English literature regarding his spiritual accomplishments. This book examines his spiritual activities and unique qualities, which played a crucial role in shaping the state we now recognize as Bhutan. It complements and expands upon existing information about Zhabdrung Ngawang Namgyal in Dzongkha, the national language of Bhutan, aiming to provide an objective perspective through my experience as a foreigner.

Last, intriguing accounts of Zhabdrung, shared by those who knew him, are preserved among the stacks of ancient, weathered

Chokey texts housed in faraway Buddhist monasteries scattered across the country. The lack of easily accessible and readable information has made it challenging for many to grasp Zhabdrung's impressive qualities and achievements. Consequently, this book aims to present this information in an easy-to-read style, fostering a deeper appreciation for Zhabdrung and greater understanding of the formation of the Bhutanese state for both Bhutanese and non-Bhutanese readers.

Information Sources

The Chokey biography[5] penned by the prominent Buddhist scholar Jamyang Palden Gyatsho, more commonly known as Tsang Khenchen (1610-1684),[6] a learned master from the Tsang region, held a central place among the reference texts that guided my exploration of Zhabdrung. Drawing also upon accounts from other disciples who had the privilege of knowing this fascinating figure, as well as later writings that offered fresh perspectives, I embarked on an intense journey of understanding. However, these texts, all written in Chokey, presented a challenge that required the assistance of scholarly English-speaking monks. Together we deciphered the ancient manuscripts, not only fact-checking existing literature on Zhabdrung against the Chokey texts but also uncovering valuable truths embedded in the complex tapestry of the language.

In addition, a report filed in the Society of Jesus in Rome by two Portuguese Jesuit priests who had the good fortune of spending time with Zhabdrung provided a unique viewpoint, adding another layer to the story. After countless cups of coffee and long days and nights spent tediously teasing out the important facts, I hope to have captured a true and accurate account of Zhabdrung's life.

Tsang Khenchen's Biography

There are several standout reasons why Tsang Khenchen's biography provides crucial information for this book. A major drawcard is that Tsang Khenchen was a well-respected Buddhist practitioner who had a personal connection with Zhabdrung through family associations in Tibet, and later as a spiritual contemporary during his time in Bhutan. Tsang Khenchen wasn't a typical reliant student; he was already an accomplished scholar in his own right. This aspect lends itself to a more objective account of Zhabdrung's life, reducing the likelihood of overinflating his greatness and increasing the probability of portraying a realistic picture of his life and legacy.

Despite being ordained into the Sakya Buddhist order—one of the four major traditions in Tibetan Buddhism,[7] alongside the Nyingma, Kagyu, and Gelug—rather than the Drukpa Kargyu order to which Zhabdrung belonged, Tsang Khenchen's nonsectarian approach to Buddhism not only demonstrates his sincere reverence for diverse teachings but also plays an important role in presenting a balanced and unbiased portrayal of Zhabdrung.

Tsang Khenchen received the blessings from Zhabdrung to write his biography and played a significant role as a leading architect of the Bhutanese state alongside Zhabdrung. This further solidifies the rationale for using Tsang Khenchen's biography as a foundational and reliable source of information.

While I do not disagree with those who argue that Tsang Khenchen's biography of Zhabdrung somewhat served to justify his state-building mission, it is important to recognize that this was not its sole underlying intention. The biography fulfilled a far broader purpose—to highlight the remarkable accomplishments, both outer and inner,[8] of this esteemed Buddhist master. It aimed to reveal his character, his intentions for Bhutan and the Dharma (teachings of Buddha), and his lasting impact. By partially relying on this biography, we come as close as we can to understanding Zhabdrung the man, from someone who knew him personally. As the saying goes, we are hearing it straight from the horse's mouth.

Through Tsang Khenchen's in-depth and often poetic writing style, we get to the heart of Zhabdrung, understanding his political reasons for commissioning his biography and the compassionate motivation that lay behind it. We learn of his vision for a Buddhist kingdom governed by a bodhisattva (highly evolved spiritual being), where people could be free from religious persecution. We come to appreciate his nonsectarian views and his compassionate diplomatic approach to conflict resolution. Witnessing his miraculous spiritual abilities and his capacity to perform supernatural acts for the greater good, we are struck by his great compassion for all sentient beings.

Landing the Role as Zhabdrung's Biographer

During this period, it was customary for a close disciple to compile a biography of their Buddhist master, known as a namthar, detailing their life and great feats. Zhabdrung, known for his noncoercive demeanor and aversion to micromanagement, subtly hinted to Tsang Khenchen, with his characteristic relaxed and simple manner, that one day a biography about his life might need to be written. This significant request took place while Zhabdrung was conducting the oral transmission of Buddha's biography at Punakha Dzong, the headquarters of his administration, well before he entered permanent retreat.

This request didn't catch Tsang Khenchen entirely off guard, as Zhabdrung's crystal clear omniscience often kept him one step ahead of events. For reasons known only to him, Zhabdrung deemed documenting his life story important. Due to their close spiritual bond, Tsang Khenchen immediately grasped the significance of what he was being asked to do. Diligently noting all the information shared by Zhabdrung, Tsang Khenchen understood that he had been specifically chosen and granted permission to write the biography.

This honor likely filled him with immense joy and a profound sense of responsibility—sentiments I can certainly relate to!

It is a widely practiced tradition among Tibetan Buddhist masters to keep meticulous records of the teachings they receive and the lineages from which they originate. During a break in the oral transmission, Zhabdrung handed over to Tsang Khenchen a collection of paper scrolls containing the specific teachings and transmissions he had received from various Buddhist masters. He then requested Tsang Khenchen to organize them chronologically. Zhabdrung's firm confidence in Tsang Khenchen's ability to write an objective account of his life led him to openly share details of his personal experiences in Tibet and Bhutan as well as the identities of the individuals who had shaped his journey thus far.

By this stage, it became apparent that the absence of a direct heir to Zhabdrung's lineage and legacy necessitated the documentation of an account to strengthen the foundations of his efforts and establish legitimacy for his state-building endeavors in Bhutan. The biography, in this context, served to justify his mission and rectify any misconceptions, ensuring the continuation of his legacy and the preservation of his Dharmic lineage. Tsang Khenchen, who had sought refuge in Bhutan from religious persecution years earlier, possessed a unique and privileged perspective on Zhabdrung and wholeheartedly embraced the opportunity to contribute to the establishment of a state governed by Buddhist ideals.

It is easy to imagine Zhabdrung experiencing a surge of pride upon receiving the carefully organized teachings and transmissions. Tsang Khenchen's flawless execution of the task serving as an inspiration for them both, with Zhabdrung's enthusiasm boosting Tsang Khenchen's confidence as the author of the biography and solidifying Zhabdrung's trust in him. This compilation of teachings and insights directly gleaned from Zhabdrung formed the backbone of his biography, known in English as *The Melody of the Great Dharma Cloud*, completed in 1681, thirty years after Zhabdrung entered permanent retreat.

Fascinating Accounts

Zhabdrung's life story is filled with accounts of spiritual feats that may seem impossible or even ludicrous, especially from a modern scientific standpoint. Many might find it difficult to fully accept the authenticity of his supernatural abilities, such as leaving body prints in solid rock or casting spells from a distance. Too often, historians dismiss these feats as mere embellishments.

In our modern era, driven by scientific reasoning and empirical evidence, it seems that we have unintentionally closed ourselves off from a different reality—one grounded in the awareness of our innate spiritual potential. This alternative reality can emerge through years of dedicated spiritual practice, leading to heights of spiritual attainment beyond our everyday experience and understanding.

Claiming to possess absolute knowledge of what is achievable and what is not is undoubtedly arrogant, yet sadly such claims are sometimes made. Without attaining a certain level of spiritual mastery ourselves, it is impossible to fully grasp the depths of spiritual realization and the mind-blowing actions associated with it.

Throughout history, accounts have described saints and spiritual masters performing miracles that defy explanation. Jesus walking on water or turning water into wine readily come to mind. While skeptics argue these accounts are exaggerated and not to be taken literally, it's worth considering that individuals with such spiritual mastery might possess the ability to influence the atomic configuration of matter, aligning with principles of quantum physics.

Notably, no definitive proof has emerged to conclusively dismiss these feats as mere make-believe. Our human limitations in language and understanding often prevent us from perceiving beyond the physical world—a capability that only a handful of highly evolved individuals seem to have achieved.

Even science is constantly evolving as new discoveries are made. Hopefully, one day, compelling scientific evidence will emerge to substantiate the possibility of the extraordinary abilities displayed by these spiritual masters. So, when reading this book, it is important to realize the limitations of our own perspective and remain open to the potential existence of spiritual realities beyond our current scientific understanding.

On a final note, it's important to acknowledge that the information in this book comes from reliable texts, some dating back over three hundred years. These historical accounts are woven into the fabric of legends, and it's crucial to preserve their integrity without distortion. Who are we to judge what is real or what is not? This is Zhabdrung, and this is his life story.

CHAPTER 1

A Precursor

In the pages of history, the rise and fall of civilizations often echo tales of conquest and domination. Yet Bhutan stands as one of only a handful of countries that has remained independent for its entire history, untouched by foreign rule despite its precarious geopolitical positioning between two Asian giants.

In this book, we will explore the life of an extraordinary individual who established the temporal and spiritual foundations that became the cornerstones of Bhutan's ongoing independence. Those who are familiar with Zhabdrung Ngawang Namgyal know him as a man whose contributions to Bhutan's distinction, sanctity, and sovereignty were unfathomable. And for those who are not familiar, prepare yourself to discover the outstanding and almost mystical aspects of his life.

He is widely known as Zhabdrung Ngawang Namgyal; however, within Buddhist circles in Bhutan, he is respectfully referred to as Chabgon Ngawang Namgyal, with Chabgon serving as an honorific epithet for "His Holiness." In this book he will be referred to as Zhabdrung Ngawang Namgyal or simply Zhabdrung.

His arrival in Bhutan in 1616, the Year of the Dragon, was hardly coincidental, given his deep ties to the Thunder Dragon order (officially known as Drukpa Kargyu[9]), a branch of the great Kagyu school of Tibetan Buddhism, which is steeped in the Vajrayana tradition.[10] In fact, nothing appears surprising when it comes to this prominent spiritual figure. Zhabdrung's life story is brimming with countless tales of amazing spiritual feats, serendipitous encounters, and ancient prophecies heralding his destiny in Bhutan. It goes without saying that anyone drawn to this ancient kingdom would in some way be touched by his enduring legacy and spiritual presence, even nearly four hundred years after his death.

A rich history peppered with tales of demons and deities, Buddhist mythology, and holy masters making the impossible appear possible characterize the landscape of this small Himalayan kingdom. It is a land where human beings and the natural world are seen as intricately woven within a sacred web of interdependence. To thoroughly understand the breadth and depth of Zhabdrung's influence on the land and the psyche of its people, we need to explore his contributions from both an *inner* and *outer* context.

In the context of Tibetan Buddhism, the concepts of inner and outer are widely used to delineate distinct dimensions of one's spiritual practice and engagement with the wider world. Often shrouded in secrecy, the *inner* aspect primarily focuses on personal transformation through practices such as meditation, visualization, and spiritual instruction, leading to the cultivation of deeper levels of compassion and wisdom. In Zhabdrung's case, having already reached advanced stages on the bodhisattva path, his inner journey involved secret spiritual practices aimed at benefiting even those considered his archnemeses.

The *outer* aspect involves one's interactions with the external world, encompassing ethical conduct, rituals, offerings, and societal engagement. As a larger-than-life spiritual figure, Zhabdrung spontaneously radiated compassion to all he encountered and skillfully guided others on their spiritual paths. Despite the challenges he faced, his journey led to his destined role—the unification of the Southern Land as foretold in numerous prophecies.

Zhabdrung at a Glance

A long, neatly groomed beard extended down to his broad chest, its right curling tip serving as a secret sign of his mastery over Vajrayana practices. Thick, prominent eyebrows arched across his wide forehead, lending an air of authority. From afar, Zhabdrung's presence was dignified and brilliantly captivating, akin to a scintillating precious jewel.

Those who approached him experienced a deep sense of wonder and reverence, undoubtedly stirred by his spiritual presence. Yet upon closer contact, an overwhelming sense of peace enveloped them. Accounts describe him as welcoming, friendly, and genuinely interested in everyone he met. His gaze, honed through years of meditative concentration, bore a powerful intensity, while his complexion shone with the brilliance of a glowing sun.

Frequent smiles adorned his face, and his words, spoken in a melodious voice, often contained deeper meaning, echoing teachings from Buddhist scriptures. His delight was noticeable when people approached him to receive Dharma teachings and empowerments, particularly those who expressed a genuine motivation to practice. He selflessly imparted his wisdom in a humble and honest manner without expecting anything in return, engaging in conversations about the Dharma with those seeking his counsel well into the night.

For thirty-five years, Bhutan had the good fortune of being nurtured by his compassionate touch. However, it is worth noting that he was not always calm and welcoming. In moments of great adversity, his temperament could instantaneously transform into the fierce, resolute demeanor of a dragon, with witnesses recounting his displays of wrathful emotion when the Dharma teachings and the nation were under threat. Such was his unyielding loyalty to the teachings of Buddha and his commitment to protecting this sacred Himalayan Buddhist kingdom and its people.

This was Zhabdrung, a man destined to forever alter the course of Bhutan's history.

Bhutan in a Nutshell

There has been some speculation that Bhutan was under the influence of the Tibetan Empire between the seventh to ninth centuries.

This assumption, though understandable—considering this was the period when Buddhism was introduced to both Tibet and Bhutan from India—is incorrect. Such misunderstandings have often arisen because of their shared religious heritages causing some accounts to lump Bhutan in with its Tibetan neighbor. Despite the similarities and ties between the two nations from a religious standpoint, there are many differences that begin to emerge on closer investigation.

The earliest written records demonstrate Bhutan's staunch defense of its sovereignty, disproving any notion of subjugation. Furthermore, its cultural traditions exhibit uniqueness compared to its neighboring countries. These distinctions are seen in Bhutan's customs, traditions, attire, language, and more. While all countries possess their own distinct cultures, many have been colonized at some point during their history. Remarkably, Bhutan has not, which begs the question: Why not?

Over the course of thirty-five years, Zhabdrung unified Bhutan under a singular political, territorial, and spiritual authority, establishing a distinct state known as Drukyul, or the Land of the Thunder Dragon.[11] Its inhabitants, the Drukpas, revered him for this monumental achievement, which not only safeguarded Bhutan from external threats but also solidified its national identity.

Although Zhabdrung was well versed in the governance style of Tibet's Tsang region, he opted for a distinct approach in Drukyul. He introduced the dual system of governance, known as *chosi nyiden*, which translates to "Dharma and secular." Under Zhabdrung's leadership, both the religious and secular aspects of governance were balanced, ensuring a unique and stable administration for the newly unified state.

He appointed a Druk Desi to handle secular responsibilities and a Je Khenpo (chief abbot) for spiritual affairs. He positioned himself as the overseer and protector of the nation, providing wise counsel during times of indecision, and answered to no higher authority, earning the title Dharma Raja ("Dharma King" or "Dharma Ruler") from the Indians.

From the inception of his nation-building efforts, it is reasonable to assume that he foresaw the need to distinguish Bhutan from its

Zhabdrung Ngawang Namgyal as an elder inspired by an original mural (Artwork © 2024 Karma Tshering Wangchuk)

northern neighbor, where power was decentralized among ruling feudal lords. By implementing a new centralized system of governance, he strategically prevented any one party from dominating, thus securing the nation's sovereignty and averting internal instability.

Zhabdrung's implementation of the dual system of governance was notable for its emphasis on meritocracy. Spiritual and secular leaders were selected primarily based on their capabilities, effectively reducing corruption and nepotism while introducing an early form of democracy.

Apart from introducing a unique dual-system arrangement, Zhabdrung's activities and achievements extended well beyond what is humanly possible and into the realm of the spiritual. Zhabdrung was a highly evolved spiritual being, and Buddhists believe he made a conscious decision to take rebirth into an ordinary human body for the benefit of others, a decision that mirrored the wisdom of Buddha and reflected the motivations of a true bodhisattva. Zhabdrung was a recognized emanation of Chenrezig, the bodhisattva of compassion (Skt. Avalokiteshvara), and his life illustrated superior achievements for the benefit of not only the people of Bhutan but for all sentient beings, a legacy that lives on in the hearts and minds of many alive today.

In 1651, Zhabdrung entered a permanent meditation retreat deep inside the chambers of a fortress known as Punakha Dzong, where he died. There are several theories surrounding his death: Some suggest he entered *thukdam*[12] on the day he entered his retreat, while others propose he was sick and died shortly thereafter. Another theory posits he embarked on a long-term meditation retreat and lived for some time before passing. Regardless, it is evident that from 1651, he was no longer able to actively serve as the preeminent head of Bhutan. Whether this was by choice or circumstance is unknown, but what is certain is that the intrigue surrounding his death is probably the best-kept secret that Bhutan has ever known!

Zhabdrung's story is certainly inspiring and at times challenges the limits of our ordinary perception. Whether from the seventeenth century or twenty-first century, narratives like his carry immense value, embodying universal themes of hardship, disappointment, and triumph. The way individuals navigate these challenges offers invaluable lessons, making Zhabdrung's story a timeless source of both inspiration and profound wisdom.

Setting the Scene

Before exploring Zhabdrung's life and times in detail, we must understand the context in which he operated. This section will provide an overview of the historical landscape, explain the two Buddhist lineages that appear in the narrative, and investigate the relevance of reincarnation—a central concept in Tibetan Buddhism that features prominently in Zhabdrung's life story.

Introducing the Buddhist lineages at the outset is crucial as it establishes the context for understanding the internal conflicts—particularly the dispute over the rightful reincarnation of Pema Karpo, the recently deceased leader of the Drukpa Kargyu order. These tensions ultimately compelled Zhabdrung to journey to Bhutan and fulfill the ancient prophecies.

The petty quarrels, conflicts, and hardships of Zhabdrung's lifetime pale in comparison to his monumental achievements: uniting a lawless land and preserving the precious spiritual teachings of the Drukpa Kargyu order. From a Buddhist perspective, these challenges served as vital catalysts that enabled Zhabdrung to realize his destiny, clearly reflecting the significance of his spiritual mission.

Understanding reincarnation is also equally important, as this concept is a recurring theme throughout Zhabdrung's life story. While justifying reincarnation from a rational standpoint is challenging due to the lack of scientific proof, emphasizing its importance in Buddha's teachings is key. Without believing in, understanding, and acknowledging that the concept of reincarnation forms the very premise of Buddha's teachings, it is impossible to technically call oneself a Buddhist. For those who are reincarnation skeptics, this section will provide an explanation. Without this understanding, certain aspects of this book will not make logical sense and may be relegated to the realm of make-believe—which they most certainly are not.

The Historical Context

Although the historical progression of Zhabdrung's early life and the events that followed in Tibet and Bhutan will be documented in later chapters, it is important to paint a brief picture of what life was like during this period in history to understand the trials and tribulations he faced.

LIFE IN TIBET

Tibet lies on a stark, grassy plateau surrounded by the world's highest mountain peaks from where several major rivers originate. The

resulting alluvial soil is topped with a light grayish-brown sprin-
kling of windblown sand, carried by the sudden gusts of cold, dry
air that cascade down from the snowy peaks that stand sentinel
over the harsh and uncompromising treeless landscape. Fleeting
summers give way to endless winters, when rivers freeze over and
bitter winds whip the barren terrain into a swirling haze of dust,
sending creatures scuttling deep into the earth.

The land where the nomadic yak herders came and went was the
same land where battles were won and lost. In particular, the region
of U-Tsang, where Zhabdrung spent his early life, was marred by
tensions and great turbulence over the centuries.

Ralung Monastery, situated in the U-Tsang region of Tibet, served
as the primary seat of Zhabdrung's lineage—the Drukpa Kargyu
order. Perched at an altitude of 4,700 meters above sea level, nestled
south of the Karo Pass, the monastery is surrounded by towering
icy glaciers and windswept mountain peaks. Those who possess
the gift of spiritual sight have reported that the mountains and
meadows encircling Ralung appear as sacred Buddhist symbols.
It is in this very region that the captivating story of Zhabdrung
begins.

Located slightly to the northwest is the ancient capital of Shigatse, situated at an elevation of around 3,800 meters—the seat of
the secular ruler of the Tsang region, the Tsang Desi. The Shigatse
region encompasses a diverse landscape, ranging from flat agricultural areas to rugged mountains. It is situated at the confluence
of the Nyang River and the Yarlung Tsangpo River, the latter of
which originates not far from the sacred gorges of Mount Kailash
to the west. Highland barley stands as the primary crop, thriving in
the area's cold and harsh climate, while other agricultural produce
struggles to flourish. The region is also home to yaks and sheep,
which yield prized resources such as milk, butter, yogurt, cheese,
and occasionally meat.

Tibet served as the citadel of monasticism, where the Buddhist
clergy wielded significant influence over both spiritual and civil matters. The governance of the land was deeply integrated with Bud-

dhist principles, a cultural norm since the reign of King Songtsen Gampo in the seventh century.

Between 629 and 842 C.E., Tibet was ruled by a series of emperors, three of whom were famously known as Dharma kings due to their great devotion to the Buddhist teachings. These ancestral Buddhist kings were King Songtsen Gampo, who brought Buddhism to Tibet from India; King Trisong Detsen; and Tritsuk Detsen, also known as King Tri Ralpachen. Following the death of King Tri Ralpachen (apparently assassinated by his brother Langdarma), Langdarma acceded to the throne (thri).[13] Historical accounts depict him as aligned with the Bon tradition, an indigenous, animistic form of worship. Considered by many as anti-Buddhist, his reign was blamed for the demise of the Buddhist teachings in Tibet during this period. Following Langdarma's death, Tibet plunged into a state of lawlessness lasting several centuries, marked by the absence of central political authority.

In the early thirteenth century, the Mongols wielded considerable influence over various regions of Tibet. Around 1240, Prince Koton, the grandson of Ghengis Khan, made a fateful journey into Tibet. Serendipitously he crossed paths with the revered Sakya master Sakya Pandita Kunga Gyaltshen (1182-1251) and his nephew Drogon Chogyal Phagpa (1235-1280), who bestowed upon him profound Buddhist teachings. Deeply moved by Buddhism, he subsequently granted the regions of U-Tsang and Ngari to Sakya Pandita. This marked the beginning of a ninety-six-year period during which the Sakya masters governed these territories.

In 1349, authority over these Tibetan regions shifted from the Sakyas to a succession of feudal lords, a dynamic that persisted for nearly two centuries. Subsequently, from 1565 to 1642, U, Tsang, and Ngari came under the governance of the Tsang Desis. This era saw the rise of the Tsang Desis, a Buddhist dynasty based in Shigatse, which controlled a substantial portion of Tibet. Among the key figures of this seventy-seven-year period were Tsang Desi Karma Tensung Wangpo (r. 1599-1611), Tsang Desi Karma Phuntsok Namgyal (r. 1611-1621), and Tsang Desi Karma Tenchong Wangpo (r.

1619–1642). It was during the reign of the second and third Tsang Desis that the epic tale of Zhabdrung began to unfurl.

The dominant Tibetan Buddhist school in this region was the Kagyu school. Unfortunately, religious rivalry erupted among the Drukpa Kargyu order (a branch of the great Kagyu school), following the death of their head, Pema Karpo. The search to identify their master's reincarnation led to two contenders: Zhabdrung Ngawang Namgyal and Pagsam Wangpo, causing a significant schism in the Drukpa Kargyu community at the time. The recognized reincarnation of Pema Karpo would gain widespread respect and considerable authority over a large area of Tibet, thanks to the extensive network of Drukpa Kargyu followers. As tensions rose and the issue became increasingly contentious, the situation prompted Zhabdrung to depart for Bhutan in 1616.

Zhabdrung's decision to leave Tibet for Bhutan was not entirely driven by the external turmoil surrounding the reincarnation drama. It was also guided by an inner spiritual impetus prophesied centuries earlier by great Buddhist masters. As we will soon discover, Zhabdrung emerged as a destined spiritual leader who unified the nation of Bhutan and significantly contributed to the flourishing of the Dharma. However, following Zhabdrung's departure, clashes between the two nations persisted for many years, fueled by jealousy and power struggles.

LIFE IN BHUTAN

The topography of Bhutan exhibits extreme differences in altitude, ranging from the remote settlements in the Lunana region of the Gasa district in northwestern Bhutan, situated at vertiginous altitudes approaching 4,800 meters, to the subtropical town of Gelephu on the Indian border, at an altitude of around two hundred meters. In the temperate valleys of Paro and Punakha, rice, millet, maize, and wheat are cultivated alongside a diverse range of fruits and vegetables. Moving to the lower subtropical areas of Samtse and Pasakha in the Chukha district, one finds the landscape adorned with lush plantations of bananas and betel nut trees.

In the higher alpine regions of Bhutan, an abundance of medicinal plants, trees, shrubs, and flowering species such as rhododendrons thrive alongside hundreds of species of bird life. The cool alpine air is infused with the sweet scent emitted by incense-bearing shrubs and medicinal herbal plants, creating an atmosphere of extreme sanctity, befitting a land blessed by many great masters. Bhutan is, in fact, known as a *beyul*—a sacred, hidden land blessed by Guru Rinpoche, a great Buddhist saint from the eighth century.

Until the seventeenth century, Bhutan was governed by noble clans and families, each exerting control over different valleys. The political landscape was unstable, lacking a universally recognized national figure or centralized authority, with no formal written code of law. Persistent fears of domination by rival clans, coupled with competition for land and water resources, remained constant concerns, bearing a striking resemblance to the political landscape in Tibet after the rule of the three Dharma kings.

An intriguing account from this period comes from the fourth Panchen Lama, Lobzang Chokyi Gyaltshen, who visited Bhutan in 1612. He described the region as a Wild West frontier characterized by rampant violence, offering a glimpse of the hostile environment Zhabdrung encountered upon his arrival:

After the manner of the proverbial big fish eating the little fish, vicious men rose up to fight and kill one another. Escorts were needed to go from the upper part of the village to the lower. The rich robbed the poor of their wealth and homes and forced them into involuntary servitude. Interfamily disputes, fighting, and injury went on unabated.

Tsang Khenchen similarly describes Bhutan as the lawless south where conflicts between relatives were common and even minor disputes led to deadly outcomes. Sacred mound-like shrines called *stupas* and Buddhist statues were plundered, while children and domesticated animals were stolen for sale. Neighborly jealousy often resulted in the destruction of bumper harvests before they could ripen. Deliberate misunderstandings were manufactured to sabo-tage relationships and undermine meritorious deeds. Overcoming such rampant lawlessness was an immense challenge, highlighting the truly remarkable nature of Zhabdrung's accomplishments.

In the face of the harsh environment, loyalty among the various family clans to the Drukpa Kargyu order remained steadfast. The origin of this loyalty dates back to the thirteenth century with the arrival of Phajo Drukgom Zhigpo, an early pioneer of the Drukpa Kargyu tradition, and was heightened by Zhabdrung's arrival in 1616. The clans of western Bhutan, committed to the Drukpa Kargyu order, not only extended invitations to numerous Drukpa Kargyu masters from Ralung but also sent their sons there for educa-tion. These families fostered spiritual connections to Ralung and forged marital ties,[14] thereby perpetuating the Drukpa hereditary lineage. These extensive marital alliances and monastic patron-ages significantly strengthened the Drukpa Kargyu order by facil-itating the dissemination of teachings in Bhutan and establishing a solid foundation of loyalty and support for Zhabdrung's unifi-cation efforts upon his arrival. Furthermore, the relationships between these patron families and the Drukpa Kargyu masters played a central role in the political governance of their respective regions.

In 1627, two Portuguese Jesuit priests, Father Estevao Cacella and Father Joao Cabral, made history by becoming the first recorded Westerners to set foot in Bhutan. Their firsthand account of life in the country, acquired during their roughly eight-month stay, offers invaluable insights. Their writings afford us a unique window into Bhutanese life during that era.

The priests recount being robbed and deceived by their guide, an experience that aligns with the fourth Panchen Lama's descrip-tion. However, amid these challenges, they also shed light on the country's positive aspects. They speak highly of Zhabdrung, their host, and note the exceptional health of the populace. Few instances of illness were observed, with many elderly individuals enjoying robust health. There was an abundance of food, including a diverse array of fruits such as pears, peaches, apples, nuts, and quinces, as well as an extensive selection of vegetables including tasty turnips and peas. Trade with neighboring countries provided goods such as salt, grapes, silk, gold, and porcelain. While wheat, rice, and meat were abundant, the priests observed a conspicuous absence of local fish, suggesting a potential restriction on fishing activities perhaps for religious reasons or certain local practices.

The climate, described as temperate, lacked extremes of heat and cold throughout their stay, which spanned from late February to well before the onset of winter. The locals seemed to possess good-quality woolen garments, although they appeared unkempt and often moved about barefoot, resorting to leather boots only on longer journeys. Notably, the absence of traditional temples suggests that local Buddhist practices may have been centered around private homes rather than grand architectural edifices, a contrast to later structures commissioned by Zhabdrung. Despite factional disputes and encounters with robbers, life in Bhutan appeared relatively comfortable on a material level.

From Zhabdrung's arrival in 1616 until the mid-1700s, however, tensions between Bhutan and Tibet remained palpable, marked by power struggles, jealousies, and unresolved disputes, particularly surrounding the reincarnation of Pema Karpo.

Another contentious side issue, driven largely by the legitimacy it conferred, revolved around the desire to possess the sacred topmost vertebra of Tsangpa Gyare, the founder of the Drukpa Kargyu Buddhist order. This vertebra, known as the Rangjung Kharsapani, contains the self-arisen standing image of Chenrezig, the bodhisattva of compassion.

Objects such as bone fragments found in the cremated remains of highly realized masters, known as *ringsel*, are highly prized possessions in the Buddhist world for their perceived power to emit blessings. The Rangjung Kharsapani was no different. Apart from these blessings, its predictive powers and capacity to confer legitimacy to its possessor over the seat of Ralung made it highly sought after, leading to its closely guarded protection by the Ralung hierarchs.

The two nations remained at loggerheads for over a century, grappling with various issues. These issues and their underlying causes will be detailed later in the book. What's crucial to understand now is that Zhabdrung's arrival and life in Bhutan unfolded against a backdrop of potential conflict and subterfuge despite steadfast support from his patrons, primarily residing in the western regions of Bhutan.

Buddhist Lineages in Zhabdrung's Story

Zhabdrung held a revered position within the Drukpa Kargyu order since he bore dual Buddhist lineages: the hereditary lineage known as the Drukpa (Gya), and the reincarnation lineage from Tsangpa Gyare, the founder of the Drukpa Kargyu order. While Zhabdrung's story prominently features his reincarnation lineage, the hereditary lineage also holds significance, reflecting the importance placed on bloodlines during that era.

The Drukpa (Gya) hereditary lineage traces its origins to the seventh century, beginning with a man called Lhaga, who was granted land in the Ralung estate for transporting a sacred statue of Shakyamuni Buddha from China to Lhasa. Originally called the Gya lineage, it gained prominence in the eighth century when Gya Jampel Sangwa, a descendant of Lhaga, prophesied the emergence of eighty-four emanations of Chenrezig within the lineage. In the early thirteenth century, Tsangpa Gyare, a member of this ancient bloodline, founded the Drukpa Kargyu order and eventually established Ralung Monastery as its main seat. The Gya hereditary lineage later became known as the Drukpa hereditary lineage, reflecting the name of Tsangpa Gyare's Buddhist order—the Drukpa Kargyu.

In contrast, the reincarnation lineage consists of successive reincarnations of Tsangpa Gyare, each holding the title of Palden Drukpa Rinpoche. These reincarnations are Kunga Peljor, Jamyang Chokyi Dragpa, Pema Karpo, and Zhabdrung Ngawang Namgyal. The dispute over Pema Karpo's reincarnation led to a significant rift among the Drukpa Kargyu followers, ultimately leading to Zhabdrung's departure for Bhutan.

If you're new to Bhutan and Buddhist concepts, the story of Zhabdrung may appear complex. To help you navigate this narrative, here are some key points to keep in mind as you read:

- In Tibetan Buddhism, storytelling often incorporates embellishments, metaphors, and allegorical elements to convey spiritual insights. Western narratives, on the other hand, emphasize linear storytelling and historical context.[15]
- The central conflict in Zhabdrung's story revolves around the Drukpa Kargyu reincarnation lineage and the recognition of Pema Karpo's reincarnation—the third reincarnation of Tsangpa Gyare—who had recently passed away.
- Two candidates for the position of Pema Karpo's reincarnation, Zhabdrung Ngawang Namgyal and Pagsam Wangpo, were embroiled in the reincarnation dispute.
- Zhabdrung's arrival in Bhutan marked the beginning of the spiritual work he was destined to accomplish, as foretold by centuries-old prophecies.
- The Drukpa (Gya) hereditary lineage, of which Zhabdrung was a throne holder, held a deep and sacred history dating back to the seventh century. Zhabdrung's efforts to ensure the continuation of this hereditary lineage were motivated by the importance people attached to bloodlines during that era.
- The confirmation of a Drukpa reincarnation was the responsibility of the Drukpa hereditary lineage hierarchs. Interference by individuals outside of the official Drukpa leadership led to the division within the Drukpa community.
- The Rangjung Kharsapani, the sacred topmost backbone relic of Tsangpa Gyare containing the standing image of Chenrezig, salvaged from his cremated remains, was closely guarded by the Ralung throne holder and the hereditary hierarchs. This relic famously guided Zhabdrung throughout his life, manifesting various spiritual signs.
- Tsangpa Gyare (1161–1211), Kunga Peljor (1428–1476), and Zhabdrung Ngawang Namgyal (1594–1651) held both lineages, granting them a revered position within the Drukpa Kargyu order.

Their dual lineage connections are visually depicted in the following diagram.

The conflict over Pema Karpo's rightful reincarnation served as the "outer" reason for Zhabdrung's journey to Bhutan, yet a deeper, "inner" purpose was at work. Centuries earlier, Zhabdrung's destiny had been prophesied, foreseeing the crucial role he would play in Bhutan's history.

Masters of the Drukpa (Gya) Hereditary Lineage Showing Collateral Lines and Reincarnations of Tsangpa Gyare

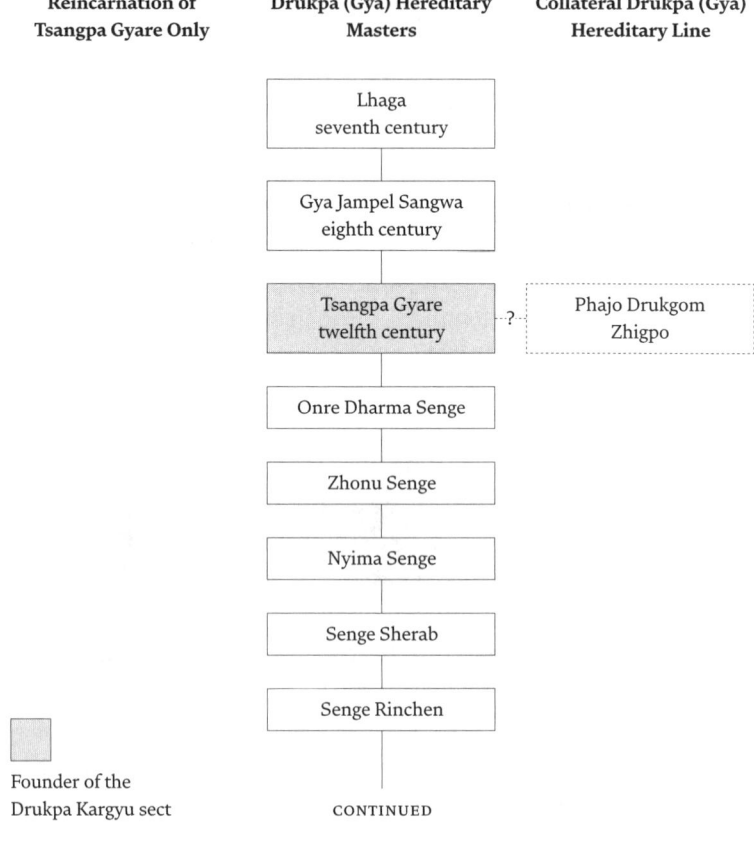

Reincarnation of Tsangpa Gyare Only	Drukpa (Gya) Hereditary Masters	Collateral Drukpa (Gya) Hereditary Line
	Lhaga seventh century	
	Gya Jampel Sangwa eighth century	
	Tsangpa Gyare twelfth century ..?..	Phajo Drukgom Zhigpo
	Onre Dharma Senge	
	Zhonu Senge	
	Nyima Senge	
	Senge Sherab	
	Senge Rinchen	

Founder of the
Drukpa Kargyu sect   CONTINUED

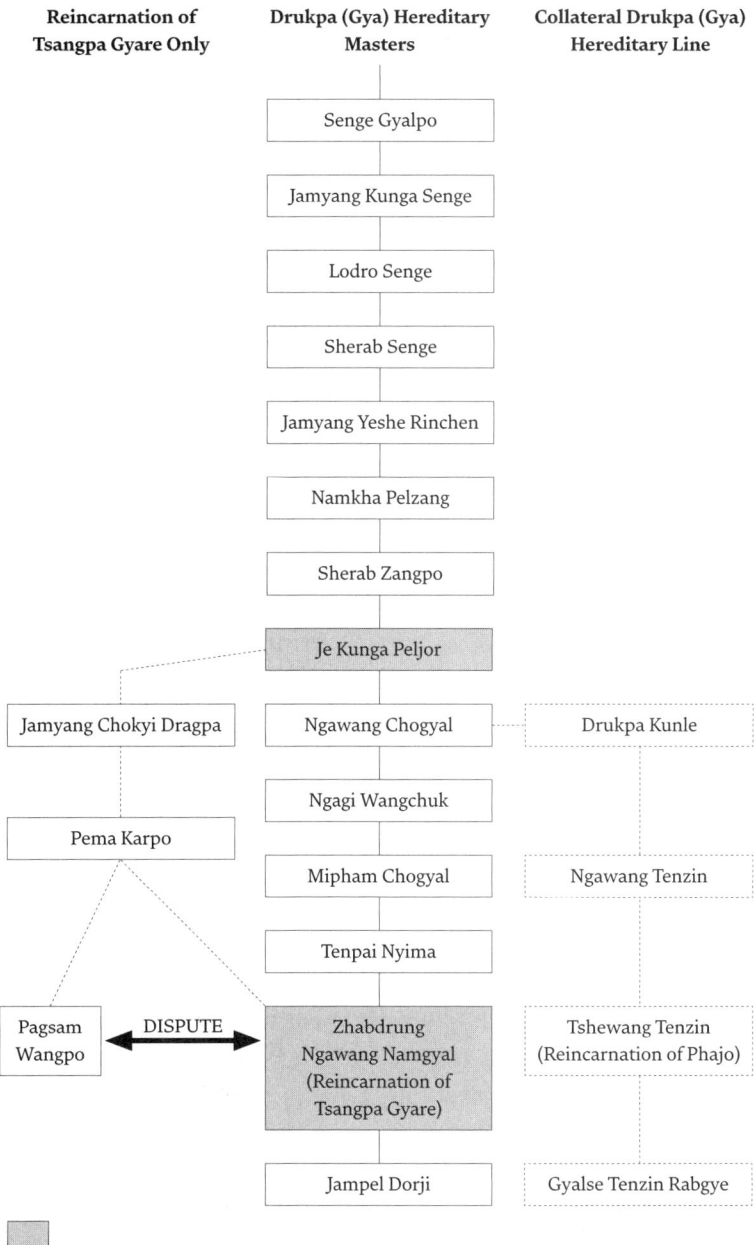

Reincarnation of Tsangpa Gyare Only	Drukpa (Gya) Hereditary Masters	Collateral Drukpa (Gya) Hereditary Line
	Senge Gyalpo	
	Jamyang Kunga Senge	
	Lodro Senge	
	Sherab Senge	
	Jamyang Yeshe Rinchen	
	Namkha Pelzang	
	Sherab Zangpo	
	Je Kunga Peljor	
Jamyang Chokyi Dragpa	Ngawang Chogyal	Drukpa Kunle
	Ngagi Wangchuk	
Pema Karpo	Mipham Chogyal	Ngawang Tenzin
	Tenpai Nyima	
Pagsam Wangpo ◄DISPUTE►	Zhabdrung Ngawang Namgyal (Reincarnation of Tsangpa Gyare)	Tshewang Tenzin (Reincarnation of Phajo)
	Jampel Dorji	Gyalse Tenzin Rabgye

Both a hereditary lineage holder and reincarnation of Tsangpa Gyare

Unraveling the Mystery of Reincarnation

The concept of reincarnation has intrigued New Age circles for decades and is a central theme in the story of Zhabdrung. References to reincarnation can be traced back to the early Hindu scriptures known as the Vedas, dating from approximately 1500 to 500 B.C.E. Reincarnation is integral to religions and philosophies such as Buddhism, Hinduism, Jainism, and Theosophy, forming a foundational belief without which these doctrines would make no sense at all.

From an early age, I held a belief that we somehow survive physical death. Death, to me, was more of a curiosity than something to be feared. I vividly recall a moment when I was around ten years old, telling my mother in all seriousness that I was looking forward to dying as it would be a great adventure. I was dead serious (no pun intended!). Needless to say, my declaration did not go over well with her, nor were my lectures to my parents at the dinner table about how, when we die, we just transition to another body and that there's nothing to worry about. Looking back, I realize that this belief must have stemmed from a knowingness of reincarnation from a previous life.

My belief was further strengthened when I had the good fortune of meeting a real-life reincarnation in Bhutan. For the Bhutanese, encountering the reincarnation of a revered spiritual teacher, a *tulku*, is no big deal—it's part of their DNA. But for me, it was a moment brimming with anticipation.

I distinctly remember being ushered into a long, narrow, dimly lit room furnished with simple, though chunky, teak furniture typical of the Bhutanese households I had visited many times before. The mundane surroundings contrasted with my expectations. My monk friend, who had taken me, sent a text message to the tulku informing him of our arrival.

"Oh, hi....Can you give me a sec? I have to finish doing something," came the voice from behind the curtain that separated the reception area from the adjacent room. My interest piqued. To my amazement, he spoke perfect colloquial English! After a few minutes, a short, stout figure emerged, looking no older than seventeen years old.

With my friend seated next to me, the tulku and I effortlessly launched into conversation, as if we were long-lost friends. There were no airs and graces, just the ease of introductory talk. That I was an "outsider" seemed to break down barriers. When I asked him about his impressive English skills, he humbly confessed that he had picked up the language by watching English movies. Strangely, I felt like I was conversing with a wise seventy-year-old man, not a teenage boy! Time seemed to warp; what felt like an hour turned into a shocking realization that four hours had passed as I stared at my watch in disbelief. My friend was outstretched on the sofa, fast asleep. The now cold tea remained untouched, the sole witness to our unusual, though spiritually charged meeting. A wave of confusion washed over me as I pondered the depth of our conversation. What had we discussed for all those hours? I had absolutely no recollection. As we rose from our seats, I extended a firm handshake. The tulku ushered us to our car. "See you again!" he yelled out as our car sped off down the steep driveway.

As our friendship deepened over the years, I grew increasingly intrigued by him. He was not only highly disciplined and devoted to his studies but also extremely intelligent, effortlessly memorizing scriptures while his peers struggled with the mental rigor. He could explain complex Buddhist philosophical principles in a simple yet effective manner. I owe a lot to the tulku. Our discussions and debates on Buddhism often lasted for hours, but what I cherished the most about our friendship was the raw honesty; there were no formalities or facades.

Buddha taught that the mind carries with it karmic seeds, or imprints, that accompany us as we transition between lifetimes of existences. I remember attending a talk on Buddhism where they spoke about looking forward to the opportunity that death presents, which drew me back to my childhood utterances and caused me to reflect further on this aspect.

What Exactly Is Reincarnation?

Reincarnation (or rebirth) is the belief that an aspect of our mind (consciousness) survives physical death and keeps on being reborn into other existences until enlightenment. This aspect of the mind is unconsciously and uncontrollably propelled forth by the law of karma, where an action is always accompanied by its consequences. In other words, the law of cause and effect.

Those who believe in reincarnation merely view the body as a temporary vessel for the mind, allowing it to undergo experiences and change, and hopefully act as a vehicle for the benefit of others. Upon death, the mind continues to transform as it moves from existence to existence, resembling the law of conservation of energy in physics, which states that energy cannot be created or destroyed; it just changes form.

In Buddhist philosophy, the mind is not permanently contained within a system. It is believed that upon reaching enlightenment, the mind ceases to exist, leaving only the ultimate buddha nature in its true, naked form. Buddha nature refers to the qualities of Buddha that every sentient being possesses. Buddhist spiritual practice involves the peeling away of layers of negative emotions such as anger, greed, desire, and jealousy to unveil one's buddha nature.

So that's the principle of reincarnation in a nutshell.

Embracing this concept wholeheartedly may bring meaning and spiritual fulfillment, as life is perceived as a continuum rather than a finality. For those who reject this belief due to a lack of scientific evidence, I encourage you to investigate the many contemporary accounts of young children recalling places and people from another lifetime, speaking foreign languages they have never heard, or displaying exceptional artistic and musical abilities without training. While no single case may be conclusive, the accumulation of thousands of cases presents a compelling argument for the existence of reincarnation.

Furthermore, the reincarnation system of succession in Tibetan Buddhism, which involves the selection of tulkus, can empower those on the spiritual path even if they initially may doubt its validity. The recollections by these tulkus of events, people, items, and places from their previous lives—details that a young child could not possibly know—raise thought-provoking questions about the nature of the mind and its potential to survive physical death. It must be emphasized, however, that continued existence should not be seen as something to look forward to but rather a cycle to be transcended in the pursuit of total enlightenment—the ultimate goal of the Buddhist practitioner.

The intricacies and implications of a system such as selecting tulkus are beyond the scope of this book and are mentioned here because Zhabdrung himself was a tulku of remarkable accomplishments. While the revelations by tulkus cannot be considered irrefutable scientific proof of reincarnation, they suggest that something beyond our limited understanding of life is at play. In fact, attempting to rationalize the spiritual by seeking scientific evidence can divert one away from the spiritual path. According to Buddhist teachings, being on the spiritual path involves a different dimension of knowledge—one that doesn't solely arise from the rational mind but from inner knowing and conscious unlearning, rooted in one's buddha nature.

As we will uncover, Zhabdrung was considered a reincarnation of Pema Karpo and an emanation of Chenrezig and Guru Rinpoche, as evidenced by his remarkable deeds and behavior. Naturally, anything not scientifically proven will have its detractors. But is it wise to judge what we don't fully understand? For those even slightly interested in the spiritual path, it might be more sensible to maintain an open, inquisitive mind rather than getting bogged down in rationalizing the existence or nonexistence of reincarnation. This perspective can be challenging to appreciate in the modern world, where rationality is often deemed essential for belief. However, rationalization, while an intellectual exercise, frequently falls short of capturing the full spectrum of spiritual dimensions and experiences.

Individuals are born with a range of attributes influenced by genetics, a concept also reflected in Buddhist philosophy through the notion of karma. While some may perceive certain traits as less favorable, it is important to recognize that our physical and mental characteristics do not determine the potential for spiritual growth. The mind, unlike these characteristics, remains adaptable and capable of cultivating compassion and understanding. For example, those with disabilities, far from being limitations, can offer profound lessons in empathy and resilience, challenging us to prioritize compassion over material accumulation.

Here are a few key takeaways to consider when contemplating the concept of reincarnation:

- Keep an open mind.
- Just because the concept has not been proven by current modern science does not render it untrue.
- Our intellect arises from our physical brain whereas the spiritual arises from the inner knowingness that is contained within our mind (Note that the mind in Buddhism is a very sophisticated idea based on many hundreds of years of investigation.) Buddhist teachings clearly distinguish consciousness from the responsiveness of the physical brain.
- Buddhist teachings describe the mind as a formless essence riding on the wind, known as *lung* in Tibetan—the vital life force that flows through the energy centers in our body. The physical brain and the mind are not the same thing; rather, they are interdependent, with the mind expressing itself through the physical body. Upon death, the body disintegrates, and the mind is released and survives.
- Our intellectual development in this lifetime may have its limitations and cannot be drastically transformed; however, our spiritual growth knows no bounds and can be continually nurtured. This underscores the empowering nature of embracing the concept of reincarnation.
- It is the mind (consciousness) that reincarnates from existence to existence, and because the mind can be changed, we have the capacity to progress further along the spiritual path toward enlightenment. By simply practicing compassion and kindness for others, we can inch our way forward on the spiritual path.

- For Buddhist practitioners on the path to enlightenment, intellectual acknowledgment of reincarnation must be integrated with an embodied knowingness and confidence in the concept.
- Ultimately Buddhists believe in the continuity of the mindstream upon physical death; the continuity of awareness that carries forward from one lifetime to the next. This is what is understood as reincarnation.

REINCARNATION (INCARNATION) VERSUS EMANATION

When discussing reincarnation, it is important to distinguish between reincarnation and emanation, as Zhabdrung was a reincarnation of great masters such as Pema Karpo and Tsangpa Gyare, as well as an emanation of Chenrezig, the bodhisattva of compassion, and Guru Rinpoche.

Reincarnation is the process of rebirth, where a sentient being's mindstream, the flow of consciousness, takes rebirth into another existence after physical death. This act of reincarnating can occur in one of two ways—uncontrolled or controlled—depending on one's level of spiritual awareness. Those who have transcended the law of karma and delusion can consciously choose their place of rebirth for the benefit of others—an ability that is a feature of a bodhisattva. However, the majority reincarnate unconsciously, as they have not reached this level of spiritual mastery.

Emanation is an energetic manifestation of a highly evolved being. Someone can be a reincarnation of another person, solely an emanation, or both, as in Zhabdrung's case.

A simple definition of an emanation in Buddhism is an energetic manifestation that can appear multiple times across time and even concurrently, benefiting others through their enlightened qualities. Chenrezig, representing the energetic vibration of compassion, can manifest in various forms to benefit others. Therefore, in the Buddhist sense, individuals who have spread compassion and peace throughout the world could be seen as embodiments or emanations of Chenrezig.

Karma: Where Does It Fit In?

Karma, a Sanskrit word for "action," is concerned with the moral intentions arising from the universal law of cause and effect. Intentional actions, both good and bad, generate consequences that affect one's present and future lives. Though karma is an extremely complex concept—beyond the grasp of the ordinary human mind—on some level, we can understand that karma underpins reincarnation.

Karma prepares and shapes our mind, serving as the ultimate driver of our future. Every thought and action, whether positive or negative, is believed to have a corresponding effect on the rest of our present life and our future lives. Therefore it logically follows that if karma impacts our future lives, it also determines our place of rebirth. Buddhists believe that if many negative deeds are committed in this life and are not remedied by positive actions and feelings of regret, an unfortunate rebirth is likely to follow. In summary, karma can be viewed as a tally of one's actions, both positive and negative, that significantly impacts our future.

I firmly believe we all possess an inherent sense of goodness and therefore an unconscious knowingness of the law of karma hidden underneath our ignorance and conditioning. As I wrote the preceding section on karma, one childhood memory, tinged with both innocence and abhorrence, came flooding back to me.

I still remember the event as if it were yesterday. The midday sun blazed overhead, its rays streaming down over the long blades of grass, enveloping me in a warm embrace. Grasshoppers leaped with glee, their wings snapping loudly as they hopped past, brushing against my bare legs and tickling my skin.

There I was, in my element, dressed in a bright-red pinafore hotpants suit with a yellow appliquéd apple on the front panel—a remnant of the 1970s fashion craze—sitting amid the overgrown grass on the embankment near our family home. As a tomboy, I preferred outdoor adventures to playing indoors with dolls and makeup. Most weekends you would find me immersed in nature, climbing trees and seeking out more adventurous pursuits. On that particular day, I was out to catch some grasshoppers with my Globite suitcase, an essential item carried by countless Australian schoolchildren at the end of the twentieth century.

As I sat in the searing sun, I eagerly caught grasshoppers and carefully placed them, one by one, in my suitcase as "pets." Each time I placed one inside, another would inevitably jump out, quickly testing my patience. Frustration mounting, I did the unimaginable—a decision that still weighs heavily on my conscience. I began tearing off the back legs and wings of each grasshopper before placing them inside the suitcase.

Initially there was silence, and I felt a twisted sense of satisfaction. Soon, however, a wave of realization washed over me, accompanied by panic and shame. The full extent of the pain and suffering I had inflicted on these creatures became excruciatingly clear.

The horror of my actions peaked as overwhelming regret consumed me for the suffering I had caused. The grasshoppers deserved to live freely in nature, yet I, a cruel and insensitive girl, had deprived them of their freedom by removing their back legs and wings, confining them to an unfamiliar, dark space.

Recognizing the cruelty of my actions, I swiftly released the grasshoppers into the long grass and hurried home. I kept the afternoon's horrors to myself, sitting on my bed, consumed by guilt and remorse for the senseless harm I had caused on such innocent creatures. In that moment, I made a solemn promise never to intentionally harm another living being.

Even at a very young age, I had an innate sense of the law of cause and effect, albeit at a rudimentary level; I believe most of us do. The law of karma is an inescapable universal principle operating in the background of our everyday lives, whether we are aware of it or not.

Understanding the concepts of karma and reincarnation is crucial to grasping Zhabdrung's story. Yet to truly appreciate Zhabdrung himself, one must understand the mysteries surrounding him, beginning with three fundamental concepts: bodhisattva, buddha, and enlightenment. After all, he was no ordinary individual; he was an emanation of Chenrezig, the bodhisattva of compassion, who stood on the cusp of attaining buddhahood.

To fully comprehend his significance, it is essential to consider the vast stretches of time in Buddhist cosmology needed to attain such spiritual heights. Figures such as Zhabdrung are incredibly rare and precious, underscoring the extraordinary nature of his journey and the immense fortune bestowed upon Bhutan to encounter such a remarkable being.

CHAPTER 2

The Path to Enlightenment: Bodhisattvas, Buddhas, and Buddhist Cosmology

Zhabdrung was recognized as an emanation of bodhisattva Chenrezig, a spiritual being known for embodying the qualities of compassion in all his actions and interactions. The essence of compassion plays a vital role in spiritual growth and is a fundamental ingredient in achieving enlightenment, highlighting the significance of Chenrezig in the Buddhist tradition. Therefore, to fully understand Zhabdrung, we must first understand the concepts of bodhisattva, buddha, and enlightenment, as this is what he was and was on the verge of becoming.

What Is a Bodhisattva?

A bodhisattva is an individual driven by a profound aspiration to reach enlightenment and dedication to the betterment of all living beings. The term *bodhisattva* derives from the Sanskrit words *bodhi* (wisdom, awakened) and *sattva* (being). The mission of a bodhisattva is to selflessly guide the spiritually unawakened toward enlightenment while remaining spiritually awakened themselves and willingly sacrificing their own place in nirvana. As beautifully expressed by H. P. Blavatsky, a central figure in the establishment of the Theosophical Society,

"There is more courage to accept being than non-being, life than death," there are those among the Bodhisattwas and the Lha[16] — "and as rare as the flower of udambara[17] are they to meet with"— who voluntarily relinquish the blessing of the attainment of perfect freedom,[18] and remain in their personal selves, whether in forms visible or invisible to mortal sight—to teach and help their weaker brothers.

Moreover, the idea of a bodhisattva is inherently connected to *bodhicitta*, the deep-seated aspiration to achieve enlightenment for the benefit of all sentient beings. In this sense, a bodhisattva is an individual who postpones achieving full enlightenment out of compassion for the suffering of sentient beings trapped in the cycle of birth, death, and rebirth, a state known as samsara.

In Mahayana Buddhism, a bodhisattva progresses through ten higher stages known as *bhumis*, the final rungs before one becomes a buddha. This branch of Buddhism not only seeks personal liberation but also aims to guide others toward enlightenment. Those who attain the higher bhumis are believed to possess profound spiritual powers and the ability to communicate with spiritual beings. Zhabdrung, having reached the tenth bhumi, just one rung away from buddhahood, was famed for communing with the three Drukpa spiritual guardians: Yeshe Gonpo (Mahakala), Palden Lhamo (Mahakali), and Legon Jarog Dongchen (Karma Mahakala). In Buddhist scriptures, the tenth bhumi is described as "the cloud of Dharma," a theme echoed in Tsang Khenchen's title choice for his biography on Zhabdrung: *The Melody of the Great Dharma Cloud*.

Gampopa, a great Buddhist luminary of whom Zhabdrung was a reincarnation, extensively described the ten bhumis in his magnum opus, *The Jewel Ornament of Liberation*. His detailed descriptions of the ten bhumis offer a structured framework for understanding the spiritual qualities one must cultivate in the pursuit of enlightenment.

According to Gampopa, beings such as Zhabdrung, who have reached the tenth bhumi, effortlessly shower the rain of Dharma upon others, like raindrops falling from a cloud, by dedicating themselves to pacifying the afflictive emotions of sentient beings. As we will discover, Zhabdrung exhibited these qualities through his utter joy in engaging in Dharmic conversations, disseminating the teachings of the Buddha, and selflessly serving others.

At the tenth bhumi, beings transcend the influence of karma and commit themselves entirely to the welfare of others. Endowed with unparalleled supernatural powers, they can employ these abilities for the greater good when needed, taking on various forms such as deities and human beings. They can also manifest ominous signs to avert evil, a feat exhibited by Zhabdrung during the numerous conflicts he encountered in Bhutan.

Shortly after Zhabdrung's arrival in Bhutan, a remarkable event occurred during the initial Tibetan invasion. Clad in yogic attire, an apparition of Zhabdrung emerged, leading an army of fearsome beings that dominated the sky, brandishing swords and shields. Though physically absent from the battlefield, Zhabdrung wielded his spiritual prowess to command the guardian deities of the land to manifest as fierce specters.

The Dharmic texts extensively document the mastery of bodhisattvas over a range of *inner* spiritual activities, which can be likened to a "spiritual toolbox." These activities or spiritual powers, as opposed to black magic used for evil intent, play a crucial role in helping sentient beings to break free from the cycle of birth, death, and suffering.

As we trace Zhabdrung's life story, we uncover numerous instances where he uses his "spiritual toolbox" to administer remedies driven solely by compassion for others. The spiritual tools employed by bodhisattvas can be categorized under four activities:

1. Pacifying activities, such as resolving conflicts and fostering unity, promote peace and harmony in the lives of others.
2. Increasing activities, such as aiding the needy, offering prayers for a person's long life, or healing the sick, enrich and enhance the lives of sentient beings.

3. Magnetizing activities draw sentient beings closer, evoking trust and devotion to guide them along the spiritual path.
4. Wrathful activities are a last resort if all other remedies prove ineffective. These actions, which may involve stern words, disciplinary action, or even severe physical harm, are always motivated by compassion, akin to a parent disciplining a child for their own benefit.

Zhabdrung found himself accused of using sorcery to harm others, an allegation that some saw as contradictory to his role as a bodhisattva. In his defense, he cited the teachings of Buddha regarding the use of wrathful actions to combat evil. Zhabdrung maintained that these activities represented spiritual powers granted to bodhisattvas and should not be misconstrued as sorcery. He famously challenged his accusers, stating, "If I am wrong, then the entire teachings of Buddha are wrong."

Tsang Khenchen supports Zhabdrung's reasoning by quoting Buddha's teachings in the sutras on the conduct of bodhisattvas:

A great king should not be too compassionate. The reason being, if a prosperous king becomes too compassionate, he will fail to carry out the responsibilities of a king and will be undermined by some people. He will even fail to suppress the act of robbery and theft.

Zhabdrung was remarkably skilled at applying a range of techniques to effectively engage with individuals of diverse temperaments and personalities. Like a master shape-shifter, he possessed the ability to embody the energies of each of the four spiritual activities. When employing wrathful activities, he could take on the appearance of a fierce demon; for pacifying activities, he exuded the warmth and kindness of a gentle lamb.

While certain aspects of Zhabdrung's behavior and abilities may challenge the beliefs of some readers, it is essential to remember that the conduct of a bodhisattva transcends our limited human understanding. Bodhisattvas continually work for the betterment of all sentient beings, often displaying actions that might seem unorthodox from a conventional standpoint. As stated in the tantric text *The Attainments Fully Expressed by the Vajra Family*,[19] even the buddhas are pleased when individuals uphold the teachings of Buddha and work for the benefit of others. This holds true even if it requires the use of esoteric practices that might be perceived as wrathful. Zhabdrung embodied this principle in every aspect of his being. His unique approach to serving others is a testament to the profound spiritual wisdom he possessed and his thorough understanding of the human condition.

The life of Zhabdrung serves as a prime example of the compassionate activities of a bodhisattva. Following the death of Pema Karpo in 1592, circumstances required someone with superior spiritual qualities to continue his vital unfinished work. By drawing upon quotes from Buddha Maitreya, Tsang Khenchen lists three reasons to illustrate why Pema Karpo reincarnated in the form of Zhabdrung.

First, fervent prayers from numerous highly advanced beings, including Zhabdrung's grandfather Mipham Chogyal, played an important role in attracting Pema Karpo's rebirth. In Buddhist belief, such prayers exert a potent magnetic force for the rebirth of great masters. Tantric scriptures emphasize the importance of prayers, specifically for requesting the rebirth of a bodhisattva, since bodhisattvas possess the ability to choose if and in what form they will be reborn.

Second, prior to his passing, Pema Karpo, despite not belonging to the Drukpa bloodline, expressed his intention to be reborn as the son of Tenpai Nyima (Zhabdrung's father) within the Drukpa hereditary lineage. According to the teachings of Buddha Maitreya, bodhisattvas always fulfill their promises when it benefits others.

Last, as a tenth-bhumi bodhisattva, Pema Karpo had transcended the influence of karma and gained the power to determine his rebirth into the Drukpa hereditary lineage, illustrating his immense spiritual power and altruistic motivation. When bodhisattvas choose to be reborn, they carefully select the beings they can benefit the most, as well as the circumstances of their birth, including their parents and birthplace. It appears that Pema Karpo chose to be reborn as Zhabdrung in a setting where he could serve the people of Bhutan, propagate the teachings of Buddha, and create favorable conditions for the continuity of these endeavors well into the future.

You may even know someone who exhibits some of the qualities described above. Bodhisattvas defy stereotypes. They need not be a high lama, adhere to a particular dress code, or even identify with a specific religion. These labels are merely social constructs. Bodhisattvas navigate the world with the singular goal of benefiting others and liberating sentient beings from the cycle of birth and death. According to Tsang Khenchen, bodhisattvas who manifest as ordinary individuals during times of profound turmoil or in eras marked by spiritual neglect—such as our present age—are considered far superior to those existing solely in the spiritual realm.

A highly advanced spiritual being could take the form of a tramp on the streets of New York or a beggar in the slums of Calcutta. They might identify as Buddhist, Jewish, Hindu, Christian, Muslim, or with no religion at all. They could be your local cashier or door-to-door salesperson. It is possible. But one thing is for sure: These highly evolved spiritual beings manifest in incarnations where they can provide the most benefit to others. Rather than be captivated by outer appearances and labels, it is important to observe a person's actions and behavior. You never know; you might be staring a bodhisattva in the face.

What Is a Buddha?

Buddha means "awakened one"—a being who has transcended the ten bhumis, reaching the highest level of realization where there is nothing left to attain. This enlightened state, known in Mahayana Buddhism as the path of perfection or no more learning, involves the purification of all negative aspects, known as obscurations. A buddha has transcended the influence of emotions such as desire, anger, and jealousy, and attained a timeless state of spiritual liberation, free from the effects of karma. A buddha simply is.

In contrast, unenlightened beings are both physically and mentally bound by their karma. According to Buddhism, beings are born, then they live, die, and are reborn into realms determined by their actions and thoughts. Since it is impossible for an unenlightened being to perceive a reality beyond the constraints of karma, understanding certain spiritual concepts may require suspending one's disbelief.

The historical Buddha of our time was born as Prince Siddhartha Gautama, who later became Shakyamuni Buddha, the sage from the Shakya clan, after attaining enlightenment. He was born approximately 2,600 years ago in the ancient Indian village of Lumbini, now a sacred site nestled in the lush Terai region of present-day Nepal. According to the Pali canon, the oldest known transcript of Buddha's teachings, Shakyamuni Buddha was the twenty-eighth buddha in a line of enlightened beings. Born into a Hindu family and belonging to a prominent and respected clan in ancient India, he laid the groundwork for what we now recognize as Buddhism. At the heart of his teachings lies the realization that life is inherently marked by suffering. Shakyamuni Buddha identified that both negative and positive emotions and experiences contribute to this suffering. Attachments to people, desires, and material possessions inevitably lead to loss, decay, and thus change—a concept in Buddhism known as impermanence. From this understanding, he unveiled a path to transcend this cycle of suffering and attain enlightenment, or buddhahood. These foundational teachings, encapsulated in the Four Noble Truths,[20] form the bedrock of Buddhist philosophy.

What Is Enlightenment?

This is the burning question! How can one possibly put into words an experience that one has no experiential knowledge of? It's like expecting a blind person to understand color or a deaf person to know what music sounds like. Impossible, right? What we can do is illuminate the concept from various angles, painting a picture that offers glimpses into a state that seekers on the Buddhist path and certain other spiritual traditions strive to attain.

But let's momentarily digress to examine my own encounter with an otherworldly state of mind, an occurrence I'm sure is a lot more common than we realize but is often dismissed and rarely spoken about. In the early 2000s during my first visit to Bodhgaya, India—the place where Buddha gained enlightenment—I had an unusual experience that made me contemplate whether there was actually more to this life than meets the eye. Was I seeing things clearly or was my vision obscured? Ever since that trip, such questions have arisen within my mind from time to time. I was neither a spiritual pilgrim nor a Buddhist when I first set foot in Bodhgaya. I had come because it was one of the places highlighted in my Indian guidebook. I loved everything about India—the vibrant colors, the constant harassment by beggars, the cacophony of sounds blended with the mix of smells both sweet and pungent. It made me feel exhilaratingly alive and completely free.

While loitering around the dusty streets, drinking chai (sweet, spicy Indian tea) from handmade clay cups, and devouring the scrumptious Indian curries that I couldn't get enough of, I befriended Krishna, a taxi driver who could speak English. He was a relatively tall, lanky guy with a small angular face, a leathery complexion, and hair slicked back with spicy-scented hair oil, which looked more like he hadn't washed his hair in months—maybe he hadn't! Despite this, he wore a glowing smile, and I intuitively trusted him. When he offered to take me to a cave on the outskirts of the town of Bodhgaya, where he claimed Buddha had meditated, it sounded interesting, so off I went, not questioning his intentions or claims. Fortunately he ended up being an honest, friendly guy. He took me to where he promised, did not try to sell me any of the tacky souvenirs, and did not try to overcharge me for the ride!

The bumpy road snaked its way through mud-brick hamlets frozen in time since the era of Buddha. Excited groups of children with perpetual runny noses caught a glimpse of us and dashed outside, flashing their innocent smiles and furiously waving as we rushed by. For a fleeting moment I felt like a celebrity! After thirty minutes we arrived at a very barren rocky landscape. Krishna parked his taxi in the shade of a neem tree and pointed to the top of a long pathway. "You walk up here, and you find Buddha meditation cave," he said in a matter-of-fact tone. As I made my way up the winding, narrow path, I sensed that I was being trailed by a group of silent beggars. I knew I would leave the place much poorer than when I arrived, but the experience was all part and parcel of being a visitor to India.

Once I reached the destination and the beggars had gotten what they wanted, we parted ways, and I entered the dimly lit cave. Luckily the area was devoid of tourists, so I had the place to myself, probably because it was the height of summer and no one—other than myself—was brave enough to book a trip at this time! I made myself comfortable in front of a statue of an emaciated golden Buddha. The atmosphere seemed extremely holy, so I decided to honor the present moment and sit in meditation, recalling the techniques I had been taught in meditation classes that I had attended during my university days.

Time seemed to be irrelevant as I was engulfed in a cocoon of all-consuming peace. What I remember of this experience was the absence of thoughts and emotions. I was floating in a kind of space or void, a vacuum of timelessness with no past and no future—purely the now. Then in what felt like the opening of a window and the letting in of a gust of crisp, clean air, I sensed that clouds were being swept aside to reveal a vivid blue sky, radiating in all its brilliance. The feelings I felt were of pure joy and peace with a razor-sharp awareness that I had never experienced before—a spaciousness that was both boundless and liberating. There was no fear, just pure bliss.

I wished to remain indefinitely in this heightened sense of awareness, since it felt good. Then as quickly as my mind had entered this space, I exited it with the sound of Indian music coming from my right side. I sank into distraction. I hadn't noticed the disheveled young man who had been lurking in the shadows when I entered the cave. Suddenly emotions of annoyance and anger arose, and my awareness crumbled. *Who is this man? Why is he disturbing my peace? Just go away and leave me alone to meditate.* Thoughts of disdain flooded my mind. I was back to square one, though with the additional, inexplicable experience in the cave, the memories of which have never left me.

Many years later, after I had entered onto the Buddhist path, I would learn that the essence of meditation was awareness and that the feelings of joy and peace were mere by-products. We must never try to seek these states. We should just relax and let go, since the more we rationalize what should happen, the more our capacity to recognize our own awareness dwindles. I have often wondered if I had had a glimpse of pure perception, of nonconceptual awareness, or what is called enlightenment. Is this what highly realized masters rest in for long periods of time? This question often plagued my thoughts. Had I experienced a momentary glimpse of naked awareness, or what Buddhists call the buddha nature or the union of emptiness and clarity? That spontaneous experience certainly caught me by surprise, and at the time, I did not know if it was a beneficial experience or not. It created more perplexity in my mind than clarity, but over time, this and other experiences have made more sense. What I encountered in the cave has certainly informed my views of what enlightenment might possibly look like.

I later discovered that this cave was the final place Buddha spent meditating in extreme asceticism before he descended to the plains of Bodhgaya and gained enlightenment under the famous bodhi tree. The cave is known as Dungeshwari, or the Mahakala cave, and sits high on Pragbodhi hill. I attributed my experience there to the sacred nature of the place rather than any contribution from my side. The heightened energetic vibration of the spiritual site seemed to be the primary contributing factor to my experience, leaving an indelible imprint on my mind as to what was possible. It showed me that if I, a carefree non-Buddhist traveler, could enter a cave and experience such a state of euphoria, then we all can. It is within our grasp if only we could rid our mind of all expectations and spend some time just letting go and sitting still in the now.

Buddhism teaches that the key to liberation lies inside ourselves. Holy places, items of worship, and spiritual teachers merely serve as inspiration or tools to uncover the wisdom and potential inherent in each one of us.

Many of us understand enlightenment as "something to get," as if it were something to possess or a state outside of ourselves—a heightened awareness we strive for. Yes and no. It certainly represents a higher state of awareness. Buddha realized, however, that the notion of enlightenment should not be grasped. While meditating in the Mahakala cave, he deprived his body of all essential nourishment as he was trying too hard to reach the end goal. He noticed his mind grasping for this outcome, lacking relaxation and practicing an imbalanced approach. He had too much expectation. He eventually realized he was following an extreme path, which he concluded was not the correct path to follow.

The Buddhist master Chögyam Trungpa Rinpoche speaks about not forgetting those glimpses of enlightenment when you go back to samsaric normality. I certainly didn't! He further emphasizes that if you try to nurse and cultivate those glimpses, you actually push them further away. In fact, whatever glimpses or experiences we get of an enlightened state, we should let them go. The grabbing onto these temporary experiences (known as *nyam* in Tibetan), or what some call "spiritual candy," and the desire to recreate them, then becomes a major obstacle. It is like you have expectations of a result, or try too hard, just as Buddha had done in the Mahakala cave, and you wander further away from your goal of enlightenment. Instead, reaching enlightenment requires genuine realization (known as *tokpa* in Tibetan), which can be attained through meditational guidance provided by an authentic spiritual master. He states that each and every one of us has the potential to experience glimpses of pure awareness or enlightenment. The trick is to remain open in the present moment, void of any expectations.

Buddha ultimately realized that he needed to simply rest in the present moment, free from doubt, ego, and expectation. This realization is somewhat paradoxical as our perception of life often involves moving from point A to point B in a linear sequence rather than delving directly into the depths of the present moment. He then left the cave and meditated beneath the legendary bodhi tree, where he carefully investigated his mind. Through this practice he achieved enlightenment and uncovered what had been inside him all along—buddha nature. The rest, as they say, is history!

I firmly believe that each of us possesses buddha nature, that spark that is an integral part of the divine whole. It is the aspect of ourselves that is all-knowing, inherently compassionate, innately pure, and exists spontaneously. Uncovering this nature is within our reach—we can peel away the layers of masks we've hidden behind for countless lifetimes. By practicing stillness—without overanalyzing or relying solely on our intellect—we can access fleeting glimpses of this buddha nature. These snapshots into the enlightened mind, even if for a moment, gradually become longer by following the teachings of Buddha. This is the core of Buddha's teachings.

As we calm our minds, heighten our awareness, and shed our masks, our ability to reside in a state of ultimate bliss lengthens. This is a state where we perceive the true nature of reality without passing judgment or making comparisons of good and bad, beautiful and ugly, or rich and poor. We see beyond projections, judgments, and false beliefs, and glimpse the unadulterated truth. This is why practicing—not just reading books, sitting on a fancy meditation cushion at Dharma teachings, or donning a maroon shawl bought from our spiritual jaunts to Kathmandu—is crucial. It is through authentic Buddhist meditation practices that we can begin to peel away the layers that have long concealed our buddha nature. Enlightenment is achieved through the transformative power of meditation and guidance, which constitute the path to realization.

Buddha taught extensively about the importance of purging our inner defilements—such as hatred, jealousy, and greed—to transcend our ego, or "I." He emphasized the virtues of honesty, not stealing, and sincerity, urging us not to deceive others by showing two faces.

The journey to enlightenment culminates in the ten bhumis, but it begins with a conscious decision to embrace compassion. Subsequently individuals can commit to a spiritual practice that fosters acceptance of the world and its diverse behaviors just as they are. This awareness brings about a deeper understanding of any situation, allowing us to remain unfazed by the tumultuous nature of life.

Take a step back and observe, be humble and practice, and surely you'll get longer glimpses of what is commonly referred to as the state of enlightenment. Don't forget to laugh and not take things too seriously, including yourself! If we can apply a humorous perspective to attacks on our ego—such as when we are hurt, offended, or embarrassed—we can harness this pain and transform it into wisdom. Becoming enlightened is simply being without judgment. It's a return to our true essence—a spark of the infinite within everyone's reach.

As the late-afternoon sun bathed the landscape in a warm golden hue and cast long shadows over the distant hills, I made my way down the rocky pathway to the welcoming smile of Krishna, who had escaped the scorching heat by napping in the shade for most of the day. During the bouncy ride along the deeply rutted dirt roads and back through the clusters of mud-brick houses to my hotel, I felt the undercurrents of both confusion and wonder bubbling to the surface of my mind. I remember glancing down at the dog-eared guidebook that had been my trusty companion, my only companion, since entering India. The book's title was *Incredible India*. I let out a faint laugh. Life is certainly full of twists and turns, and little did I know what was in store for me then—Bhutan, and finally, finding my spiritual teacher.

A Glimpse of Buddhist Cosmology

The world is an infinite sphere, whose center is everywhere and whose circumference is nowhere.

BLAISE PASCAL, French mathematician and philosopher

Understanding the depth of Zhabdrung's spiritual accomplishment requires recognizing the extensive time frame needed to progress along the bodhisattva path to the tenth bhumi. To do so, it's essential to touch on Buddhist cosmology, examining the formation of universes and the cycles within cycles. Through this exploration, the magnitude of Zhabdrung's attainment becomes abundantly clear, showcasing the exceptional individual that he was.

In Buddhist cosmology, mandala-like universes are described as concentric oceans and mountains surrounding a central peak known as Mount Meru, which Buddhists, Hindus, and Jains believe is Mount Kailash in western Tibet. These universes follow a cyclical expansion, growth, contraction, and degeneration, resembling certain contemporary scientific thought such as the big bounce hypothesis, which suggests that the universe could have originated from a single point, expanded, then contracted, and cycled through eons. Just as individual sentient beings undergo cycles of birth, death, and rebirth, so do entire universes.

According to Buddhist thought, there exist countless world systems or universes, each undergoing an eternal cycle of formation, existence, disintegration, and destruction. This perpetual process involves the continuous existence, disintegration, and annihilation of these worlds, followed by their re-formation in an endless cycle. These distinct stages or time periods are referred to as kalpas in Sanskrit, or eons/cosmic cycles in English. It is important to note that Buddhist cosmology acknowledges various lengths of kalpas, corresponding to different durations of time, a concept also present in Hindu cosmology.

However, the birth and destruction of universes do not occur simultaneously. When one universe reaches its end, another emerges, while countless others are at various stages of evolution or dissolution. Additionally, the mindstream of beings reincarnating across these universes and planes of existence persists, undergoing transformation rather than annihilation. Thus, even if the bodies they inhabit are destroyed, they are reborn, determined by their karma, in different realms. This process, known as reincarnation, can occur in the same universe or even in entirely different universes.

A kalpa represents an inconceivably vast stretch of time, beyond the grasp of ordinary human comprehension. To illustrate this, Buddhist scriptures employ metaphors. The largest known kalpa, a mahakalpa, is said to be the time it takes an individual to empty a walled city (the circular distance that a royal army can march in a day) full of poppy seeds by removing one seed every one hundred years! This largest unit of time is estimated to be around 1.28 trillion Earth years.

At the culmination of a mahakalpa, the universe undergoes complete destruction, initiating a new mahakalpa and perpetuating the cycle of expansion and destruction indefinitely. To put this into perspective, texts originating from the historic Buddha assert that reaching the highest level of a bodhisattva, the tenth bhumi, requires the accumulation of merit and wisdom of three mahakalpas, equivalent to a staggering 3.84 trillion years!

It is essential to recognize that the human mind, in its unenlightened state, perceives reality through a dualistic lens. We tend to categorize phenomena into opposing pairs, such as good versus evil or light versus dark. This dualistic perception limits our understanding, preventing us from grasping the penetrating insights held by enlightened beings who perceive reality as an interconnected illusion, part of an infinite and indivisible whole. Furthermore, our linear conceptualization of life serves as another barrier to understanding the vast time frames depicted in Buddhist cosmology.

While these concepts may initially appear incomprehensible given our rational worldview, it is crucial to acknowledge that our resistance often stems from a lack of deep spiritual awareness. When exploring the concepts of Buddhist time periods and cosmology, it can be beneficial to momentarily set aside our preconceived notions about the formation of worlds and universes. Temporarily embracing these ideologies might facilitate a more open-minded acceptance of these profound ideas

Having invested 3.84 trillion years to reach the tenth bhumi, it is no wonder that Zhabdrung left an indelible mark on the minds of countless individuals. His captivating story as a bodhisattva with superhuman abilities is intricately interwoven with universal themes of karma and reincarnation, making his life story as relevant today as it was four centuries ago. Throughout the ages, great Buddhist masters made accurate prophecies about his appearance and remarkable achievements, affirming his karmic destiny and the profound impact he would have on Bhutan and its people.

CHAPTER 3

The Prophecies

As far back as our sources can take us, across all cultures, legends and spiritual texts have been enriched by intriguing prophecies imparted by revered spiritual figures. These prophecies often foretold the coming of a great being or a significant world event.

There is no denying that the art of prophesying forms an important aspect of Tibetan Buddhism. Of great significance is that every buddha is required to have been prophesied by another buddha while on the bodhisattva path. This includes details such as when they would become enlightened, the name they would be known by, and who their first disciples would be. Many Buddhist masters, hidden texts, objects, and teaching lineages have been validated by prophecies inspired through visions, dreams, omniscience, or favorable signs known as *tendrel*.

The significance of Zhabdrung Ngawang Namgyal, particularly his importance to Bhutan, is profoundly evident. A long trail of prophecies shed light on Zhabdrung's deep connection to Bhutan, emphasizing his spiritual greatness and ambitious nation-building efforts. These prophecies, often cryptic yet profound, reveal his destined role in shaping Bhutan's unique cultural and spiritual heritage. Remarkably, many of these prophecies were made well before his arrival in Bhutan in 1616, with some dating back as far as the eighth century. For those who hold even the slightest belief in the spiritual dimension, these prophecies leave no doubt about Zhabdrung's karmic connection to this ancient Himalayan kingdom.

Many great Buddhist masters, including Guru Rinpoche, Tsangpa Gyare, and Pema Karpo, made significant prophecies about Zhabdrung's life. These predictions highlight both Zhabdrung's repute as a skilled spiritual practitioner and his destined role in Bhutan. Their existence reveals that he was no ordinary human being but someone preordained to lay a solid foundation for Bhutan's prosperity.

By the seventeenth century, Bhutan found itself fragmented among numerous ruling clans and noble families, leading to a landscape marked by ongoing feuds and internal division. Despite the comings and goings of acclaimed Buddhist masters from Tibet, none were able to bring tranquility to the land or lead it forward. However, the arrival of Zhabdrung Ngawang Namgyal changed everything. Zhabdrung was not merely a fleeing Buddhist monk from Ralung but a figure destined to unify the land. His arrival amid political turmoil marked a pivotal moment, ushering in a new era of peace and unity. Rather than being deterred by the challenges he faced, Zhabdrung embraced his calling and seized the opportunity to settle, protect, and unite the land and its people, transforming adversity into a peaceful Buddhist nation.

Guru Rinpoche, also known as Padmasambhava, was the first to prophesy the coming of Zhabdrung. A renowned tantric Buddhist master from the eighth century, he formally introduced the teachings of Vajrayana Buddhism to Bhutan around 746 C.E. Zhabdrung is widely believed to be an emanation of Guru Rinpoche, further strengthening his connection to the spiritual heritage of the nation.

Venerated as the Second Buddha throughout the Himalayan region, Guru Rinpoche was a Buddhist saint revered by emperors and common people alike. While chapter 4 will provide a brief account of his life and deeds, our focus here is on the significant prophecies he and others made about Zhabdrung. These ancient prophecies often reference Zhabdrung using different names. To fully comprehend their meaning and deepen our understanding of Zhabdrung, we must first explore the origins and significance of the names by which he was known.

Decoding Zhabdrung's Various Names

During these ancient times, it was customary for learned Tibetan Buddhist masters to be recognized by multiple names, each highlighting distinct qualities or achievements at different stages of their lives. While this practice was common, it can lead to confusion.

Zhabdrung was linked with several names, each symbolizing unique aspects of his character. In a prophecy attributed to Guru Rinpoche, he was called Dudjom Dorji, "Indestructible Subduer of Evil," a name befitting his reputation as a skilled esoteric practitioner capable of shape-shifting to confront and tame negative forces. Guru Rinpoche also spoke of Zhabdrung's profound karmic connection with Mahakala, the spiritual guardian, whom he frequently invoked to conduct wrathful bodhisattva activities. Additionally, Zhabdrung was addressed as Druk (Thunder Dragon), a nod to his lineage. Other names such as Namgyal and Nga were used, referencing his given name, Ngawang Namgyal. Last, he was referred to as the King of Lotus, suggesting his identification as Chenrezig, a bodhisattva often symbolized by a lotus flower.

Furthermore, Pema Karpo, Zhabdrung's previous incarnation, referred to him as the Dharma king. Interestingly this title was also adopted for him by the two Portuguese Jesuit missionaries during their visit to Bhutan in 1627. They were hosted by Zhabdrung for many months, addressing him as Dharma Raja. Their use of *raja*, an Indian term for a hereditary king or ruler, suggests their admiration for Zhabdrung's diplomatic prowess, charisma, and leadership in Bhutan's predominant Buddhist faith. Additionally, Pema Karpo also referred to him as Ngagi Wangpo Nampar Gyalwai De, meaning "the All-Victorious Lord of Speech," a title that was also conferred upon Zhabdrung by a distinguished Sakya master during his enthronement.

As a young child, Zhabdrung often declared himself to be Drukchen Thamche Khyenpa, "All-Knowing Great Drukpa," a title previously held by Pema Karpo, whom many believed Zhabdrung to be a reincarnation of. Ancient texts mention a figure called Drukgyal

Drung, believed to be Tenzin Drukgyal, who recalls hearing from those who cared for Zhabdrung as a child that his nature closely resembled that of Pema Karpo.

At the time of his birth, Zhabdrung was named Mipham Tenzin Dorji by his father and grandfather who was the sixteenth hereditary throne holder of Ralung, the main seat of the Drukpa Kargyu order. This name translates to "Invincible Dharma Holder." As Zhabdrung matured and received his lay Buddhist vows at the age of eight, his grandfather bestowed upon him the name Ngawang Tenzin Nampar Gyalwa Jigme Drakpa Chog Thamche Le Nampar Gyalwa Pal Zangpo, meaning "Fearless Lord of Speech, Renowned Dharma Holder in all Directions, All Victorious, Glorious, and Excellent," in recognition of his exceptional proficiency in Buddhist studies. Eventually these elaborate names, along with the name foretold in Guru Rinpoche's prophecies, were simplified, and he came to be known as Ngawang Tenzin Namgyal or simply Ngawang Namgyal.

In 1606, at nearly thirteen years of age, Zhabdrung ascended the throne of Ralung, succeeding his grandfather who had passed away a few years earlier. During this time, Sakya Dagchen Wangpo, a prominent Sakya master and head of the Sakya school, offered a long-life prayer in Zhabdrung's honor. In this prayer he bestowed upon Zhabdrung the elaborate name Gyalwai Se Chog Ngagi Wang-chuk Chog Thamche Le Nampar Gyalwa Tashi Drakpai Gyaltshen Pal Zangpo, meaning "the Supreme Son of the Buddhas, Lord of Speech Victorious from all Directions, and a Banner of Auspicious Fame and Glory." Grounded in the teachings of Buddha, this elaborate name was believed to confer blessings upon those who heard it. Tenzin Drukgyal, the *umze* (chant master) of Ralung at the time, even carried this name in a charm box around his neck as a form of protection.

During this period, it was customary in the regions of Tibet and Bhutan to use specific titles for prominent spiritual figures. In Tibetan Buddhist culture, the title Zhabdrung was tradition-ally reserved for highly respected lamas, particularly those with a hereditary lineage connection. In the Khon lineage of the Sakya school of Tibetan Buddhism, it served as a general honorific title for senior lamas. However, in Bhutan it held a more nuanced meaning, signifying great reverence and spiritual authority, translating to "At Whose Feet One Submits."

The great Sakya master who bestowed the elaborate title on Zhabdrung during his enthronement also conferred the title of Zhabdrung upon both Ngawang Namgyal and his father at the consecration ceremony of a statue of Pema Karpo. This marked the beginning of the widespread use of the name Zhabdrung Ngawang Namgyal for the son.

The intense dispute over the reincarnation of Pema Karpo led one of the Tsang Desis, Karma Tenchong Wangpo, to designate Zhabdrung as the throne holder of the Drukpas, while the other candidate, Pagsam Wangpo, was named Drukpa tulku. This led to considerable tension between their respective followers, each side firmly maintaining that their own candidate was the true reincarnation of their revered master, Pema Karpo.

The Drukpa Kargyu order, established by Tsangpa Gyare, extended its influence across three regions of the Tibetan Plateau: Upper, Middle, and Lower. The Middle Drukpa branch, which later flourished in Bhutan, was led by Tsangpa Gyare's nephew and student, Onre Dharma Senge, following the uncle-nephew succession system common in many Tibetan Buddhist traditions of the time. This branch became known as the Palden Drukpa Kargyu order in Bhutan, and the title Palden Drukpa Rinpoche was bestowed upon Tsangpa Gyare and his subsequent reincarnations, including Zhabdrung. Therefore, another name Zhabdrung was known by was Palden Drukpa Rinpoche or Palden Drukpa Rinpoche, Zhabdrung Ngawang Namgyal.

Upon Zhabdrung's arrival in Bhutan, he encountered opposition from various quarters, including the Tsang Desi Phuntsok Namgyal, the secular leader of the U-Tsang region, and a group of dissident lamas known as the Lama Khag Nga (a group of lamas with ancestry stemming from five lamas). These members of the Lama Khag Nga originated from ancestors with origins in five Buddhist sects in

Tibet[21] who had established their presence in Bhutan between the twelfth and fifteenth centuries. Despite these challenges, Zhabdrung eventually overcame their opposition through his superior spiritual powers, earning him the title Thuchen Chokyi Gyalpo Ngawang Namgyal, which translates to "the Dharma King Ngawang Namgyal, the One with Great Power."

Before exploring Zhadbdrung's story, it is important to understand that the miraculous and at times assertive powers that Zhabdrung displayed were the result of his absolute dedication to and mastery of meditative and yogic practices. These powers were not used for malevolent purposes but rather as means to convey spiritual messages to his followers and adversaries. As discussed in the section on bodhisattvas, manifesting wrathful activities is a "skillful means"[22] of assisting others.

The preceding account provides an overview of the names and titles attributed to Zhabdrung at various points in his lifetime, providing a preliminary insight into this remarkable figure. Although he is commonly known as Zhabdrung, it is important to recognize his formal title to honor his significance in both historic and spiritual contexts. This title symbolizes the utmost respect accorded to him.

His formal title is Palden (Pal) Drukpa Rinpoche Chabgon Ngawang Namgyal. In the name Palden, *pal* is an honorific term meaning "glorious." *Drukpa* in this context refers to the lineage holder of the Drukpa Kargyu order, the Thunder Dragon school of Buddhism. *Rinpoche* means "precious one," and *Chabgon* means "His Holiness" or "the source of refuge and protection." Ngawang Namgyal is the name he had been known by since his youth and the name prophesied by Guru Rinpoche. For the purposes of familiarity and uniformity, Zhabdrung Ngawang Namgyal (Zhabdrung for short) will be used throughout the book.

Let's now uncover these fascinating prophecies that shed light on this historical figure, hinting at Zhabdrung's destined role in Bhutan.

Prophecies by Guru Rinpoche (Eighth Century)

Guru Rinpoche is widely revered as an emanation of bodhisattva Chenrezig, a belief affirmed in ancient texts such as those by Pema Karpo praising Guru Rinpoche. In his brief autobiography, the *Kathang Duepa*, Guru Rinpoche unequivocally identifies himself as Chenrezig. Therefore it is not surprising that Guru Rinpoche made several significant prophecies about the arrival of Zhabdrung, who was also recognized as an emanation of Chenrezig. Remarkably these prophecies were made centuries before Zhabdrung's arrival in Bhutan.

The prophecies attributed to Guru Rinpoche provide compelling evidence of Zhabdrung's predestined spiritual role in Bhutan. They highlight that his manifestation was intended solely to benefit sentient beings, serve as a conduit for disseminating the precious teachings of the Buddha, and unify the sacred land, referred to as Lhomon or Lhorong at the time these prophecies were made (see glossary of names).

Below is a list of prophecies attributed to Guru Rinpoche, found in various scriptural texts:

1. In the *Tantra of the Great Compassionate One Who Liberates All from Samsara*, Guru Rinpoche states,

> Known as Dudjom Dorji,
> The lord of the secret teachings
> A great liberator will appear,
> A mere sight of him will close the doors of suffering to the
> lower realms.

2. From the *Dudul Ter Lung* (*Predictions from the Treasure Text Subduing Maras*), Guru Rinpoche states,

> An emanation of Naropa[23] by the name of Nga will arise,
> By the teaching of the Mahamudra, sentient beings will be
> ripened.

3. Guru Rinpoche further states,

> On the trunk of the mountain that resembles an elephant,
> A great being by the name of Namgyal will appear.

The prophecy most likely refers to Punakha, a district in western Bhutan. As depicted in the accompanying photo, the mountain in question bears a striking resemblance to an elephant's head and trunk. It was precisely at this point, at the confluence of two rivers, that Zhabdrung went on to construct Punakha Dzong in 1637. Also known as Pungthang Dewachenpoi Phodrang, or "the Celestial Palace of Great Bliss Resting on the Ground of Heaps," it served as the main seat of the Drukpa Kargyu order in Bhutan during Zhabdrung's time.

4. In the *Tagsham Gongdu* liturgy, Guru Rinpoche states,

> Known as Druk, self-illuminating essence of the sky (referring to the sun),
> A renowned being by the name Nga [Ngawang] will appear in the direction of Lhorong [Bhutan].

5. In the text known as the *Kulu Khari*, Guru Rinpoche states,

> Prominent in the lineage of Gya, famous also in the Tsang region,
> The wisdom emanation of the Lotus King,[24] Flashing like lightning in the region of Ngari and Tsang,
> To the south of U-Tsang his fame will spread like the dragon's roar of thunder.[25]
> Possessing these birthmarks on his body such as a *vajra*[26] on his head, a double vajra on his palms, the Dharma wheel on his hands and feet, and the syllable Hung (ཧཱུྃ) on his leg, and a mole in his navel,
> He is undeterred by unpredictable behavior and possesses a resolute meditative concentration as solid as a diamond.

Mountain resembling an elephant head and trunk in Punakha (Photo © 2024 Sasha Wakefield)

> He will always seek counsel from me [Guru Rinpoche],
> Anyone encountering his presence will be born in the blissful realm.[27]

In the same text, Guru Rinpoche prophesied the appearance of an emanation of Chenrezig in Bhutan, commonly believed to be Zhabdrung. This belief is reinforced by the well-documented connection between Zhabdrung and Mahakala:

> In the degenerative times, the southern valley will be subdued by an emanation of Chenrezig who will have a strong karmic connection to the spiritual guardian Yeshe Gonpo (Mahakala) and, as a result, this great being will successfully abate the fear of foreign invasion and spread the buddhadharma.

6. Yet another prophecy by Guru Rinpoche states,

A renowned being by the name of Ngawang who is accomplished in divine powers, who holds the throne of Mon,[28] will benefit both the people from Tibet and Druk [Bhutan].

7. Similarly, in the text known as *Gathering of Victorious Ones: The Accomplishment of Life*, Guru Rinpoche states,

The one from Ralung, named Ngawang, who is an emanation of great bliss, will divert wars from the surrounding areas. Merely seeing his face will close the door to the lower realms.

8. In Guru Rinpoche's prophecies on both Taktsang Monastery in Paro, and Punakha Dzong, he respectively states that "Taktsang will be cared for by a vajra holder" (an accomplished Vajrayana practitioner) of which he was, and in the Punakha area…"on the front side of a majestic mountain that looks like an elephant, a great being with the name Namgyal will appear at a palace of great bliss" (referring to Punakha Dzong, known as the Celestial Palace of Great Bliss).

9. A treasure text (*terma*) composed by Guru Rinpoche states, "In between two rivers, the life-force castle of the Drukpas will appear" (referring either to Cheri Monastery where Zhabdrung established the first Drukpa Kargyu monastic body in Bhutan around 1621 in northern Thimphu or Punakha Dzong, the seat of his rule).

10. Numerous tales have been written about Guru Rinpoche's clairvoyant powers. The incident below serves as an indication of Zhabdrung's destined role and work in Bhutan.

While meditating in Maratika cave in eastern Nepal, Guru Rinpoche engaged in a sacred long-life practice alongside his consort. Accompanied by spiritually powerful female celestial beings known as *dakinis*, he proclaimed, "If a fortress is built between two rivers, the dual system of governance of the Drukpas will remain forever."

Zhabdrung Rinpoche's dual system of governance became one of his hallmark contributions. Interestingly, he built a fortress between two rivers, which served as the spiritual and administrative center of his newly formed state. Even before Guru Rinpoche's time, the seventh-century Tibetan Dharma king Songtsen Gampo prophesied that "at the end of time, when the teachings of Chenrezig flourish, a person of destiny and karmic merit will bring immense benefit to beings. His activities will extend from the south to the center." When considering all the prophecies, these words, though ambiguous, appear to point to Zhabdrung. Many prophecies were urging Dharma practitioners to go to the south (Bhutan) where the teachings of the Buddha would take hold, but it was Zhabdrung who ultimately made a lasting impact.

Finally, according to a prophecy by Gya Jampel Sangwa, a devoted disciple (heart disciple) of Guru Rinpoche, it was foretold that the Gya hereditary lineage, to which Zhabdrung belonged, would witness the birth of eighty-four manifestations of Chenrezig. This revelation further supports the probability of Zhabdrung being an emanation of Chenrezig (the significance of Chenrezig will be elaborated in chapter 4).

The collection of prophecies by Guru Rinpoche, along with those of other great masters of the time, preserved in ancient texts dating back over eight hundred years before Zhabdrung's birth, underscores his significance as not only a revered Buddhist master but also a figure destined to achieve remarkable accomplishments in Bhutan.

Prophecies by Tsangpa Gyare (1161–1211)

Tsangpa Gyare, the lineage founder of the Drukpa Kargyu order, prophesied his own reappearance, declaring that he would return when the lineage needed him the most. His prophecies, revealed almost four hundred years prior to Zhabdrung's birth, centered around his reincarnation as Zhabdrung and the missed encounter with a revered Buddhist lama from the Kham region just before his passing. Though these prophecies may appear enigmatic, they possess an undeniable allure that hints at a deeper reality beyond our ordinary comprehension.

During Zhabdrung's formative years in Tibet, disputes over the reincarnation of Pema Karpo sparked significant political turmoil among the Drukpas. True to Tsangpa Gyare's prophecy of returning when the lineage needed him most, it is believed that he fulfilled this prophecy by reincarnating as Zhabdrung, thus fortifying the Drukpa Kargyu lineage.

Zhabdrung held a unique position as both a Drukpa hereditary lineage holder and a reincarnation lineage holder in the Drukpa Kargyu tradition. His blood lineage can be directly traced back to Tsangpa Gyare and his nephew Onre Dharma Senge (1177-1237). Before the appearance of Tsangpa Gyare's reincarnations, the Drukpa lineage from Ralung relied solely on hereditary succession. However, with Zhabdrung's birth, as with Kunga Peljor before him, the hereditary and reincarnation lineages merged, bestowing upon Zhabdrung immense significance among the Drukpas.

A prophecy attributed to Tsangpa Gyare, documented in several reliable texts and conveyed to his nephew Onre Dharma Senge, foretells his reincarnation in Bhutan. It expressed a desire to meet a revered lama named Phajo from the Kham region of Tibet, whom he had missed encountering during his lifetime. The prophecy reads as follows:

> In the future I will also come there
> And establish the dual system [an inference that Tsangpa
>   Gyare would reincarnate as Zhabdrung],
> And at that time, tell him [Phajo] to pray for our meeting!

Phajo Drukgom Zhigpo (?1184-?1251), affectionately known as Phajo, was a significant Tibetan Buddhist saint who preceded Zhabdrung and introduced the Drukpa Kargyu teachings to Bhutan. His descendants played a vital supportive role in Zhabdrung's unification efforts and in spreading the Drukpa Kargyu teachings in western Bhutan.

This prophecy suggests that Tsangpa Gyare foresaw himself as reincarnating as Zhabdrung, underscoring the intertwined destinies of these two figures.

Tsangpa Gyare further prophesied,

> In the future, in the place of U-Tsang [central Tibet], the teachings of Buddha will not flourish in its purest form; however, in the place known as Lhorong [Bhutan], it will sustain.

He further disclosed to his nephew Onre Dharma Senge a prophecy regarding a destined individual from the Kham region of Tibet who would journey to Bhutan to propagate the Dharma, foreseeing that his teachings would greatly benefit the Buddhist tradition:

> A son from Kham is coming to Ralung but he will not meet me. You care for and teach him, then direct him to the southern valley [Bhutan] that has been blessed by Guru Rinpoche. He will be of great benefit to the buddhadharma there.

As foretold, a distinguished master indeed arrived in Bhutan from the Kham region of Tibet during the thirteenth century, introducing the Drukpa Kargyu teachings from Ralung. This revered figure was none other than Phajo Drukgom Zhigpo.

While the precise dates of Phajo's birth and passing are debated, his contributions to the spread of the Drukpa Kargyu teachings in Bhutan are undeniable. Given the name Phajo Drukgom Zhigpo (Liberated Meditator of the Druk Lineage) by his teacher Onre Dharma Senge, he excelled in the Drukpa Kargyu practice of meditation, leaving an indelible mark on Bhutanese Buddhist history.[29]

Prophecies by Pema Karpo (1527–1592)

Pema Karpo, the head of the Drukpa Kargyu lineage during his time and the reincarnation of Tsangpa Gyare, made insightful prophecies about his future reincarnation. In the solemn moments preceding Pema Karpo's passing, a hushed atmosphere enveloped the room as he imparted his last prophecy. In a tender exchange between devoted disciple and master, Zhabdrung's father, Tenpai Nyima, leaned in closely to the ailing Pema Karpo, seeking a sign of his next incarnation. In a moment that would reverberate through the ages, Pema Karpo revealed the astonishing prophecy: "I will return as your [Tenpai Nyima's] own son, destined to become a Dharma king to strengthen the Drukpa lineage."

Interestingly, Zhabdrung exhibited a striking resemblance to Pema Karpo, not only in temperament but also in intelligence. Accounts indicate that even before acquiring fluent speech, Zhabdrung would frequently declare, "I am Drukchen Thamche Khyenpa" (the All-Knowing Great Drukpa), and "I am the Drukpa lineage holder, the omniscient one." These utterances strongly imply a connection to Pema Karpo, also known as Drukchen Thamche Khyenpa, suggesting that Zhabdrung was, in all likelihood, a genuine reincarnation of Pema Karpo.

Quoting Tsang Khenchen, the following excerpt is drawn from the long-life prayer composed by Pema Karpo prior to his passing, referring to his reincarnation. It foreshadows the rise of a Dharma king and praises his exceptional spiritual qualities—a clear prophecy of the emergence of Zhabdrung.

> The foundation for the emanation of all the past victorious ones
> And the source of all future buddhas
> No different from all the present buddhas
> Is the Dharma king, may he live long.

In a passage from Pema Karpo's self-commentary, *The Magical Display of the Compassionate One*, he refers to an individual, most likely Zhabdrung, as the "second one." Within the Drukpa Kargyu lineage, only two figures, aside from the founder Tsangpa Gyare, could claim both a hereditary and reincarnation lineage connection. The first was Kunga Peljor, followed by Zhabdrung—the "second one." Pema Karpo's reference hints at Zhabdrung's crucial role in preserving and strengthening the teachings of the Drukpa Kargyu order. The passage reads as follows:

> In the future, the emanated being who holds the lineage, namely one who has power over speech and is victorious over evil (the exact meaning of the name Ngawang Namgyal), is the second one who will illuminate the essence of the teachings.

Furthermore, Tsang Khenchen extracts the following from the biography of Pema Karpo, which clearly relates to Zhabdrung:

> He is the ground from which many previous manifestations of the great compassionate Chenrezig appeared. Likewise, I [Pema Karpo] will appear as a son of the great bodhisattva, King of Yogis [Tenpai Nyima], as an emanation of the future Buddha Avalokiteshvara [Chenrezig]. I will be reborn as Prince Ngawang Namgyal, who is the source of the future generation of this [Drukpa] family. The secret qualities of his body, speech, and mind are no different from that of me (Pema Karpo). He will introduce the enlightened activities of the dual system of governance.

A Prophetic Dream

Tibetan Buddhists believe that important events are foretold in dreams. Before Zhabdrung made his way to Bhutan, he had a significant dream in which a raven appeared and flew southward, landing in an unfamiliar place. Upon his arrival in Bhutan, Zhabdrung recognized the exact location from his dream as Druk Phodrangding Lhakhang (the Castle of the Thunder Dragon), located in Pangri Zampa on the northern outskirts of Thimphu.

Sure enough, as he entered Bhutan, a raven accompanied him down the steep mountainous region and flew into an ancient cypress tree in the grounds of this temple. This raven was viewed as a spiritual guide, with many believing it to be the manifestation of the spiritual guardian Legon Jarog Dongchen, also known as Karma Mahakala, an emanation of Mahakala himself. This tale, undoubtedly foreshadowing Zhabdrung's fate in Bhutan, has become a prominent part of Bhutanese folklore, with the raven and the cypress tree now symbolizing Bhutan's national bird and tree.

Druk Phodrangding Lhakhang was established by Zhabdrung's great-great-grandfather, Ngawang Chogyal. Located in an area called Pangri Zampa, which means "an opening beside a bridge," the temple holds great historical significance. Zhabdrung's living quarters were adjacent to the main temple and comprised four floors, with his meditation chamber located on the uppermost floor. At the entrance to the temple grounds stands a towering cypress tree, believed to be the very one into whose branches the raven that guided Zhabdrung to Bhutan disappeared.

When we collectively review these prophecies, meticulously documented by revered masters in ancient Chokey texts centuries before Zhabdrung's birth, a compelling case emerges for his central role in shaping the nation-state and advancing the teachings of the

Druk Phodrangding Lhakhang, Thimphu (Photo © 2024 Sasha Wakefield)

Bridge beside
Zhabdrung's
residence at
Pangri Zampa
(Photo ©
2024 Sasha
Wakefield)

esteemed Drukpa Kargyu lineage. These prophetic insights offer strong evidence of Zhabdrung's extraordinary spiritual qualities and his destined place in the annals of history. There thus remains little doubt regarding his identity as the reincarnation of Pema Karpo and an emanation of Chenrezig—a bodhisattva teetering on the brink of enlightenment.

Equally intriguing is the recollection by his previous incarnation, Pema Karpo, of his own past lives, deepening our understanding of Zhabdrung's character and spiritual greatness, which we will now explore.

CHAPTER 4

Previous Incarnations

In my quest to learn more about Zhabdrung, I uncovered a fascinating revelation attributed to his previous incarnation, Pema Karpo. This renowned spiritual master not only prophesied his own rebirth as Zhabdrung but also recounted his previous ten lives. This insight proved essential in understanding the depth of Zhabdrung's spiritual nature, as these reincarnations and emanations signify the continuity of the same mindstream in new physical forms.

The six prominent biographies of Zhabdrung written in Chokey offer captivating glimpses into these past lives. Known in Buddhist circles as the *Thungrab Phunsum Tshogpa* (previous incarnations of Zhabdrung), these recollections are a treasure trove of spiritual insights into Zhabdrung—so much so that I found it hard to contain my excitement at the discovery!

To truly appreciate Zhabdrung's unique attributes, it is important to examine his previous lives, each being a great bodhisattva and an emanation of Chenrezig. Seeing these past lives as aspects of a single consciousness deepens our understanding of his essence, freeing us from being distracted by different names and time periods. If you prefer to jump straight into the narrative, however, you may skip this section and return to it later. For a more profound insight into Zhabdrung's spiritual nature and extraordinary capabilities, viewing these previous lives through this unified perspective is invaluable. As we will now discover, the demeanor, motivations, and accomplishments of these eleven great masters (inclusive of Pema Karpo) reveal a striking resemblance to Zhabdrung.

Chenrezig

Chenrezig (Skt. Avalokiteshvara), the bodhisattva of compassion, serves as the source of all Zhabdrung's previous incarnations. This thread of compassionate energy runs through his diverse lifetimes and is the same energy inherent in all the buddhas that have ever existed.

In the Buddhist world, Chenrezig appears in many forms: two arms, four arms, standing, sitting, male, and female. Chenrezig is even depicted with one thousand arms, one thousand eyes, and eleven heads. But what is a constant is the ever-present essence of compassion. Throughout history, Chenrezig has taken on various manifestations—including teachers, philosophers, religious leaders, kings, and ministers—to address the specific needs of sentient beings.

The story of Chenrezig is intricate and expansive, extending well beyond the scope of a single book. However, a distinct connection between Chenrezig and Zhabdrung stands out—the embodiment of Chenrezig as a figure known as Dha Yo Zhonu.

Imagine a young monk named Dha Yo Zhonu, believed to be an emanation of Chenrezig, and a disciple of Shakyamuni Buddha. Around 500 B.C.E., Buddha prophesied that Dha Yo Zhonu would be reborn in Tibet to spread the Dharma. Fast-forward to the year 1079 C.E., when a child was born who would later grow up to become a monk named Gampopa, rising to prominence as one of the most celebrated spiritual practitioners of his time. Among his various titles, one particularly relevant to the story of Chenrezig is Dha Yo Zhonu. He would later reincarnate as Zhabdrung.

Adding support to this claim, in the *Kulu Khari*, Guru Rinpoche foretold the emergence of a spiritually powerful figure in the form of Chenrezig who would bring peace to Bhutan by taming its people and averting conflicts.

Rigden Pema Karpo (176–76 B.C.E.)

The second of Zhabdrung's eleven past lives was King Rigden Pema Karpo. He was born and raised in the mythical kingdom of Shambhala, a paradise believed to exist on the edge of physical reality, accessible only to those who have attained a certain level of spiritual development. He is considered a human manifestation of enlightened qualities rather than an ordinary individual in the conventional sense.

This emanation of Chenrezig made significant contributions to both the teaching and composition of commentaries on sutras (direct teachings from the historic Buddha) and tantras (esoteric spiritual teachings), particularly those related to the bodhisattva path. He initiated the system of hereditary kingship and authored a comprehensive commentary on the Kalachakra, a complex system of Buddhist philosophy and practices encompassing various subjects such as cosmology, astrology, philosophy, meditation, and ritual practice.

Rigden Pema Karpo's contributions to the Kalachakra teachings were continued by Pema Karpo and Zhabdrung, both of whom unsurprisingly displayed a deep fascination with this field of study.

King Songtsen Gampo (c. 605–650 C.E.)

The third of Zhabdrung's eleven past lives was as King Songtsen Gampo, a central figure in Tibetan history. His reign marked a dynamic period characterized by the establishment of a robust cultural and political framework that laid the groundwork for the flourishing of Buddhism in Tibet. Songtsen Gampo was born around 605 C.E. in central Tibet, and his era coincided with a phase of imperialism in Tibetan history. Foreseen by Shakyamuni Buddha himself, Songtsen Gampo's arrival was prophesied as an emanation of Chenrezig destined to spread the Dharma in the region. He is revered as the first of the three Dharma kings of Tibet, succeeded by King Trisong Detsen and later Tritsuk Detsen (King Tri Ralpachen).

King Songtsen Gampo ascended to the throne around the age of twelve, a time when the Bon religion, an ancient animistic religion of Tibet, held sway as the dominant spiritual practice. Renowned for unifying several kingdoms into a cohesive nation, he ushered in a period where Buddhism flourished under his enlightened leadership. His diplomatic efforts extended to the neighboring regions of present-day Nepal, India, and China, fostering the spread of Buddhism and enriching Tibet culture. These societies boasted rich Buddhist traditions and advanced knowledge in science and the arts, which he recognized as valuable assets in his vision for nation-building. It is for these reasons that he was hailed as the founder or first king of the modern Tibetan Empire.

During the early years of his rule, he made a strategic move driven by spiritual and political considerations rather than romantic ideals—he married two princesses, both regarded as emanations of the goddess Tara, a female bodhisattva. These marriages were instrumental in elevating the king's cultural awareness and played a vital role in the modernization of his newly established state.

He married the first one, Princess Bhrikuti of Nepal, around 634 C.E. She brought with her the rich traditions of Himalayan Buddhism. According to legend, King Songtsen Gampo dreamed of this Nepalese princess, believed to be the emanation of Green Tara. Acting on this vision, he dispatched two of his ministers, Garab Tongtsen and Thonmi Sambhota, to seek her hand in marriage from her father.

Princess Bhrikuti's arrival came bearing a valuable dowry, including numerous Buddhist statues. Among them, the most famous was the statue of an eight-year-old Shakyamuni Buddha, known as Jowo Mikyo Dorji, which is now prominently housed in the Ramoche Temple in Lhasa. Additionally she brought a team of skilled artisans to construct Buddhist temples. With her presence, King Songtsen Gampo initiated the unification process. Encouraged by his new wife, he relocated the capital to Lhasa, which rapidly emerged as the political, economic, and cultural epicenter of the Tibetan Empire

Some time after marrying Princess Bhrikuti, King Songtsen

Gampo married Princess Wencheng, the daughter of the Tang emperor of China. She was believed to be an emanation of White Tara. Princess Wencheng's arrival brought a wealth of ancient Chinese wisdom, including sacred astrology, geomancy, literature, and medicine. She also brought with her the revered Jowo Shakyamuni statue, carried by two men, Lhaga and Luga. This statue is now housed in the Jokhang Temple in Lhasa. Princess Wencheng's presence greatly contributed to the realization of the king's vision for a modernized Tibetan Empire, encompassing social, cultural, political, and spiritual aspects.

King Songtsen Gampo was not only a skilled diplomat but also a brilliant strategist in dealing with opposing forces. He undertook the study of the Chinese language, honed his leadership skills, and significantly embraced the sacred principles found in Buddhist scriptures. During his reign, Buddhism gradually supplanted the shamanistic rituals of the Bonpas, who practiced the Bon religion.

His visionary leadership in the service of the Dharma led him to dispatch one of his ministers, Thonmi Sambhota, to the northern Indian region of Kashmir to acquire the art of writing. Inspired by this expedition, he commissioned a unique script known as *uchen*, which became the primary script for writing the Tibetan language. The introduction of this writing system facilitated the translation of numerous invaluable Buddhist texts from Sanskrit into Tibetan, thereby advancing the propagation of the Dharma and fortifying the security of his Buddhist kingdom.

According to folklore, King Songtsen Gampo undertook the monumental task of constructing 108 sacred Buddhist temples in a single day to subdue a colossal demon believed to be obstructing the spread of Buddhism across Tibet and its neighboring lands. Among these temples, Kyichu Lhakhang in Paro and Jampa Lhakhang in Bumthang, Bhutan, were strategically erected on the demon's left foot and left kneecap, respectively. According to legend, the king multiplied himself 108 times to accomplish this mind-boggling feat, a level of greatness reserved only for those who have attained the tenth bhumi.

King Songtsen Gampo is revered for his role in introducing Buddhism to Tibet and catalyzing the formation of the nascent Tibetan Empire. Under his wise leadership, Buddhism flourished, becoming deeply ingrained in Tibetan culture. He established comprehensive political, economic, cultural, and legal systems based on Buddhist principles. His visionary leadership not only unified the Tibetan Empire but also enriched its cultural and educational milieu through an appreciation of diverse foreign influences.

Shantarakshita (725–788 C.E.)

Shantarakshita (Tib. Zhiwatsho), recognized as the fourth of Zhabdrung's eleven past lives, was an eight-century Buddhist scholar from India. He was the son of the ruling king of the ancient Buddhist kingdom of Zahor, located in what is now the modern-day East Indian states of West Bengal and Bihar.

As an ordained monk with a profound understanding of Vajrayana practices, Shantarakshita served as the chief abbot of Nalanda University in Bihar, India, renowned as the largest and most prestigious among the ancient Indian Buddhist universities.

Upon arriving in Tibet at the invitation of King Trisong Detsen, Shantarakshita encountered a region marked by internal strife and opposition to the Dharma, particularly from the Bon priests. Rather than imposing his beliefs on those who resisted, he collaborated with King Trisong Detsen to invite Guru Rinpoche to Tibet with the aim of defending the Buddhist teachings and overcoming obstacles. Guru Rinpoche employed his supernatural abilities to subdue negative forces while skillfully integrating certain Bon traditions into Buddhist thought and practices to win over the people and facilitate the transition. Amid these challenges, Shantarakshita's diplomatic skills and resourcefulness shone through.

Shantarakshita collaborated with Guru Rinpoche in founding the Samye Monastery, where he ordained the first seven monks from Tibet. This monastery quickly emerged as one of the premier centers for Buddhist studies, playing a crucial role in disseminating Buddhist teachings throughout the region.

His influence, however, extended well beyond Tibet, propagating the Dharma across India, Nepal, and various Himalayan areas. Renowned for his sharp intellect and exemplary moral conduct, he was instrumental in spreading Buddhist teachings far and wide.

An intriguing legend links Shantarakshita to bodhisattva Chenrezig through a tale associated with the renowned stupa of Boudhanath in Kathmandu. According to folklore, the daughter of a Nepalese chicken keeper, inspired by Chenrezig's compassion, began the construction of this stupa with the support of her four sons. Despite her untimely demise before its completion, her sons fulfilled her dying wish to finish the stupa.

It is believed that these four sons, who prayed fervently for rebirth to serve the Dharma, were reborn as Shantarakshita, King Trisong Detsen, Guru Rinpoche, and a Tibetan minister during the same period. They are thought to have been emanations of Chenrezig, each greatly benefiting the Dharma.

Naropa (1016–1100 C.E.)

The fifth of Zhabdrung's eleven past lives was the mystic Naropa, a revered eleventh-century Buddhist scholar. Born into a Brahmin family in the northeastern part of the Indian subcontinent, Naropa renounced his life of privilege at a young age to embark on a profound spiritual journey, mirroring aspects of Shakyamuni Buddha's path. Under the guidance of the esteemed master Gaganakirti, he studied Buddhist logic, science, art, and grammar, receiving lay Buddhist ordination vows at the tender age of eight.

Upon returning home, in accordance with noble tradition, Naropa entered into an arranged marriage. He and his wife lived together for a time before mutually agreeing to pursue separate spiritual paths. Remarkably, his ex-wife would later become one of his most devoted disciples.

Having mastered various Mahayana and Vajrayana philosophies and authored numerous spiritual commentaries, he rose to prominence as one of Nalanda University's most famous scholars, following in the footsteps of his predecessor, Shantarakshita. During his eight years at Nalanda, he gained recognition for his sharp intellect, spiritual wisdom, and exceptional oratory and debating skills.

Naropa's unwavering focus on intellectual pursuits shifted dramatically around his fortieth year when an old hag materialized before him, triggering an epiphany. This mysterious woman was believed to be a dakini, the emanation of Vajrayogini, embodying complete buddhahood in female form.

After hearing the name Tilopa from this woman, Naropa was struck by an inexplicable and intense devotion toward him. Following her guidance, he embarked on a transformative journey to seek out Tilopa. This mystical encounter led Naropa to a profound realization: he understood that his comprehension of Buddhist teachings had been limited to mere intellectual understanding, devoid of a deeper spiritual realization. Recognizing the inadequacy of words to convey the essence of the spiritual path, he made the courageous decision to relinquish his prestigious position at Nalanda and abruptly abandoned his pursuit of intellectual knowledge.

As he traveled eastward, Naropa eventually encountered his root guru (primary spiritual teacher), a mere fisherman. At first Tilopa ignored him, subjecting him to a series of tests to purify his negative karma and assess his determination to tread the rigorous spiritual path. After enduring these trials, Naropa spent twelve transformative years under Tilopa's guidance, a journey that concluded with the passing of his revered guru.

Having attained the highest level of a bodhisattva, Naropa went on to teach extensively throughout the region, focusing on a meditational wisdom method known as the Six Yogas of Naropa. Today these teachings stand as core principles of yogic practice in Tibetan Buddhism, particularly in the Kagyu school, and form the basis of the three-year retreat, known as Losum Chogsum, in the Drukpa Kargyu order in Bhutan.

Naropa's teachings found their way to diverse places, from Kashmir in northern India to Zanskar in Ladakh, where he established numerous monasteries. His impact rippled across India, Nepal, and Tibet, thanks to the efforts of one of his closest disciples, Marpa.

Charged with upholding this practice lineage, Marpa facilitated the introduction of Naropa's teachings to Tibet. Through translation and dissemination efforts, he earned the name Marpa the Translator and emerged as a seminal figure in the establishment of the Kagyu school of Buddhism in Tibet.

Later, in the Kagyu school, differences arose, leading to the formation of several offshoot orders by various disciples. One of these offshoots was the Drukpa Kargyu order, although they all shared the same foundational teachings. Tilopa is recognized as the root source for the teachings of the Kagyu school, having received these teachings directly from the primordial Vajradhara Buddha through spiritual means.

Naropa's spiritual journey culminated in his enlightenment, often symbolized as the realization of Vajradhara. In some Tibetan traditions, this level of realization is also associated with the attainment of the rainbow body—a state in which the practitioner's body dissolves into light at death, leaving little or no physical remains.

The Six Yogas of Naropa, a set of practices which he pioneered, stands as a fundamental pillar of the Vajrayana Buddhist tradition. These teachings persist in an unbroken lineage passed down from Tilopa to Naropa, Marpa, and Milarepa, continuing through numerous accomplished practitioners alive today, including those in the Drukpa Kargyu tradition in Bhutan.

Gampopa (1079-1153 C.E.)

In sixth position, we find Gampopa. Among the two main disciples of the famed yogi Milarepa, Gampopa was often regarded as the sun, while the other, Rechungpa, was known as the moon.

Before committing himself to the spiritual path, Gampopa had already gained the reputation as a proficient physician, skilled in Tibetan, Chinese, and Ayurvedic medicine and was known as Dagpo Lhaje (physician from Dagpo). While he bore several names, he is most famously known as Gampopa. Remarkably he was also referred to as Dha Yo Zhonu, highlighting his recognition as the incarnation of the youthful disciple of Shakyamuni Buddha and emanation of Chenrezig mentioned earlier.

Gampopa was born in the lower Nyel Valley in eastern Tibet. When he was around the age of thirty-two, tragedy struck when disease claimed the lives of his wife and two children, propelling him toward a monastic life. However, it was his life-altering encounter with Milarepa that reshaped his destiny, elevating him to the status of Milarepa's foremost disciple.

Gampopa's celebrated text *The Jewel Ornament of Liberation* harmoniously integrated two distinct traditions: the *lamrim* teachings of the Gelug school and the Mahamudra meditative practices propagated by Milarepa. In 1121 C.E., he founded the first Kagyu monastery, Dagla Gampo, situated in Dagpo in southern Tibet, three hundred kilometers southwest of Lhasa, now part of present-day Gyantse region, marking the beginnings of the Palden Dagpo Kagyu tradition.

Historical sources document a revealing dialogue between Milarepa and Gampopa upon their first meeting. When Milarepa inquired about his name and qualities, Gampopa humbly responded, "My name is Sonam Rinchen. I am not sure whether what I know are qualities or mistakes. I can go without food for ten days without feeling hunger, walk on the water of lakes without wetting my feet, and enter a house without using the door or being obstructed by walls." This illustrates that Gampopa had already achieved a high level of realization before encountering Milarepa. Under his guru's guidance, he likely advanced to the tenth bhumi.

Centuries later, a well-known master from Tibet by the name of Jamgon Kongtrul Lodro Thaye also acknowledged Gampopa's realization, referring to him as the Second Buddha who attained the tenth bhumi. Furthermore, Shakyamuni Buddha had himself prophesied Gampopa's appearance in the world for the benefit of sentient beings, envisioning a dedicated *bhikshu* (fully ordained Buddhist monk) doctor who had undergone numerous lifetimes of committed Dharma practice.

Gampopa himself shared a significant recollection, revealing that he had sat before Shakyamuni Buddha during his time as the bodhisattva Dha Yo Zhonu, an emanation of Chenrezig. Tsang Khenchen pointed to this testimony as compelling evidence of Gampopa's emanation as Chenrezig. Another prophecy by Guru Rinpoche further emphasized Gampopa's role, foretelling that he would be born as a physician known as Dagpo Lhaje in the Nyel region and would establish a flourishing community of practitioners at Dagpo Hill—a clear indication that Gampopa was his reincarnation.

During his lifetime, Gampopa attracted over ten thousand disciples, including eighteen close disciples known as heart sons. Marpa (1012-1097), Milarepa (1040-1123), and Gampopa (Dagpo Lhaje) (1079-1153) are collectively referred to as Mar Mi Dag Sum (an abbreviation of their names) and are recognized as the formal founders of the Kagyu school of Buddhism.

Tsangpa Gyare (1161-1211 C.E.)

Yeshe Dorji, commonly known as Tsangpa Gyare, recognized as the seventh of Zhabdrung's eleven past lives, occupies a significant place in history as the founder of the Drukpa Kargyu order, which became Bhutan's predominant religion under Zhabdrung's leadership. Born into the Gya hereditary lineage in Tibet's Tsang region, Tsangpa Gyare was identified as the reincarnation of Naropa, as prophesied by Guru Rinpoche and Shakyamuni Buddha. Like Zhabdrung, he embodied a dual greatness: inheriting the Drukpa (Gya) hereditary lineage while representing the reincarnation lineage as its source.

His journey commenced under the tutelage of Lingchen Repa Pema Dorji, fondly known as Lingrepa, whom he encountered at the age of twenty-one by Western count,[30] amid the windswept plains of Ralung and who eventually became his root guru. This serendipitous meeting laid the foundation for the establishment of the Drukpa Kargyu order, with Tsangpa Gyare assuming the role of its founder, known as the inaugural Palden Drukpa Rinpoche.

Before exploring Tsangpa Gyare's groundbreaking contributions to Buddhism, it is worth exploring the unusual circumstances surrounding his birth, foretelling the extraordinary trajectory of his life.

Tsangpa Gyare belonged to an ancient bloodline Buddhist lineage, with his father originating from the Gya lineage. He was born into a humble family of seven sons in upper Nyang, located in the Tsang province of central Tibet. He entered the world on the fifteenth day of the first month of summer in the Year of the Snake. His name, Tsangpa Gyare, can be interpreted as "the man from the Tsang region (Tsangpa) of the Gya lineage (Gya), clad in cloth (Re)."

Throughout her pregnancy, his mother experienced significant dreams. In one, she witnessed a prince entering her body from the right side, holding a white lotus flower—a symbol associated with both Shakyamuni Buddha and Guru Rinpoche. In another dream, the sun emerged from her navel, accompanied by celestial music and the chanting of Dharma teachings.

Tsangpa Gyare's birth occurred in a nomadic tent on the desolate Tibetan Plateau and was heralded by remarkable signs. His mother, alone during labor while her husband and children were herding yaks, was initially alarmed to find the baby enclosed in the amniotic sac. However, upon closer examination, she discovered that the baby had miraculously ruptured the sac, leaving a footprint on a nearby rock. The baby's body also displayed favorable markings associated with enlightened beings.

Despite these miraculous occurrences, Tsangpa Gyare's uneducated and impoverished parents failed to recognize these favorable omens, and they handed him over to a local Bon family, who named him Yungdrungpal. From an early age, he displayed a strong renunciation of worldly life, entering the monastic order at the tender age of eight and achieving remarkable scholarship in a short period of time.

Under Lingrepa's guidance, Tsangpa Gyare had profound realizations. Following Lingrepa's instructions, he established a monastery at the site of their first meeting in Ralung. This monastery eventually became the central seat of the Drukpa Kargyu tradition.

Lingrepa advised him to embark on a journey to spread the Dharma. During a mission to establish a monastic center, Tsangpa

Gyare and his followers paused at a place known as Namgyi Phu (Nam, for short). It was during this rest stop that an extraordinary event unfolded. He received a vision of thirteen dragons[31] sleeping in a forest, who then took flight, unleashing a roar of thunder across the sky, leading to the place being renamed Namdruk (Sky Dragon). Tsangpa Gyare saw this event as a good omen that thirteen *mahasiddhas* would come in his lineage, as indeed they did.[32] The ground trembled, flocks of birds took flight, and an eerie silence followed—the gods had spoken.

It was at this location in 1205 that Tsangpa Gyare founded the (Nam) Druk Sewa Jangchubling Monastery, also known as Druk, while the Buddhist order he established was named Drukpa Kargyu.[33] Although Druk Sewa Jangchubling initially served as the principal seat of the Drukpa Kargyu order, Ralung Monastery— located near the northern border of western Bhutan and the site of his first meeting with Lingrepa—eventually took its place as the main seat.

In addition to establishing the Drukpa Kargyu order and disseminating the Dharma extensively across Tibet, Tsangpa Gyare gained renown as a *terton*—one who uncovers hidden spiritual treasures (*terma*). He experienced a clear vision of his guru advising him to journey to the sacred site of Chakrasamvara at Tsari, a mountain in southern Tibet, which he subsequently rediscovered. He then revealed the esoteric teachings of Rechungpa, based on the *Chakrasamvara Tantra*, and integrated them as central tenets in the Drukpa Kargyu teachings.

Chakrasamvara, the emanation of Vajradhara Buddha, remains a core aspect of the Kagyu school's teachings.

Numerous prophecies heralded the arrival of this great being. Two of the most prominent prophecies were made by Shakyamuni Buddha:

After my *parinirvana*,
My monk, Sonam Nyingpo,[34]
will be born in the Land of Snows.[35]

And

> In the clan of Gya, in a place called Tsa,
> A person by the name of Gya will be born
> who is the emanation of Naropa.[36]

The next notable prophecy came from Guru Rinpoche, reaffirming his reincarnation as Naropa and naming two of the monasteries where the Drukpa Kargyu order would flourish—Druk Sewa Jangchubling (Druk) and Ralung. The prophecy reads,

> An emanation of Pandit Naropa,
> Tsangpa Gyare, will come to Druk and Ralung.

With recognition as the undeniable emanation of Naropa by both Shakyamuni Buddha and Guru Rinpoche, we can confidently assume that Tsangpa Gyare was an emanation of the great bodhisattva Chenrezig.

As his fame grew and his following rapidly expanded, stories of his greatness and the popularity of the Drukpa Kargyu teachings spread far and wide. Two sayings that are often recounted in relation to Tsangpa Gyare are:

> His teachings spanned an area that would take a vulture eighteen days of continuous flight to cover.

And

> Half of the people were Drukpas [Drukpa Kargyu followers], with half the Drukpas being mendicants, and among these mendicants, half were enlightened.

Tsangpa Gyare counted eighty-eight thousand devoted disciples as his followers, including twenty-eight thousand highly realized yogis and yoginis among them. His popularity arose from his humble lifestyle and skillful way of imparting the Dharma. Famed for his ascetic ways, he was often referred to as the Cotton-Clad Yogi. As with Tsangpa Gyare's birth, his passing at age fifty was marked by favorable signs. A vivid rainbow appeared alongside a shower of white flowers. Sweet smells wafted far and wide, accompanied by celestial music that seemed to come out of nowhere. Among his cremated ashes, many relics were found. His eyes, tongue, and heart remained intact, while his skull bore images of the bodhisattvas Chenrezig, Vajrapani, and Manjushri. Notably, twenty-one vertebrae transformed into twenty-one images of various Buddhist deities, with the uppermost vertebra representing the standing form of Chenrezig, known as the Rangjung Kharsapani.

The Rangjung Kharsapani became the most famous and highly contested sacred relic of the Drukpa Kargyu order and was brought to Bhutan by Zhabdrung in 1616. According to an explanation provided by Lodro Rinchen, an attendant of Pema Karpo, the Rangjung Kharsapani disappeared for a few days following Pema Karpo's death—a likely sign of the sadness felt upon losing such a great bodhisattva. Also, the color of the vertebra relic turned dark before negative events and became luminous before significant events, as it did at the time of Zhabdrung's conception, indicating to many that the birth of an emanation of Chenrezig was imminent.

This sacred vertebra relic of the Drukpa Kargyu lineage has been vigilantly safeguarded in Bhutan ever since. It is a widely held belief among followers that merely catching a glimpse of this relic is equivalent to seeing Chenrezig in the flesh.

Following Tsangpa Gyare's passing, his disciples established three subbranches within the Drukpa Kargyu tradition: Upper Druk (Todruk), Middle Druk (Bardruk), and Lower Druk (Medruk). The Middle Druk branch was founded by Tsangpa Gyare's nephew Onre Dharma Senge and eventually became Bhutan's predominant religion on Zhabdrung's arrival.

Nangwa Dudrel Sempa

The eighth of Zhabdrung's eleven past lives was the bodhisattva Nangwa Dudrel Sempa, who resided in the spiritual realm. Although records of his activities are limited, it is known that he originated from the eastern pure land known as Abhirati, associated with Buddha Akshobhya. He devoted himself tirelessly to the welfare of all sentient beings during his 217-year stay in this realm.

Kunga Peljor (1428–1476 C.E.)

The ninth of Zhabdrung's eleven past lives was once again reborn in human form, this time as Kunga Peljor. He was recognized as the first and undisputed reincarnation of Tsangpa Gyare and therefore known as the second Palden Drukpa Rinpoche. He held exceptional significance in the Drukpa Kargyu lineage, possessing both lineages: the Drukpa (Gya) hereditary lineage and the reincarnation lineage.

As foretold by Tsangpa Gyare, his birth would occur after nine hereditary lineage holders bearing the name Senge (referred to as the Nine Senges) and three bodhisattva emanations (known as Rigsum Namtrul). True to the prophecy, Kunga Peljor was born (refer to the list of throne holders in the appendix).

Even Guru Rinpoche prophesied his arrival in the world and his greatness as a spiritual being, stating,

> In the sacred place called Ralung,
> A bodhisattva named Kunga,
> With richness and glory [Peljor] of various knowledge,
> Will subdue and benefit many sentient beings.

Under the intensive guidance of his father, Sherab Zangpo, Kunga Peljor ascended to the throne of Ralung at the age of eleven. He received extensive Dharma teachings from numerous eminent masters, achieving proficiency in Buddhist philosophy, Sanskrit, and translation. Additionally he received divine visions and teachings from Guru Rinpoche and Gampopa from the spiritual realm. Among his notable disciples from Tibet were Drukpa Kunle (the Divine Madman), Thangthong Gyalpo (the Iron-Bridge Builder) and Unyon and Tsangnyon (referred to as the madmen from the U and Tsang regions). It is worth noting that many enlightened masters of the time were perceived as behaving strangely, leading to them being labeled as "mad."

Kunga Peljor also played a significant role in propagating the Drukpa Kargyu teachings in present-day Bhutan, making several visits to the country. He imparted numerous teachings and empowerments, as well as oversaw the construction of numerous temples and meditation centers.

Jamyang Chokyi Dragpa (1478–1523 C.E.)

The Third Palden Drukpa Rinpoche, the tenth of Zhabdrung's eleven past lives, was born as Jamyang Chokyi Dragpa in the Jayul region of southern Tibet. He started his life as a prince and eventually ascended to become the king of the region. Despite recognition from Zhabdrung's great-great-grandfather, Ngawang Chogyal, and many spiritual masters as the reincarnation of his predecessor, Kunga Peljor, he did not belong to the Drukpa hereditary lineage. Consequently some members of the Drukpa lineage family did not accept him as the successor of the Ralung establishment and prevented him from holding the throne. In response, his family, members of the Ja family, constructed another monastery, Tashi Thongmon, in southeast Tibet, where he assumed the throne.

Despite these family disputes, Jamyang Chokyi Dragpa remained committed to the spiritual path. He received Drukpa Kargyu teachings from Drukpa Kunle and tantric teachings from a close disciple of Kunga Peljor.

Throughout his life, he actively promoted the teachings of the Drukpa Kargyu order and was a highly accomplished spiritual practitioner. He left numerous handprints and footprints in rocks as symbols of his great spiritual accomplishments. Legend has it that

Rechungpa, one of the two main disciples of Milarepa, appeared before him and imparted the essential esoteric instructions of the Whispering Dakini teachings. Jamyang Chokyi Dragpa also played a crucial role in disseminating teachings and practices compiled by Renchungpa.

Pema Karpo (1527–1592 C.E.)

The last of Zhabdrung's eleven past lives was Pema Karpo, known as the fourth Palden Drukpa Rinpoche[37] and the head of the Drukpa Kargyu order. He was born in the Kongpo region of southeast Tibet. His birth had been prophesied by Chenrezig, who foretold the emergence of a great being in Kong Yul. Remarkably, at only twenty-one days old, he was heard chanting the six-syllable Chenrezig mantra, OM MANI PADME HUM, further confirming his status as a genuine emanation of Chenrezig.

At the age of nine, he was recognized as the reincarnation of his predecessor, Jamyang Chokyi Dragpa, and enthroned at Tashi Thongmon Monastery. Throughout his lifetime he was known by many names, including Kunkhyen Pema Karpo (the Omniscient Pema Karpo), Ngawang Norbu, and Drukchen Thamche Khyenpa (the All-Knowing Great Drukpa).

He received intensive teachings from Zhabdrung's great-grandfather, Ngagi Wangchuk, the fifteenth throne holder of Ralung. Among his disciples were prominent figures such as Tenpai Nyima, Zhabdrung's father; Lhawang Lodro, one of Zhabdrung's main tutors; and Tulku Pekar Wangpo, who served as a tutor to Zhabdrung and was recognized as the reincarnation of Ngagi Wangchuk.

When Zhabdrung's father requested the dying Pema Karpo to reveal who he would be reincarnated as, he prophesied that he would be reborn as his son—a Drukpa hereditary lineage holder and a Dharma king.

Pema Karpo lived a distinguished life, dedicated entirely to advancing and enriching the teachings of the Drukpa Kargyu order. His legacy includes the composition of twenty-four volumes of commentaries on the sutras and tantras, which highlight his profound understanding of Buddhist philosophy. Beyond theoretical Buddhist knowledge, he mastered logic, history, and astrology. However, it was in the practical realm of meditation where he excelled, attaining profound realizations and earning acclaim for his extraordinary supernatural abilities. Throughout his life, he often experienced numerous visions and prophetic dreams.

Pema Karpo's legacy extended to the establishment of many monasteries, including a total of thirteen meditation centers known as *lings*. Notable among these was Druk Sangag Choling, meaning "Dharma Garden of the Drukpa Secret Mantrayana." Situated in the Jayul province of southern Tibet, it later evolved into the principal seat of the Gyalwang Drukpa order of the Bodruk—that is, the northern branch of the Drukpa Kargyu order—during this time.

The reincarnation lineage of the Drukpa Kargyu order, the Palden Drukpa Rinpoches of Ralung, continued until 1616. That year, Zhabdrung left Tibet for Bhutan due to the dispute over the reincarnation of Pema Karpo, the fourth Palden Drukpa Rinpoche, marking a turning point in his spiritual destiny. This event led to the split of the Drukpa Kargyu order: the northern Drukpa Kargyu branch (Bodruk) consisted of followers remaining in Tibet, while the southern Drukpa Kargyu branch (Lhodruk), under the leadership of Zhabdrung, established itself in Bhutan. Over time, due to Zhabdrung's tireless unification efforts, the southern seat holders of the Drukpa Kargyu branch were bestowed with the title of Je Khenpo, a meritocratic position recognizing their spiritual leadership as the heads of the Drukpa Kargyu order in Bhutan.

Guru Rinpoche (Eighth Century)

It is important to recognize another significant figure whom Zhabdrung is believed to be an emanation of. He is none other than Guru Rinpoche, who needs no introduction to the Bhutanese. Guru Rinpoche's presence is ubiquitous in Bhutan, where his statue adorns almost all homes and temples across the country.

Guru Padmasambhava, popularly known as Guru Rinpoche, is a historic Buddhist figure from the eighth century. Born in Oddiyana, which some believe to be in the Swat Valley of modern-day Pakistan, he is revered as the Second Buddha who introduced Buddhism to Tibet and founded the Nyingma school of Tibetan Buddhism. While various biographies offer differing accounts of Guru Rinpoche's birth, the treasure teachings of Guru Rinpoche indicate that he was born on the tenth day of the fifth month according to the Bhutanese calendar. He emerged as an extraordinary figure, reportedly appearing spontaneously as an eight-year-old boy from a lotus flower in Lake Danakosha, earning him the epithet Lotus-Born.

Although nurtured by royalty, he renounced his worldly life and embraced the path of a wandering yogi. Guru Rinpoche sought teachings from esteemed tantric masters, engaged in extensive meditation retreats, and gained recognition for subduing demonic beings and making accurate prophecies; his journey closely mirrored that of Zhabdrung. However, it is crucial not to perceive him as an ordinary human being. Doing so might hinder our ability to fully recognize and appreciate his enlightened qualities and awe-inspiring deeds.

Zhabdrung is regarded as an emanation of Guru Rinpoche, with both recognized as emanations of bodhisattva Chenrezig. As different expressions of the same essence, studying Guru Rinpoche offers deeper insight into Zhabdrung.

Guru Rinpoche himself prophesied his rebirth as Gampopa, as cited in Tsang Khenchen's biography:

I, Ugyen (Ugyen Guru Rinpoche), shall be born as a physician (Gampopa was known as Dagpo Lhaje, a physician) in Nyel,
    And lead a community of practitioners to flourish at Dagpo Hill.

Given their shared mindstream (Zhabdrung being a reincarnation of Gampopa), Zhabdrung can convincingly be regarded as an emanation of Guru Rinpoche.

Guru Rinpoche's influence on Bhutan's history and culture was immense. Prior to his arrival in Bhutan in the eighth century, Bhutan's spiritual practices were a mix of Bon, animism, and shamanism. While Buddhism had begun to enter Bhutan as early as the second century, it did not gain significant traction until Guru Rinpoche arrived around 746 C.E.

According to several Buddhist sutras and tantras, Shakyamuni Buddha prophesied the coming of a great being after his passing, known as Lotus-Born or the Second Buddha. It was foretold that this figure would spread the Dharma widely, especially the Vajrayana teachings.

After meditating in what is now modern-day Nepal, Guru Rinpoche entered Bhutan at the invitation of King Sindhu of Bumthang. The exiled Indian king, having established his rule there, sought Guru Rinpoche's help after falling seriously ill—an illness believed to have arisen from neglecting the proper appeasement rites to the local deity, Shelging Karpo.

Guru Rinpoche demonstrated his miraculous powers by swiftly subduing the troublesome deity, leading to King Sindhu's miraculous recovery. This event had a profound impact not only on King Sindhu but also on his rival, King Naoche, with whom he was in conflict in southern Bhutan. In response, both kings immediately embraced Buddhism, resulting in the restoration of peace.

Guru Rinpoche's displays of supernatural abilities, particularly in subduing demons and malevolent spirits, played a central role in spreading Buddhism throughout the region, and his influence continues to be deeply revered in Bhutan.

Guru Rinpoche's second visit to Bhutan occurred after establishing Buddhism in Tibet at the request of Tibetan King Trisong Detsen. According to King Sindhu's biography, Guru Rinpoche arrived in Bumthang through the Monkha Nering cave in Senge Dzong, located in northeastern Bhutan. This cave holds profound significance as the site where Guru Rinpoche meditated for three months, performing transformative actions central to his spiritual journey.

In the Senge Dzong area, there are eight solitary locations where

Guru Rinpoche attained profound realizations, including Monkha Nering cave. Another renowned sanctuary is Taktsang cave, famously known as the Tiger's Nest, nestled in the Paro Valley of western Bhutan. These caves served as repositories for spiritual treasures and are revered as sites conducive to receiving prophecies and spiritual insights. It is believed that Guru Rinpoche's consort, Yeshe Tshogyal, achieved exceptional spiritual realizations through the practice of Vajrakilaya in the Monkha Nering cave. Guru Rinpoche emphasized the inherent spiritual potency of Bhutan's landscape, once remarking that meditating for seven days in Bhutan is equivalent to seven years of meditation in Tibet.

His third and supposedly final visit to Bhutan is said to have occurred during the reign of Muthri Tsenpo (c. 764–817 C.E.), the son of Tibetan King Trisong Detsen, although scant information exists regarding this visit. Throughout his visits, Guru Rinpoche traveled to every corner of Bhutan, bestowing blessings upon the land, seeking solace in remote caves, and subduing malevolent spirits and demons along the way. He proclaimed Bhutan as a sacred land (beyul) destined for the flourishing of the sacred Vajrayana teachings.

Guru Rinpoche is credited with concealing spiritual treasures (terma), which include texts of meditational instructions, rituals, and sacred artifacts. He entrusted their eventual discovery to highly evolved spiritual beings known as tertons, depending on the ripening of essential causes and conditions.

Concluding the investigation into Zhabdrung's past lives, it becomes evident that these incarnations share remarkable similarities in character and achievements with Zhabdrung himself. The essence of compassion, embodied by Chenrezig, flows through all these lives, strongly suggesting that Zhabdrung was indeed an emanation of Chenrezig. This belief is supported by declarations from notable figures such as Gya Jampel Sangwa, a close disciple of Guru Rinpoche, and Tsangpa Gyare centuries earlier. Both prophesied the emergence of eighty-four emanations of Chenrezig in the Gya hereditary lineage, among which Zhabdrung played a significant role. Guru Rinpoche himself foresaw the rise of a spiritually influential figure in the form of Chenrezig, destined to bring peace to Bhutan by guiding its people and preventing conflicts.

Not surprisingly, Zhabdrung shared a mutual passion for the Kalachakra teachings with both Rigden Pema Karpo and Pema Karpo. And much like King Songtsen Gampo, who established a comprehensive system founded on Buddhist principles to unify a lawless land. Zhabdrung played a similar role in Bhutan; they both laid the foundation for political, economic, cultural, and legal systems to flourish that were deeply embedded in the Dharma. Zhabdrung's lifelong fascination with herbal medicine, nurturing a close bond with his personal physician, mirrors the path of Gampopa.

All these accomplished masters possessed remarkable qualities, including razor-sharp intellect, unwavering moral integrity, and compassionate resilience when confronting challenges—traits seen in Zhabdrung himself. They also shared an unwavering dedication to safeguarding and spreading the teachings of Buddha. Like Guru Rinpoche before him, Zhabdrung did not hesitate to call upon his spiritual powers to pacify malevolent forces and individuals intent on causing havoc.

The lives of these great masters offer invaluable insights into Zhabdrung's multifaceted capabilities, revealing his compassionate purpose on Earth. With this understanding, we are now able to confidently grasp the complex layers of Zhabdrung's life story. The pages that follow will trace his extraordinary journey of hardship and triumph through the landscapes of Tibet and Bhutan—a life prophesied and a precious legacy destined to endure.

PART TWO

The Story

CHAPTER 5

Fortunate Birth and Rivalry

Destiny seemed to have set its sights on Zhabdrung from the very start. His birth, which took place amid great turbulence for the Drukpa Kargyu order, fulfilled an ancient prophecy by Tsangpa Gyare that he would return when the Drukpa lineage needed him the most. In this prophecy he foretold of his birth in the form of Zhabdrung and his mission to establish the dual system of governance in Bhutan. It was as though the universe had conspired to bring forth an extraordinary individual destined to shape the course of Bhutan's history forever.

The Early Years

Zhabdrung's birth marked a crucial moment in history, coinciding with the waning influence of the Tsang Desi court and the rising prominence of the Gelug school, which would later come under the leadership of the Fifth Dalai Lama, Ngawang Lobsang Gyatsho (1617–1682). Recognizing the impending challenges, the Ralung hierarchs prayed fervently for the preservation of the precious teachings of the Drukpa Kargyu order.

Zhabdrung's mother, Sonam Palgyi Buthri, came from Lhasa's ruling family, boasting an aristocratic lineage dating back centuries. A devoted Dharma practitioner, she resided near Druk Sewa Jangchubling, the monastic seat of the Drukpa Kargyu order in the Tsang region. There she met Tenpai Nyima, a prominent holder of the Drukpa (Gya) hereditary lineage, and became his consort.

Renowned as a skilled practitioner and Buddhist scholar, Tenpai Nyima was widely recognized throughout Tibet, India, and Mongolia.

Like many great spiritual figures, Zhabdrung's gestation period and birth were marked by numerous auspicious signs. During her pregnancy, his mother had a significant dream. In this dream she found herself bathing in a beautiful, flower-adorned pond, where she was greeted by dakinis who crowned her head with flowers. A vajra then merged into her heart, granting her the ability to visualize realms beyond the human dimension.

The spiritual guardian Palden Lhamo (Mahakali) watched over her in the form of a cuckoo from the moment she conceived. She found great solace in the warmth and contentment of pregnancy, while the landscape around her seemed unusually vibrant. Animals approached her without fear, and melodious tunes from larks near the palace filled the air.

In the picturesque valley of Gardrong, not far from the Drukpa Kargyu monastery of Druk Sewa Jangchubling, encircled by majestic peaks, a great day had arrived: the eleventh day of the eleventh month in the Year of the Wood Horse, according to the ancient Tibetan calendar. On this day in 1594, Zhabdrung Ngawang Namgyal was born.

As the newborn's first cries echoed through the valley, the air carried a sweet floral scent while he was bathed in saffron-infused water symbolizing purity, prosperity, and auspiciousness. Meanwhile, his father and grandfather performed elaborate thanksgiving rituals to honor the spiritual guardians who had safeguarded him since conception. As Zhabdrung grew, he learned to call upon these guardians during moments of great peril to the Drukpa Kargyu order—a skill granted only to those of the highest spiritual attainment.

His birth was celebrated not only by the patrons and followers of the Drukpa Kargyu order but also by the chieftains from the U and Tsang regions, who recognized its significance. As the long-awaited hereditary lineage holder of the Drukpa Kargyu order, he arrived at a crucial point in time, when the order's future lay in the balance. During the grand festivities, a long-life prayer composed by Pema Karpo for his reincarnation was recited, expressing heartfelt aspirations and prophesying the emergence of a great Dharma king:

> The foundation for the emanation of all the past victorious
>   ones
> And the source of all future buddhas
> No different from the present protector [Pema Karpo]
> Is the Dharma king, may he live long.

Zhabdrung was no ordinary child. In the months and years that followed, he displayed wisdom and power beyond his years. His first word was the sacred syllable AH, a sound associated with enlightened speech.

He defied normal development; what others accomplished in a year, he achieved in a month, which astounded those around him. At an extraordinarily young age, he introduced himself as Drukchen Thamche Khyenpa, a name synonymous with Pema Karpo, signaling his destined greatness.

Zhabdrung exuded exceptional composure and maturity, showing little interest in childish play. He rarely cried, displayed minimal hunger, and required little sleep—characteristics often associated with bodhisattvas. To everyone's surprise, he began reading and writing around the age of two without any prompting or formal teaching.

Visitors who came to see him did not bring offerings of red rice, yet this variety, not native to the region, inexplicably sprouted in his bedroom. Red rice even appeared between his teeth and under his tongue, leading devotees to believe it was an offering from celestial beings. Much later, Zhabdrung confirmed the rice's appearance to Tsang Khenchen. Even when Zhabdrung was very young, it became evident that he was being guided from a higher realm, preparing him for his noble earthly duties. Birds not typically found in Tibet congregated at his birthplace. Later it was discovered that these birds, along with grains, were common to Bhutan. They were interpreted as auspicious signs, hinting that his spiritual destiny lay to the south.

Following the tradition for supposed reincarnate lamas, Zhabdrung commenced his moral and spiritual education early, around the age of four. He was fortunate to have several highly learned teachers, including his father, Tenpai Nyima, his root guru; his grandfather, Mipham Chogyal; Lhawang Lodro, an eminent Drukpa Kargyu scholar and accomplished Buddhist astrologer; and Pekar Wangpo, the reincarnation of his great-grandfather, Ngagi Wangchuk. He also received instruction from the Sakya master Sonam Wangpo.

For twelve years Zhabdrung resided at Druk Sewa Jangchubling Monastery, where, as a tenth-bhumi bodhisattva, the lines between the spiritual and physical realms were blurred, allowing him to commune with spiritual guardians and wield influence over their actions. By the age of five he had already mastered many Buddhist prayers and rituals. In a few more years he could articulate the intricate meanings of tantric scriptures with astonishing precision, leaving seasoned Buddhist scholars in utter disbelief. At the tender age of eight he received the lay Buddhist vows from his grandfather, marking the formal commencement of his spiritual journey.

While Zhabdrung was presiding over a ritual dedicated to the spiritual guardian Palden Lhamo, a remarkable phenomenon occurred. Sparks of fire, akin to celestial blessings, danced forth from the meticulously arranged ritual sculptures (*torma*) adorning the altar. Startled eyewitnesses were taken aback by this spellbinding display of divine power. Impressed by Zhabdrung's supernatural abilities, the Ralung hierarchs duly honored him with the title Lord of Power. What follows is Tsang Khenchen's description from that time:

> The anticipation in the prayer hall was palpable as the conch shell was blown, heralding the arrival of Zhabdrung before a congregation of over one hundred Buddhist scholars, yogis, monks, and lay practitioners. The scent of burning juniper and

butter lamps permeated the air, accompanied by the resonant clang of cymbals. Adorned in the finest silks and surrounded by a grand mandala depicting the universe, all offered in tribute to his spiritual prowess, the young master stood as a beacon of reverence. Devotees, recognizing him not as an ordinary child but as a highly realized bodhisattva with a mind as enlightened as their previous master, Pema Karpo, were moved to tears of devotion as they prostrated before him. They then proceeded to circumambulate the throne on which he sat, demonstrating their reverence and deep respect.

As he matured, Zhabdrung reached deeper into the esoteric teachings of the Drukpa Kargyu tradition. He received the most sacred Vajrayana teachings, empowerments, and oral transmissions—closely guarded secrets passed down through generations of masters. He tirelessly devoted himself to perfecting his understanding of the sutras and tantras, his intellect likened to the blazing pinnacle of a flame. Visitors from far and wide embarked on pilgrimages to his doorstep, humbly prostrating themselves in admiration and deeply moved by his unwavering insights and mastery of the teachings.

Zhabdrung exhibited remarkable independence and self-assurance, wholeheartedly embracing his destined purpose and remaining unaffected by criticism. His sharp intellect rivaled that of Pema Karpo, astonishing his parents and filling them with hope that he was the one—his reincarnation. He effortlessly grasped the meaning of complex Dharma texts and teachings, as demonstrated by his ability to provide detailed explanations of Buddhist cosmology without any formal instruction, leaving those present in disbelief. He simply asserted that he had acquired this knowledge in his early years, alluding to his past lifetimes.

Despite his inherent knowledge, he insisted on formal instruction in all Buddhist philosophical subjects, sciences, and the arts—a trait common among bodhisattvas, who seek to inspire their peers by actively learning alongside them. He studied astrological texts with such diligence that his iron pencil wore down to a mere stump.

Impressed by his dedication, his teacher, Lhawang Lodro, likened him to the embodiment of the qualities of the one thousand buddhas of the fortunate eon and a manifestation of Chenrezig. This praise sparked speculation among his followers, igniting whispers that he might indeed be the earthly manifestation of Chenrezig.

His thirteenth year was significant. He left Druk Sewa Jangchubling for Ralung Monastery, and during a grand celebration around 1606, he was enthroned as the seventeenth hereditary throne holder of Ralung.[38] On this momentous day, numerous inexplicable and favorable signs arose. A sudden shower of flower petals appeared out of nowhere, the celestial resonance of cymbals filled the sky, a vibrant rainbow canopy adorned the heavens, and the pervasive fragrance of incense wafted from every direction.

Crazy, right? But no. These mystical experiences still occur—even in modern times! I have no idea how or why, but they do. I encountered two such moments in Bhutan.

The first experience happened while I was trekking to a sacred site in Paro, known as Bumdra, situated nearly four thousand meters above sea level. This place, blessed by Guru Rinpoche, is believed to be where one hundred thousand dakinis left their footprints in a rock over eight hundred years ago. I had organized an overnight adventure for my husband and son's visit, and as I effortlessly made my way up the steep mountainside, they struggled with the altitude, jokingly comparing me to an uncompassionate mountain goat.

As I approached the open plain of Bumdra, bathed in dappled light, I entered a canopy of trees. Suddenly a gentle shower of pale-pink petals floated gently down upon me, seemingly out of nowhere, leaving a carpet of delicate blush. Surprised, I looked up at the trees, but there were no flowers in sight. I reached for my phone only to realize I had left it in my backpack with the guide who was assisting the stragglers.

To this day, I have found no scientific explanation for this phenomenon. Neither did my husband nor son see any traces of petals along the way. Had I entered a parallel reality? Who knows! Over the years I've learned to simply be present and avoid overanalyzing, especially when in Bhutan.

The second experience occurred when my spiritual teacher came to visit my assistant and me in our new office. He had found premises for us deep in the woods on the outskirts of Thimphu. Secluded would be an understatement—isolated is more fitting; as Australians would say, it was "in the middle of Woop Woop." I suppose he thought the tranquility would be conducive to writing, but we often found ourselves overwhelmed by the fear of encountering a bear or the blustering icy-cold Himalayan winds that buffeted the windows, causing them to rattle as if a spirit were trying to enter.

After settling into our new office, my teacher arrived to bless the space, accompanied by his attendant and two family members. After exchanging formal greetings, we sat and enjoyed the customary sweet, milky tea with *zow*—roasted rice. The day appeared to be unfolding as planned. It was early spring; the alpine flowers were beginning to bloom and the Himalayan vista stretched before us under a cobalt sky unmarred by a single cloud.

What followed will be etched in my mind forever. Just as my teacher stepped out onto the balcony, a deafening roar of thunder erupted from the heavens, unlike any I had ever heard before. We jumped back, startled. Bewildered glances were exchanged, while he remained unperturbed. But there were no clouds in sight! In that moment I was transported back to the tale of Tsangpa Gyare. Could my teacher be a reincarnation of Tsangpa Gyare, the great Buddhist master, the founder of the Drukpa Kargyu order who had a vision of dragons flying up into the sky at Namdruk amid thunderous echoes through the valley? Or perhaps a mahasiddha concealed within the guise of an ordinary human? Many monks claim him to be a bodhisattva; that day, for me, served as compelling evidence that he may well be one.

The celebration of Zhabdrung's enthronement was a lavish affair, adorned with a splendid array of offerings ranging from honey, sugar, rice, horses, and cotton to silver, tiger skins, and leopard skins. Dignitaries from various monastic orders, monasteries, and elite families made the arduous journey across Tibet to pay homage. Among them were Buddhist luminaries from the south, such as Tshewang Tenzin from Tango, the reincarnation of Phajo Drukgom

Zhigpo; and the Obtsho Lama, representing the lineage of Drubthob Terkhungpa. Additionally, the occasion attracted attention from afar, with kings from different nations sending their heartfelt felicitations. Patrons and descendants of the noble Hungral clan from Paro were also in attendance, adding to the sense of camaraderie and solidarity among attendees.

At Ralung, under his father's guidance, the young Zhabdrung deepened his spiritual practices. He mastered Buddhist initiations, advanced teachings, and sacred rituals involving the spiritual guardians. His command over these powerful protectors was unrivaled, a testament to his strong karmic connection with them, and echoing Guru Rinpoche's prophetic visions foretelling his greatness. As Zhabdrung's journey unfolds, we will witness how these mighty protectors shielded him from harm and paved the way for his destiny as a true spiritual leader of the people of the Southern Land.[39]

Signs of Zhabdrung's dedication to the teachings of the Drukpa Kargyu tradition began to emerge during his teenage years. It was during this time that he established a community of lay practitioners known as a *chogdra*. To lead this community as the *umze* (chant master), Zhabdrung appointed Tenzin Drukgyal, a prominent figure from Bhutan who would later serve as the first Druk Desi (civil head) under Zhabdrung's leadership. Additionally, Zhabdrung took the initiative to create a comprehensive code of conduct for this community, showcasing his commitment to expanding the influence of the Drukpa Kargyu tradition beyond the confines of monastic life. This code would later shape the legal framework of the newly formed state of Bhutan.

Between ages fourteen and nineteen, under the guidance of his teacher, Lhawang Lodro, Zhabdrung dedicated himself to intensive study. Delving deep into the intricacies of the Kalachakra system, he mastered its complex calculations. Additionally, he became proficient in Sanskrit grammar, a sacred language for Dharma study believed to have originated from the time of Buddha.

His understanding of Sanskrit allowed him to grasp certain Indian dialects, fostering a close friendship with an Indian yogi named Amrit Nath, who was nearly a century old. From Amrit Nath Zhabdrung learned esoteric methods to enhance vitality and lifespan. Adjusting his diet to include more herbal plants and flowers, he followed in the footsteps of Milarepa, the great yogi of centuries past.

Furthermore, Zhabdrung's talents extended to include the art of composing poetic verses imbued with profound Dharmic messages. Through these verses he eloquently praised the qualities of his lineage masters, an act revered by Buddha for its ability to generate great merit and accelerate the path to enlightenment. Simultaneously, in the realm of academia, Zhabdrung immersed himself in the study of epistemology under the guidance of esteemed scholars from the Gelug and Sakya schools, engaging in rigorous debates on Buddhist philosophy. His academic journey led to his initiation into tantric studies at the age of seventeen, under the expert guidance of Lhawang Lodro, marking the beginning of Zhabdrung's absorption into deeper spiritual practices.

Zhabdrung's medical education flourished under the tutelage of his personal physician, Athob. Athob imparted not only knowledge on the nature of illnesses but also their esoteric origins, providing him with a broader medical understanding. Zhabdrung's exploration also extended to the medicinal teachings embedded within tantric texts. He honed his skills in crafting sacred pills through invocations to the Dharma protectors and dakinis, a practice that later prompted him to confide in Tsang Khenchen about receiving medical instructions from the spirit realm during his formative years.

Yet Zhabdrung's talents weren't confined to scholarly pursuits. He blossomed into a masterful artist, diligently observing sculptors from present-day Nepal as they molded intricate copper images of buddhas. This passion paralleled that of Pema Karpo, a master craftsman in his own right. Zhabdrung expressed a deep desire to learn the exact measurements of various Buddhist statues and stupas, as well as the art of drawing mandalas. As a bodhisattva, he inherently understood the vast merit in producing images of enlightened beings and the tremendous blessing that would arise for those who laid eyes upon them.

During his time in Bhutan, he would be the driving force behind the construction of many fortresses, statues, and stupas, as well as the composition of many holy scriptures.

His innate ability to craft intricate depictions of buddhas and bodhisattvas, with impeccable proportions and precision, left observers speechless. Like a virtuoso musician blessed with perfect pitch, he effortlessly sketched and fashioned religious images, regardless of their size or complexity. His most astounding artistic feat, beyond belief for mortal humans, involved crafting an image of Shakyamuni Buddha's sixteen disciples on a single grain of rice. This achievement stood as a testament to his unparalleled skill and relentless attention to detail. It was as if the essence of enlightenment flowed effortlessly through his fingertips, manifesting itself in the brilliance of his artwork.

As word of Zhabdrung's intellectual abilities, artistic talents, and spiritual accomplishments spread throughout the land, people from far and wide began to flock to him, eager to witness firsthand the unusual wisdom of this young prodigy.

Zhabdrung's relentless pursuit of knowledge knew no bounds. By his late teens he had achieved exceptional mastery in the five major Buddhist sciences: Buddhist philosophy, grammar, traditional medicine, epistemology, and arts/crafts. In fact, he once shared with Tsang Khenchen that he had an eidetic memory, capable of memorizing entire texts from their titles to their conclusions. Zhabdrung's thorough mastery of these sciences granted him access to miraculous spiritual powers and the potential for omniscience, both of which he exhibited throughout his life.

On the topic of spiritual powers and omniscience, I recall an early incident during my initiation into Buddhist teachings under my teacher's guidance. On this occasion, the translator was running late, leaving me alone with my teacher. To break the uncomfortable silence, I fumbled through a few phrases in the local language, which only heightened my awkwardness. My teacher remained calm and composed, likely amused by my attempts at small talk.

My monkey mind then went into overdrive. I began to imagine what his toilet might look like. In that split second, he turned to me and in broken English said, "My toilet over there to look," while gesturing to its location. He had just read my mind!

The embarrassment I felt was mortifying; my face flushed crimson just as the translator entered the room.

Zhabdrung's father and grandfather were deeply moved by his exceptional abilities and believed that Pema Karpo's prophecy of his rebirth as Tenpai Nyima's son had indeed come to pass. Zhabdrung had even gone as far as personally recording his recollections of his previous life in a letter to Sangye Dorji, a scholar well versed in Pema Karpo's teachings, compounding everyone's faith in him as the genuine reincarnation of Pema Karpo.

Following the successful completion of his studies, Zhabdrung embarked on a sacred journey with his father. They visited the Drukpa Kargyu monastic estates, engaging with devotees and taking in the spiritual richness of the Tibetan Plateau. Their pilgrimage was further enriched by visits to Lhasa's major holy sites, where they took their time to offer prayers and bask in the silent piety of these revered sanctuaries.

The Rivalry Begins

The initial excitement and profound spiritual implications of their journey across Tibet gradually waned as the looming conflict over the reincarnation of Pema Karpo took center stage.[40]

The favorable signs surrounding Zhabdrung's birth, beginning at conception, along with Pema Karpo's prophecy that he would be born as the son of Tenpai Nyima, left the Ralung hierarchs convinced that Zhabdrung was the genuine reincarnation of Pema Karpo.

The responsibility for appointing a hereditary Ralung throne holder and identifying the reincarnation of a Drukpa predecessor lay with the Ralung hierarchs and other influential lamas of the Drukpa Kargyu order. At the time of Zhabdrung's birth, the hierarchs were his father, Tenpai Nyima, and his grandfather, Mipham Chogyal, who held the throne. The Ralung throne holder also served as the custodian of the sacred backbone relic of Tsangpa Gyare, the Rangjung Kharsapani.

However, on Pema Karpo's death, tensions arose within the Drukpa Kargyu order over his successor. Lhatsawa Ngawang Zangpo, a disciple of Pema Karpo and a relative of Chongye Depa, the governor of the nearby region of Chongye, who enjoyed close ties to the Tsang Desi, clandestinely recognized another candidate as the reincarnation of Pema Karpo. This candidate, Pagsam Wangpo, born in 1593 as a result of an affair between Chongye Depa and a maid, was recognized without seeking permission from the Ralung hierarchs. Thus, the contentious dispute over the reincarnation of Pema Karpo was ignited by the emergence of Pagsam Wangpo as a competing candidate.

The story as told by Zhabdrung's supporters goes as follows.

In the final weeks of his life, Pema Karpo grappled with the weighty responsibility of selecting a woman to serve as the vessel for his reincarnation. As a bodhisattva of superior realization, he possessed the ability to choose the circumstances of his rebirth.

One potential candidate, the consort of Zhabdrung's grandfather, fell out of favor due to her disrespectful behavior. To assess another candidate's suitability, Pema Karpo arranged for a cup of yogurt, which he sipped, to be sent through a messenger to the wife of Chongye Depa. If she consumed it, it would be considered an auspicious sign (*tendrel*) confirming her worthiness to bear his reincarnation. However, due to the messenger's failure to deliver the yogurt, Pema Karpo's fate hung in the balance. It wasn't until he prophesied to Tenpai Nyima, declaring that he would be reborn as his own son, none other than Zhabdrung, that his destiny was finally sealed.

A few years after Pema Karpo's passing, Lhatsawa Ngawang Zangpo manipulated the circumstances surrounding Pema Karpo's reincarnation. He succeeded in persuading Chongye Depa and many of Pema Karpo's followers that Pagsam Wangpo, the illegitimate child of Chongye Depa, was the true reincarnation. This narrative gained momentum during Zhabdrung's time at Ralung, buoyed by the endorsement of some of Pema Karpo's closest disciples who were persuaded by Lhatsawa Ngawang Zangpo's compelling promises and manipulative strategies.

Unbeknownst to Zhabdrung, who was happily leading a carefree life at Ralung, a serious challenge to his rightful claim as Pema Karpo's reincarnation loomed on the horizon. The Ralung hierarchs, confident in Zhabdrung's legitimacy, pointed to the prophecy that Pema Karpo would be reborn as Tenpai Nyima's son and noted Zhabdrung's exceptional qualities, which closely mirrored those of Pema Karpo. Furthermore, Pagsam Wangpo's failure to recognize any of Pema Karpo's possessions during a test as a young boy further solidified Zhabdrung's position.

To formalize the recognition of a reincarnation in Tibetan Buddhism, specific tests are administered to assess any potential candidate, almost always accompanied by divination. When Pagsam Wangpo was four years old, he was brought before a group of senior lamas from Ralung for recognition—an event that turned out to be disastrous for the young boy.

As he was being prepared to meet the senior lamas, the skies suddenly darkened, unleashing a vehement storm. The cutting gusts of wind and pelting rain were regarded as a foreboding sign of misfortune, the ominous atmosphere mirroring the anxiety that filled the hearts of those gathered.[41]

From this point onward, events took a turn for the worse. Pagsam Wangpo stubbornly rejected the auspicious offering of the white cotton cloth of a yogi, and the Rangjung Kharsapani failed to emit its customary glow—a sign linked with favorable outcomes. When Tenpai Nyima, wearing a pandit's hat known as a *panzha*, reminiscent of his attire during encounters with Pema Karpo, called out to the boy, Pagsam Wangpo burst into tears. Some of his supporters speculated that it was due to Tenpai Nyima's disheveled appearance after his recent completion of a three-year retreat, which they believed may have frightened the boy. However, this theory was debunked as Tenpai Nyima was meticulously groomed and possessed great splendor following the end of his retreat.

The final test was aimed at ascertaining the boy's ability to recognize three items belonging to Pema Karpo. Carefully arranged on an elaborately embroidered cloth before the boy were an exquisite image of White Manjushri, the bodhisattva of wisdom; a musty, elongated scriptural text with pages that had curled over time due to centuries of recitation; and a well-used bag woven from the finest Chinese silk. Despite the meticulous presentation, the boy showed no sign of recognition when he glanced at the items. Recalling his guru's parting words—"The one who can recognize these three items is the genuine reincarnation. Do not trust anyone else"—Tenpai Nyima realized then and there that this boy was not the reincarnation of his beloved master. Spontaneously he declared that Zhabdrung, his son, was the true reincarnation of Pema Karpo.

Despite these negative test results, the campaign to recognize Pagsam Wangpo as the reincarnation of Pema Karpo intensified as he came of age. Lhatsawa Ngawang Zangpo and his supporters led a concerted effort to have his relative recognized as the reincarnation, culminating in the secret enthronement of Pagsam Wangpo at another monastery called Tashi Thongmon—a move more resembling a power play than one driven by spiritual motives. At this time, Zhabdrung addressed the matter in a letter to the Tsang Desi, asserting that Lhatsawa Ngawang Zangpo, the primary antagonist, had deceived Pema Karpo's followers by falsifying and distorting Pema Karpo's final words.

From a broader spiritual perspective, transcending titles and egos, what holds utmost significance is how one lives one's life dedicated to serving others, guided by compassionate actions and sincere intentions. However, this broader view was not shared by those involved. Instead, the situation deepened divisions, as each side was firmly convinced that only their chosen candidate—either Zhabdrung or Pagsam Wangpo—was the rightful reincarnation of Pema Karpo, intensifying the already growing conflict.

Over the years, the Ralung hierarchs made desperate attempts to quell the growing conflict over the reincarnation issue. They sought the assistance of the governor of the Jayul region in southern Tibet and explored all possible avenues. Despite their efforts, the feud only escalated, with the increasing support of Pagsam Wangpo by the Fifth Dalai Lama compounding tensions.

Intractable and uncompromising, Chongye Depa firmly insisted that his son was the rightful reincarnation. Zhabdrung then intervened to try to broker peace, appealing to the Tsang Desi to resolve the dispute. However, heavily reliant on Chongye Depa's support, the Tsang Desi refused to listen and threw his weight behind Pagsam Wangpo, igniting a powder keg of tension between the two factions. This friction continued to escalate from around 1612 until Zhabdrung's departure from Tibet in 1616.

Throughout the tumultuous dispute over his status as the reincarnation of Pema Karpo, Zhabdrung remained steadfast in his belief that the truth would be revealed by Mahakala, the wisdom protector of the Drukpas. Zhabdrung even prophesied that the other candidate would meet his demise before the genuine reincarnation. Calling upon the spiritual guardians, he unleashed a cascade of ominous signs: ravens persistently squawked above the Tsang Desi's palace, owls hooted, and black cats and dogs made unsettling noises throughout the night, leaving the Tsang Desi trembling in fear.

In an attempt to ease tensions, the Tsang Desi extended a cordial invitation to Zhabdrung to visit his palace in Shigatse, in central Tibet, around the year 1614. Zhabdrung confidently accepted and rode into the palace courtyard on his horse. However, rather than fostering harmony, the encounter took a turn for the worse as the Tsang Desi was offended by Zhabdrung's bold entry. The discussions quickly soured, ending without resolution, marking the beginning of a strained relationship between the two men.

The tense relationship between the Tsang Desi and Zhabdrung reached a breaking point in a dramatic incident that marked the beginning of the end of their relationship. As Zhabdrung and his entourage made their way back from the meeting, they encountered trouble at a ferry crossing at a place called Tagdrukha. Attendants of Pawo Tsugla Gyatsho of the Karma Kagyu order prevented them from crossing the Tsangpo River, forcibly removing Zhabdrung from the boat. The situation escalated into violence, with fatal stabbings and drownings adding to the chaos.

Despite the aggression shown toward him, Zhabdrung responded with compassion, ordering his attendants to rescue the drowning members of the opposing party. However, the damage had been done. This incident was among the last straws in the already strained relationship between the Tsang Desi and Zhabdrung.

On their journey back from the troubled river crossing, Zhabdrung and his entourage encountered a woman who had fallen victim to a violent robbery, her jewels stolen by none other than the guards of the Tsang Desi court. Without hesitation, Zhabdrung sprang into action, dispatching his attendants to retrieve the stolen jewelry and ensuring justice was served. The resulting brawl unfortunately left the guards nursing injuries. This incident only added fuel to the conflict between Zhabdrung and the Tsang Desi, who, aligned with the Karma Kagyu order, chose to support Pawo Tsugla Gyatsho over the ferry-crossing altercation.

As news of the dispute spread, the Tsang Desi seethed with anger and vowed to punish Zhabdrung for what he saw as a disregard for the law. He demanded compensation to Pawo Tsugla Gyatsho for the loss of life and the surrender of the sacred vertebra relic of Tsangpa Gyare. However, Zhabdrung ignored these orders, further exacerbating the rift between them.

In a fiery letter to the Tsang Desi, Zhabdrung did not hold back in expressing his frustration at the Tsang Desi's rudeness. With unyielding conviction, he declared that he would not hand over the relic even if he possessed it, claiming that its existence could not be confirmed, as it was as vast as the sky and smaller than a mustard seed. Dismissing the Tsang Desi's demands as mere trifles, Zhabdrung recounted a humiliating experience suffered by his father and grandfather at the hands of the Tsang Desi's court. The two had been made to prostrate before the barely five-year-old Pagsam Wangpo, an act that had caused a deep rift within the Drukpa community at the time. With words sharper than a double-edged sword, Zhabdrung warned the Tsang Desi of the dire consequences of his actions as he invoked the name of the almighty spiritual guardian Mahakala. However, the Tsang Desi was not one to back down. The relationship between them deteriorated even further, setting the stage for further conflict.

As hostilities reached fever pitch, Zhabdrung sensed that the lineage was under threat and reached into his bodhisattva toolbox of spiritual powers. He offered a small torma (ritual sculpture made from barley flour and butter) to the fearsome Mahakala, and in response, a massive fireball materialized over the Tsang Desi's palace in Shigatse. Flocks of ravens swooped and cawed, while roving packs of dogs added to the sense of impending doom.

As a countermeasure, the Tsang Desi frantically summoned hundreds of black magicians and monastics to ward off the looming omens. Meanwhile, a strange turn of events unfolded: Chongye Depa, the original source of the dispute over Pema Karpo's reincarnation, committed suicide by stabbing himself with his own sword. His accomplice, Lhatsawa Ngawang Zangpo, died suddenly, reportedly from an epileptic attack. It seemed that the gods themselves had taken sides in the escalating conflict, leaving both parties to wonder what other twists of fate lay ahead.

Convinced that Zhabdrung's spiritual guardians were orchestrating the series of frightening events, the Tsang Desi resolved to take drastic action. He mobilized a sizable army with the intent to capture Zhabdrung, and at that moment Zhabdrung's fate appeared all but sealed. However, life had other surprises in store.

A stroke of luck came in the form of a minister from the Tsang court, Kaloen Zugpopa. He had been a supporter of the Drukpa establishment ever since Zhabdrung's father had granted him access to view the sacred relics of Ralung, and it was he who leaked the secret plan to arrest Zhabdrung. This act of betrayal would prove to be a game changer in the unfolding drama.

Just as the ancient prophecies had predicted, the karmic forces were aligning, and momentum was building for Zhabdrung to leave for Bhutan. It was during this time of uncertainty that Zhelngo Sithar, a staunch patron from the Gon Gasa region of Bhutan, came to pay his respects to Zhabdrung, unaware of the troubles Zhabdrung was facing. After Zhabdrung shared his difficulties with the Tsang Desi and the plot to assassinate him, Zhelngo Sithar advised him that he should come to Bhutan, where he would be warmly welcomed due to his extensive network of Drukpa Kargyu monastic patronages. It would be a place where he could find peace and quiet away from the antagonism and stress.

Zhabdrung initially considered seeking refuge in Mongolia. However, the night following Zhelngo Sithar's suggestion, he had a significant dream. In the dream, a cat was damaging a torma on the altar, which was not a good omen. This was followed by another dream of a raven approaching him and flying southward, leading him to a place he did not recognize. Later, upon arriving in Bhutan, he would identify this place to be Pangri Zampa on the northern fringes of Thimphu. On waking, Zhabdrung sought guidance from the Rangjung Kharsapani relic, praying fervently for a sign regarding his future direction. The relic turned southward, making his course of action unequivocal.

As Zhabdrung prepared to leave behind the treacherous plots and dangers that had been brewing, he received a letter that would alter the course of his life. The letter came from the Obtsho Lama, a revered figure from the Gon region of Gasa in northern Bhutan, with whom the Drukpa hereditary family of Ralung had a long-standing relationship. For centuries, the Obtsho family had sent their sons to Ralung for training, and now they were extending a helping hand to Zhabdrung. The invitation to come to Bhutan was a glimmer of hope in the midst of a dark storm, a promise of sanctuary and protection in a new land of unknown wonders. As Zhabdrung read the letter, a flicker of optimism ignited in his heart, for he recognized it as the path of destiny he was meant to follow.

With the sacred relics carefully packed and a party of trusted attendants assembled, Zhabdrung's secret journey to Bhutan was about to begin. Tenzin Drukgyal, the chant master and the financial overseer from the Obtsho lineage, led the way, accompanied by a disciple, Damcho Gyaltshen, and descendants of Phajo Drukgom

Zhigpo. Once in Bhutan, Tenzin Drukgyal would prove to be an invaluable ally, standing by Zhabdrung's side during countless battles against the forces from Tibet and eventually rising to become the first Druk Desi in the newly formed state. Similarly, Damcho Gyaltshen would play a vital role in the ecclesiastical affairs of Bhutan.

As the party ventured into the night, Zhabdrung's father, Tenpai Nyima, remained behind to tend to the Ralung monastic estate, his heart heavy with the weight of his son's departure. A whole new chapter in Bhutan's history was about to unfold.

CHAPTER 6

Turning the Horse Southward

Seek out repose in the southern valleys,
on the border, through the southern door.
If you do this, you will gain as much success
   in seven days of meditation,
as in seven years in the Land of Snows.

GURU RINPOCHE

In the Year of the Fire Dragon, at the age of twenty-two, Zhabdrung heeded Guru Rinpoche's advice and journeyed south to Bhutan. The year was 1616. The timing was hardly a coincidence, given his ancestral and spiritual ties dating back to the establishment of the Drukpa Kargyu order—the Thunder Dragon school.

Under the cover of darkness, a caravan of horses and mules set out, laden with essential supplies and the precious relics from Ralung. Accompanied by a retinue of around thirty devotees, Zhabdrung embarked on a perilous journey across rugged terrain, scaling mighty peaks and braving harsh weather conditions. Ravines and rocky outcroppings offered fleeting shelter as the group pressed onward, their determination fueled by the promise of reaching the pass at the present-day Tibet-Bhutan border.

As they crossed the treacherous terrain, they entered a realm where the ordinary blurred with the mystical. Strange and otherworldly phenomena seemed to haunt the Himalayan wilderness, as if hidden spirits and deities watched their every move. Tsang Khenchen meticulously documented these extraordinary encounters, drawn from years of intimate conversations with Zhabdrung.

Approaching the border, they were faced with a fierce onslaught of hail and snowstorms, shrouding the landscape in a veil of white. Undeterred by the unforgiving weather, Zhabdrung called upon his mastery of *tummo*, a Tibetan Buddhist technique for generating inner body heat, while the group sought refuge in the sanctuary of Gomdraphu, a nearby cave.

For days on end, they battled through relentless swirls of snow and biting gales, their unwavering resolve tested against nature's fury. Each obstacle became a chance for spiritual growth, a living testament to their unshakable Buddhist faith. Amid the turmoil, a truly extraordinary event unfolded: hailstones transformed into crimson stones before their eyes. This miraculous metamorphosis, attributed to Zhabdrung's revered status as a bodhisattva, left an indelible mark on all present.

Even now, the cave radiates warmth, serving as a testament to the enduring legacy of that miraculous moment. Despite its remote high-altitude location, nestled among snowcapped peaks and crystalline glaciers, the cave remains a refuge of comfort and wonder. Local nomads speak of discovering peculiar red stones scattered in and around the cave, a tangible reminder of the divine presence that once graced these sacred grounds.

During their stay in the cave, another mystical chapter unfolded, intertwining the fates of Zhabdrung and Palden Lhamo—the spiritual guardian who had once watched over his expectant mother in the guise of a cuckoo. In a vivid dream, Palden Lhamo appeared before Zhabdrung, her celestial form radiant against the darkness, urging him to heed the signs that would guide their path.

As dawn broke, a haunting cry pierced the stillness as a fox stealthily bounded through the powdery light snow. Zhabdrung sensed that the fox was Palden Lhamo in disguise and followed its lead with unwavering faith. Through treacherous terrain and over towering peaks, the fox navigated for the group, revealing hidden paths and safe passages until they reached the summit. There, amid swirling mist, the fox vanished into the ether. The pass became known as Wake La, "the Fox Pass," a testament to the divine guidance that had led them through the perilous journey.

During a brief rest stop on the challenging descent, Zhabdrung lifted his hat to shake off the snow. As the flakes fell, they inadvertently etched delicate marks onto the rock beneath, capturing the attention of the entire group. This incident became woven into the tapestry of mystical tales surrounding his southward journey. Legends also whispered of how every touch of his walking stick left indelible marks on the rocks, seen by many as a sign of his destined role in Bhutan.

Leaving imprints on rocks to inspire those on the spiritual path was an act performed by many accomplished Buddhist masters, as documented in numerous ancient spiritual biographies. Bhutan serves as a treasure trove of these imprints, adding curiosity and mystique to the land. Who knows? Perhaps it is possible to influence the atomic structure of matter through a sufficiently high spiritual vibration, transcending the boundaries of the ordinary and expected, as Zhabdrung unquestionably did.

Continuing the spiritual legacy of the Drukpa Kargyu order, spanning from the majestic peaks of Tibet to the lush valleys of Bhutan, a powerful legacy had been forged through generations of spiritual masters. Among them were Zhabdrung's forefathers, whose teachings had already taken root in the Southern Land long before his arrival.

As Zhabdrung journeyed toward Bangdekha, a grand opening below the Fox Pass, anticipation filled the air. News of the great bodhisattva's impending arrival ignited excitement among those in the know. Amid the ethereal plumes of burning incense, the Obtsho Lama, who had extended the formal invitation to Zhabdrung, stood at the forefront of a small gathering. The atmosphere was one of deep reverence and quiet celebration. While the welcoming party was relieved to see Zhabdrung arrive safely, the moment was bittersweet. He had left behind his beloved homeland and his primary spiritual guide—his father. Nevertheless, his arrival marked a momentous occasion—an opportunity to carry on the work of his ancestors and fulfill his destiny as a Dharma king and unifier of the Southern Land.

Tsang Khenchen describes Zhabdrung as possessing the spiritual ability to view the whole of Bhutan, from the lofty peaks from where he descended to the glistening plains of present-day India. As he traversed the mountains that Tsang Khenchen likens to holy crystalline stupas, wild elephants, and crouching lions, vibrant rainbows arched across the sky. Though these mountains may have seemed insubstantial to the average person, they were nonetheless stunning as they receded into the bluish-gray Himalayan haze of the late afternoon.

As Zhabdrung ventured deeper into the blue pine forests on his southward journey, he encountered a breathtaking scene. The trees had transformed into a magical playground for exotic birdlife, with birds flitting from branch to branch, displaying a kaleidoscope of colorful plumage, and filling the air with a symphony of sweet song. It was as if they were performing just for him—and perhaps they were!

But this was just the beginning of the wonderland that awaited him. The landscape was adorned with a vibrant array of scented blooms, each one more radiant than the last. This was the sacred abode of the nature spirits and deities, whose presence could be felt in every rustle of leaves and every chirp of birdsong.

As he journeyed farther, Zhabdrung encountered even more stunning vistas: rooftops adorned with bloodred chilies drying in the sun against a backdrop of lush-green rice-terraced hillslopes shimmering in the sunlight. It was a momentary glimpse of the beauty and diversity of the land that would become his new home.

As he navigated the terrain, the promise of warmer weather beckoned him onward. Villagers, who had heard of his arrival through word of mouth, eagerly offered tea and delicacies as he graciously moved among scattered dwellings, welcomed by the sweet-smelling smoke of burning juniper. It was not until he reached the village of Lungo, in the remote region of Laya, that he encountered his first established settlement.

From the moment I arrived in Laya, I was captivated by its vibrant nomadic culture, breathtaking snowcapped peaks, and the laughter of warmhearted village women filling the air. It felt like a lost paradise. Driven by the desire to experience the same stunning landscape that Zhabdrung had encountered and to immerse myself in the unique culture of the region, I had trekked there over a year before as part of my research for this book. I wanted to get as close to Zhabdrung's world as possible.

Every night I would huddle around the *bukhari*, a traditional wood-burning stove, with my hosts. I drank endless cups of smoke-flavored yak butter tea, more out of politeness than genuine fondness. Yet I found myself mesmerized by the enthralling stories of Zhabdrung, relayed to me with great enthusiasm. It felt like a friendly bidding war as to who could tell the most captivating story!

Almost every household boasted an ancestor who had met Zhabdrung during his visit in 1616. I was shown numerous shoes and pots, claimed to have been gifted by him in appreciation for their ancestors' generous hospitality. These treasured relics were proudly displayed in intricately adorned altar rooms, alongside walls piled high with luxurious yak wool blankets—a sign of wealth among the Layaps (people of Laya).

During my stay in Laya, I had the good fortune of meeting Ap Tshering, a jovial yak herder who was a walking encyclopedia on all things Zhabdrung. My host had thoughtfully invited him over once he had heard that I was writing a book about this great lama.

As I peered through the window in anticipation of his arrival, I saw the light from a flashlight cutting a brilliant white arc through the darkness. In no time, Ap Tshering strode confidently into the house, his infectious smile illuminating the room. A well-known character among the Layaps, he regaled us with riveting stories about Zhabdrung, holding us spellbound well into the night. Sadly, our conversations had to end due to an early start the next morning, but the memories lingered, providing a rich layer of insight and understanding to my research.

Zhabdrung continued his journey south until he reached Taktsekha, where his horse left a hoofprint embedded in a rock. This event led to the site becoming known as Tajekha (Display of a Hoofprint), revealing yet another testament to the significance of his passage through this sacred land.

As small crowds gathered along his path, the air became filled with the smell of delectable food while melodious tunes wafted through the air for miles. People from diverse backgrounds, ranging from nomadic herders to wealthy landlords, converged to pay their respects, offering food, incense, and riches in honor of Zhabdrung's wisdom and guidance.

Upon reaching the settlement in Gasa, Zhabdrung was welcomed by a modest procession and escorted southward to the Obtsho Dzong, the stronghold of the Obtsho Lama. There he received a heartfelt reception and was grandly hosted. The following day, he was guided to the present site of the majestic Gasa Dzong, once a sacred meditation ground of Drubthob Terkhungpa, a close disciple of Tsangpa Gyare, and an ancestor of the Obtsho family clan.

The air was heavy with the sweet aroma of burning incense as Zhabdrung made his way through the eager crowd, each person seeking a blessed glimpse while presenting traditional offerings of butter and milk. The valley resonated with horns and joyous songs, creating an electrifying, unforgettable atmosphere. At every stop, Zhabdrung methodically blessed each individual, imparting Buddhist teachings wherever he stayed, leaving a lasting impression on all he encountered.

When Zhabdrung reached the village of Damji in southern Gasa, it appears that he altered his course upon learning of potential adversaries north of Punakha. This led him on a challenging journey along an ancient nomadic trail, following the Rimmi Chu (river) and later the Lingzhi Chu. Navigating rugged terrain and passing through the small hamlets of Chebisa and Gonyul, he eventually arrived in Lingzhi in the northern part of the Thimphu district, where he was warmly welcomed.[42]

One year I trekked this same path in reverse as autumn gave way to winter. The windswept landscape, encircled by towering, snow-capped mountains, was breathtaking. The only visible difference from Zhabdrung's time was the presence of electricity poles, which guided our journey from Lingzhi to Gonyul and onward to Chebisa.

In Gonyul, a gracious family of Tibetan heritage welcomed us with

Ap Tshering
from Laya
(Photo © 2024
Sasha Wakefield)

warm butter tea and a generous spread of local dishes for lunch. From there, we continued to Chebisa, where we stayed as guests in a local home. Just as in Zhabdrung's time, the locals opened their doors to weary travelers. Their kind hospitality and bottomless cups of tea were a blessing after hours of navigating the harsh landscape, where biting winds left our skin chapped and raw.

In the spring and summer months, the air in the valleys of Lingzhi and Mentsephu, located farther south, is thick with the fragrant scents of medicinal and aromatic plants. Mentsephu, a sacred site where the cliff face is said to have manifested as the deity Chakrasamvara—an emanation of Vajradhara Buddha—to the seventh Senge of the Drukpa Kargyu lineage, became a gathering place for the spiritual guardians and wealthy patrons of the Drukpa Kargyu order upon Zhabdrung's arrival. These patrons demonstrated their devotion and respect with lavish offerings and by waving white flags. Zhabdrung's mere presence imbued the land with tranquility, quelling disputes, theft, and malevolent forces.

From this point, Zhabdrung forged his way through the untamed landscape, following ancient yak trails and winding river gorges. His path took him through Barshong, then along the well-trodden nomadic route via Tokchung and Dzongkha. He ascended the mountain pass of Zatog La, before descending to the settlements of Kabesa and Pangri Zampa in northern Thimphu.

Just as he had dreamed before leaving Tibet, Zhabdrung and his entourage were guided by Legon Jarog Dongchen, an emanation of Mahakala who appeared as a raven, across the rugged mountain terrain above Tango via the Zatog La pass. When they reached Pangri Zampa, a place he had recognized from his dream, the raven vanished into an ancient cypress tree. Everything seemed to be falling into place as planned.

Like the Lingzhi area, Pangri Zampa possessed its own unique charm, offering a distinct atmosphere and beauty that set it apart. Druk Phodrangding Lhakhang, constructed by Zhabdrung's great-great-grandfather, rests on the banks of a crystal clear river. This river, often a gushing torrent of icy water from nearby mountain peaks, provides essential irrigation for the abundant fruit orchards and grain fields surrounding the villages. Luxuriant stands of forest extend up the mountain slopes, offering a haven for a diverse array of birdlife and other fauna. The familiarity of the place gave Zhabdrung an overwhelming sense of destiny—a reassuring feeling for anyone venturing far away from home and into a foreign land.

Following long-standing tradition, patrons, monastics, and villagers from the region gathered to greet him with elaborate offerings. At Druk Phodrangding Lhakhang, he presided over sacred ceremonies dedicated to the three prominent spiritual guardians of the Drukpa Kargyu order, collectively known as Gonpo Chamdrelsum. His visit extended to nearby Dechenphu Lhakhang, where he was

warmly embraced by the community. There, amid a spirit of camaraderie, Zhabdrung received pledges of allegiance from both the local
spiritual deity, Genyen Jakpa Melen, and the spiritual guardians.

Upon Zhabdrung's return to Pangri Zampa, a bustling crowd of
devotees had gathered, each with unique stories and purposes for
seeking teachings from the great master. Excitement and anticipation radiated from the followers, their eyes fixed on the spiritually imposing figure who had come to guide them. Among the
crowd were spiritual leaders such as Tshewang Tenzin of Tango and
descendants of Phajo, all eager to receive Zhabdrung's blessings and
hear his wisdom. With an intuitive grasp of each individual's needs,
Zhabdrung imparted his teachings with precision and compassion,
following in the footsteps of Buddha himself.

Zhabdrung's journey across Bhutan was one of wonder and challenge, interwoven with tales of mythical creatures and fierce rivals.
One such legend revolves around the renowned yak Nyima Senge,
who had accompanied him on his journey from Tibet. According to
the tale, this yak alerted Zhabdrung to a rocky outcrop by bleating
from its dizzying heights. It was at this spot in 1620 that Zhabdrung founded the site of Cheri Monastery, the inaugural Drukpa
Kargyu monastic institution, heralding a sacred place from where
the teachings would swiftly spread across the land.

His arrival in Bhutan set in motion a chain reaction of positive
events. People felt safe to move between regions, and an overriding
sense of peace enveloped the land. However, not all was well. During
his travels to the various regions, he encountered numerous rival
factions determined to thwart the spread of the Drukpa Kargyu
teachings.

Meanwhile, back in Tibet, the Tsang Desi had seized control of the
Drukpa Kargyu strongholds of Druk Sewa Jangchubling and other
Drukpa monasteries, while Zhabdrung's father and community of
monks were held captive inside the Ralung estate. Fueled by his
insatiable lust for power and seething envy of Zhabdrung's growing popularity in the south, the Tsang Desi harbored deep-seated
hatred, prompting him to launch an assault.

CHAPTER 7

The First of Many Conflicts

Zhabdrung's journey to Bhutan was fraught with peril, as he navigated treacherous mountain passes in a chapter defined by profound challenges and ultimate triumphs. Undeterred by adversity,
he remained steadfast in his commitment to serve others and
uphold the unbroken Drukpa Kargyu lineage of Buddha's teachings. Guided by deep compassion for all beings, Zhabdrung forged
ahead, fulfilling ancient prophecies and leaving an unrivaled legacy.

An integral aspect of Zhabdrung's story is the skillful way he
navigated attacks fueled by jealousy and the thirst for power. As we
follow his journey through these adversities—marked by diplomacy,
compassion, and ultimate triumph over evil—an inspiring image
comes to light. He emerges as not only a skilled statesman but also a
humble Buddhist practitioner and a genuine bodhisattva, challenging the often erroneous portrayal of him as a warrior, antagonist,
or black magician.

The First Conflict

In 1617, during Zhabdrung's inaugural journey across his newfound
homeland, a confrontational letter arrived from the Tsang Desi,
Karma Phuntsok Namgyal, the authoritative figure in the U-Tsang
region of Tibet at the time. As Zhabdrung cast his eyes over the
contents of the letter, he immediately knew that trouble was brewing. The cutting tone of the letter clashed sharply with the pristine
mountain air, infused with the sweet scent of blue pine. The joy

he had felt from visiting the monastic seats of his forefathers and connecting with the local people was momentarily dampened.

As he carefully read the elegantly handwritten letter, he perceived the underlying intentions veiled behind the threats. It became unmistakably clear that the Tsang Desi aimed to formally legitimize Pagsam Wangpo as the reincarnation of Pema Karpo and lay claim to the sacred backbone relic of Tsangpa Gyare.

The letter brashly accused Zhabdrung of being an impostor, disputing his claim as the true emanation of Chenrezig by dredging up past conflicts, notably the ferry-crossing incident at Tagdrukha. The Tsang Desi boldly proclaimed his takeover of the Drukpa monastic seats, issuing a stern ultimatum for the immediate return of the sacred vertebra relic. In Buddhist circles, this relic held profound significance, symbolizing not just spiritual authority but also coveted control over the vast number of Drukpa Kargyu followers, intensifying the desire to possess it.

Zhabdrung, known for his inner confidence, delivered a stern rebuttal to the Tsang Desi's accusations and demands. He accused the Tsang Desi of hypocrisy and negligence toward the Drukpa Kargyu order while firmly asserting his identity as an emanation of Chenrezig. To substantiate his claim, Zhabdrung cited prophecies from Gya Jampel Sangwa and Tsangpa Gyare, foretelling that eighty-four descendants of the Gya hereditary lineage would be emanations of Chenrezig, a lineage where he stood as a prominent figure.

His response revealed unshakable strength and conviction. His statement to the Tsang Desi—"For those who accept me as Chenrezig, I am; and for those who do not, I am not"—underscored his self-assurance. Confident in his true identity, he was free from the need for external validation. Fearlessly confronting the Tsang Desi, he declared that if he could not stop the Tsang Desi's negative deeds, he would accept that he was not the true reincarnation of Pema Karpo and that the Drukpa Kargyu order lacked spiritual protectors. Feathers were ruffled, and rather than negotiating, the Tsang Desi began orchestrating a plan for a full-scale invasion to annihilate Zhabdrung and seize the sacred relics, setting the stage for a fierce battle.

While war cries reverberated from the north, Zhabdrung faced another threat from a different corner—the Lama Khag Nga. This group held grudges against Zhabdrung's rising influence, particularly in the western regions of Bhutan where his ancestors had established Drukpa Kargyu strongholds. Joining forces with the Tsang Desi's army, they attacked Zhabdrung's ancestral temple of Druk Choding in Paro, taking his followers by surprise despite Zhabadrung's forewarning that an assault may be imminent.

Rather than leading the army of devotees into battle, Zhabdrung made a strategic decision to retreat to Jela Dzong, an ancestral fortress built by his great-great-grandfather, Ngawang Chogyal, situated on a ridge above Paro Dzong. Eyewitnesses reported seeing his hair billowing in the wind as he hastily departed from the battlefield.

Zhabdrung chose not to directly engage in the wars he faced. Instead, he exerted his spiritual influence from afar, refraining from issuing retaliatory orders. It was the unwavering devotion of his followers that inspired them to act independently and confront the enemy.

During the attack, Zhabdrung secluded himself at Jela Dzong, performing rituals and offering prayers to the spiritual guardian Yeshe Gonpo (Mahakala). While resting on his climb to the pass summit, he had a vision of the guardian, who prophesied his victory over the invading forces. According to scriptural texts, Yeshe Gonpo symbolically offered Zhabdrung the whole of Bhutan in the palm of his hand, a promising sign of his future success in uniting the nation.

Despite the positive prophecy, Zhabdrung found himself overwhelmed by homesickness and confusion as a wave of melancholy swept over him. The stark contrast between the horrors of war—its violence and suffering—and his yearning to follow the ascetic path gripped him in that moment.

At a place called Tshalunang, nestled between Thimphu and Paro, Zhabdrung resorted to a poignant act. He blew his ritual human-thigh-bone trumpet three times in the direction of his ancestral seat of Ralung. In a moment of vulnerability, he openly confessed to his father and Tsangpa Gyare about his near desire to abandon his noble intent of establishing the prophesied dual system of governance. Expressing deep regret for the recent casualties of war and acknowledging the upheaval his presence caused his patrons in Paro, he reflected on the overwhelming challenges he faced in this foreign land.

This revelation sheds light on Zhabdrung's genuine humanity and compassion, serving as a touching reminder that despite being a tenth-bhumi bodhisattva, he navigated life's spectrum of joys and sorrows like any other ordinary human being. He existed in flesh and blood, susceptible to frustration and anguish, even though his mission was far from ordinary. It is easy to empathize with his plight, to feel his sadness and desperation, particularly considering his profound regret for the lives lost. He had reached rock bottom—chased out of his homeland, thrust into a barbaric tribal land pursued by an army hell-bent on destroying him—an ordeal few have experienced, yet one many can relate to. We've all had to contend with our own Tsang Desis in our lives—there is no doubt about that!

At this point, one might assume that Zhabdrung had fallen into depression due to the harsh realities he faced. However, his experience actually proved to be quite the opposite.

During the night, amid his inner turmoil, Zhabdrung experienced a transformative dream: A shimmering image of the wisdom dakinis materialized before him, urging him to follow his karmic destiny. This profound vision reignited his optimism and bolstered his unwavering commitment to establish the prophesied dual system of governance in the Southern Land. As a bodhisattva, he saw beyond the illusory nature of appearances, demonstrating patience toward those who caused harm and resisting worldly temptations. As Zhabdrung embraced the reality of sacrificing his own peace and happiness for the greater good, his determination solidified, his doubts evaporated, and his bodhisattva motivation surged stronger than ever.

As the battle approached its end, Tibetan forces reported witnessing a remarkable sight: an apparition of Zhabdrung, dressed as a yogi, leading a formidable army. Zhabdrung held his thigh-bone trumpet high in the air, wrapped in a blue ribbon, while warriors brandished their own thigh-bone trumpets, proudly displaying the flags of the spiritual guardians. Among these warriors were fierce-looking nonhuman beings and animals, with cawing vultures seen encircling the army from two sides, forming a protective barrier. This apparition was believed to be a manifestation resulting from Zhabdrung's invocation of the spiritual guardians, a testament to his powerful karmic connection with them.

This display of supernatural powers startled the attackers, causing them to hastily scatter in all directions, ultimately resulting in victory for the Drukpas. Zhabdrung's strategic use of these supernatural powers resolved the battle with significantly fewer casualties and less violence than an all-out war would have caused. This exemplifies the skillful actions of a real-life bodhisattva aimed at minimizing the loss of life.

During the heat of the attack, Zhabdrung had traveled to Pangri Zampa and ascended to the sacred site of Tango, nestled among the towering mountain peaks. There, for several days, he sought refuge in the company of Tshewang Tenzin, revered as the reincarnation of Phajo Drukgom Zhigpo. Tshewang Tenzin's lineage within the Drukpa Kargyu order runs deep; his father, Ngawang Tenzin, was the son of the revered Drukpa master, Drukpa Kunle.

Continuing his journey, Zhabdrung safely transported the sacred relics to the Wangdue Phodrang area, where he was warmly welcomed by the descendants of Phajo Drukgom Zhigpo. This underscored the substantial support he had gained in Bhutan. His triumph, coupled with prophetic visions of success, affirmed his important role in fulfilling the ancient prophecies and disseminating the Dharma throughout Bhutan.

Zhabdrung's embodiment of virtues such as dignity, inner confidence, grace, and wisdom stood in stark contrast to the unrestrained cruelty, aggression, and unchecked envy displayed by the Tsang Desi. It is astonishing to think that the same individual who had driven Zhabdrung from his homeland later dispatched an army to pursue him on foreign soil.

After his resounding victory against the Tsang Desi, Zhabdrung conducted a grand thanksgiving ceremony to honor the spiritual guardians for their role in the victory. He then embarked on a tour of gratitude and blessings, visiting the small hamlets scattered across the Thimphu region.

At each stop, a breathtaking spectacle unfolded: tents arranged in circular formations resonated with the melodic chants of monks and the ceremonial sounds of ritual instruments echoing across vast distances. People from far and wide converged in these makeshift towns to honor Zhabdrung and seek his blessings. His egalitarian spirit and boundless compassion were truly touching as he dedicated time to ensure that everyone had the chance to receive his blessings before he moved on to the next location.

A Man Called Phajo

Now let us take a moment to examine more closely the remarkable legacy of Phajo Drukgom Zhigpo, a thirteenth-century Buddhist figure briefly mentioned in the chapter on prophecies. While his contributions to the establishment of the Drukpa Kargyu order in Bhutan are well documented, his significance extends far beyond that. Centuries later, his karmic connection with Zhabdrung played a crucial role in the latter's efforts toward unification. It is indeed mind-boggling to contemplate how the actions of one person can create ripples across generations, shaping the course of history in profound and lasting ways.

Phajo Drukgom Zhigpo's lineage appears somewhat of an enigma. Differing claims about his family's roots persist, with some asserting their connection to a distant branch of the Drukpa (Gya) hereditary clan, while others strongly disputing this belief. The considerable geographical distance between their homeland in the Kham region of Tibet and Ralung Monastery, however, raises doubts about this alleged connection.

Phajo's spiritual journey began in the Nyingma school of Tibetan Buddhism. However, in his early thirties, he was deeply moved upon hearing of the great holy being Tsangpa Gyare. Without hesitation, he undertook the long journey to Ralung to meet him—only to discover tragically that Tsangpa Gyare had already passed away. Despite this setback, Phajo remained undaunted and continued his spiritual quest, eventually connecting with Tsangpa Gyare's nephew and successor of the Drukpa Kargyu lineage, Onre Dharma Senge. Tsangpa Gyare had prophesied that his nephew, a distinguished spiritual master in his own right, would mentor a son from Kham in the teachings of the Drukpa Kargyu order. This chosen disciple was none other than Phajo himself.

The prophecy states,

> A son from Kham is coming to Ralung but he will not meet me. You look after and teach him, then direct him to the southern valley blessed by Guru Rinpoche. He will be of great benefit to the buddhadharma there.

After fully mastering the teachings of the Drukpa Kargyu lineage, Phajo found himself in possession of a letter from Onre Dharma Senge. The letter contained prophetic words penned by Tsangpa Gyare years earlier outlining his destined role in spreading the Drukpa Kargyu teachings in the Southern Land. So, at the age of forty, he embarked on his journey southward to fulfill this prophecy. He eventually arrived at Lingzhi, nestled in the northern part of the Thimphu district, at the base of Tsherim Gang (mountain), believed to be the abode of the goddess of long life, Tashi Tsheringma.

Lingzhi, a high-altitude settlement, greeted Phajo with wind-swept landscapes and sharp, rocky escarpments adorned with fragrant medicinal plants. Its remote location, immersed in pristine natural beauty, served as a sanctuary for spiritual practitioners seeking solitude and enlightenment. The tranquility of Lingzhi, combined with its breathtaking vistas, greatly inspired Phajo as he embarked on his mission to disseminate the profound teachings of the Drukpa Kargyu lineage.

Renowned for his ability to subjugate demons and malevolent entities during his travels, Phajo swiftly gained widespread acclaim.

While at the Taktsang region of Paro, he had a dream of a young boy, believed to be Guru Rinpoche, who instructed him to meditate in twelve specific locations throughout Bhutan. Following this divine guidance and traveling throughout the western regions to set up sacred areas for meditation, Phajo made his way to Dodena,[43] the present-day site of Dorden Tashithang Buddhist University, situated on the northern fringes of Thimphu.

Soon after, near the heart of present-day Thimphu town, Phajo encountered his longtime consort, Sonam Paldron, at a bridge spanning a gushing river. Revered as a dakini and an emanation of the eleventh-century Tibetan yogini Machig Labdron, Sonam Paldron joined Phajo in laying the groundwork for the Drukpa Kargyu seat at Dodena, dedicated to propagating its teachings. The bridge became known as Lungten Zampa, "the Bridge of Prophecy."

Dodena lies near the base of two southward-facing hills, where Cheri and Tango Monasteries were built. According to the *Tantra of Mahakala*, such hills are considered conducive to the wrathful practices of Mahakala. This may explain why Zhabdrung later performed rituals from these locations to subdue the Tsang Desi:

> A tantric practitioner, holding an unbroken *samaya* [sacred Buddhist vow] must practice in a black cave with a sharp apex, in a cave facing southward, at the top of a hill.

As the story goes, Phajo crossed the river from Dodena after hearing the neighing of a horse. From the base of the hill where Cheri Monastery now stands, he gazed across to the opposite hill and saw the shape of a horse's head in the cliff face—believed to be the tantric deity Hayagriva, the wrathful manifestation of Chenrezig. Phajo, regarded as an emanation of Hayagriva, identified this site as the future location of Tango Monastery, cementing himself as its original founder.

Before meeting Sonam Paldron, Phajo was believed to have fathered a son named Dampa while meditating near the village of Wang Chudo in the Thimphu district, whom he declared as the reincarnation of the esteemed Indian spiritual master, Dampa Sangye. Following Phajo's passing, Dampa assumed responsibility for overseeing his seat at Dodena and continuing his father's legacy.

During his lifetime, Phajo established numerous meditation centers (*drubde*), firmly anchoring the teachings of the Drukpa Kargyu order in western Bhutan. This effort paved the way for the eventual arrival of Zhabdrung centuries later. Phajo's four surviving sons, born to Sonam Paldron, succeeded him, each governing different regions of western Bhutan in accordance with Buddhist principles.

Phajo's life came to an end during a retreat at Tango at the age of sixty-eight. In his final moments, he shared a significant prophecy to his sons, encouraging them to uphold the teachings of the Dharma and support the dual system of governance. Phajo foresaw that the future leaders of the Drukpa Kargyu order in Bhutan would originate from Ralung, and he urged his sons to ensure that their descendants wholeheartedly serve these future leaders.

The subsequent patronage and loyalty extended by Phajo Drukgom Zhigpo's descendants firmly embedded the seeds of the Drukpa Kargyu teachings from Ralung in Bhutan. By the end of the sixteenth century, five prominent Drukpa Kargyu families had established roots in Bhutan,[44] providing a solid foundation of support for Zhabdrung upon his arrival in 1616. This support continued during his subsequent efforts to consolidate and unify the western regions.

Now the story takes an interesting twist. As we recall, Tsangpa Gyare and Phajo never had the chance to meet in person, with Tsangpa Gyare passing away just before Phajo reached Ralung. However, Tsangpa Gyare had prophesied that Phajo would spread the Drukpa Kargyu teachings in Bhutan, a mission he successfully fulfilled. In another prophecy,[45] Tsangpa Gyare hinted at a future meeting with Phajo, suggesting that he would reincarnate when the Drukpa lineage needed him the most.

Reflecting on the meeting between Tshewang Tenzin and Zhabdrung at Tango, both recognized as the reincarnations of Phajo and Tsangpa Gyare respectively, it becomes clear that Tsangpa Gyare's prophecy of a future meeting had come to pass. Despite occurring more than four hundred years later, this encounter played a crucial role in establishing a partnership essential for uniting the Southern land. While some may dismiss the notion of predestined encounters, this ancient prophecy remains undeniably intriguing, pointing to the significance of Zhabdrung's earthly mission.

At their amicable meeting, Tshewang Tenzin made a startling gesture by gifting the entire area of Tango, along with all its sacred relics, to Zhabdrung. This spontaneous act not only revealed his deep commitment to Zhabdrung but also hinted at a profound karmic bond between them. As we have come to learn, Phajo had envisioned the cliff face at Tango as a horse's head—the deity known as Hayagriva, a wrathful manifestation of Chenrezig. Considering Tshewang Tenzin's acknowledgment as the reincarnation of Phajo and his strong karmic bond with Zhabdrung, alongside Zhabdrung's recognition as an emanation of Chenrezig, it becomes clear from a spiritual standpoint why Tshewang Tenzin would gift the entire Tango area to Zhabdrung. In Buddhist tradition, such acts of generosity toward one's spiritual teacher are believed to lead one to nirmanakaya, the emanation of Buddha in human form.

Renowned for his expert craftsmanship, Zhabdrung reciprocated by gifting Tshewang Tenzin a white sandalwood statue of the standing image of Chenrezig. Tsang Khenchen had personally held this statue while Tshewang Tenzin recounted to him how his house in Kabesa, located on the northern periphery of Thimphu, was engulfed in flames, destroying all his possessions. Surprisingly, this statue, wrapped in a thin cotton cloth, remained unscathed. This event further solidified Tshewang Tenzin's belief that Zhabdrung was truly the emanation of Chenrezig.

Given their previous lives as Phajo and Tsangpa Gyare centuries earlier, it is not surprising that Tshewang Tenzin held a profound devotion to Zhabdrung. During Zhabdrung's rule, Tshewang Tenzin emerged as a key supporter of Zhabdrung's efforts in forging a unified nation.

Back to Zhabdrung

As synchronicities unfolded, support for Zhabdrung gradually grew. However, a crucial component necessary for a specific meditation practice to protect the Drukpa Kargyu teachings and ward off the Tsang Desi's fury was missing—a sacred triangular metal box known as a *drubkhung*, which remained in Ralung. Recognizing its significance, Zhabdrung ordered its immediate retrieval.

In 1618, with all necessary materials in hand, Zhabdrung ventured into a cave just below the main site of Tango. This cave, known as Dudul Phug[46]—the "Cave Where Evil Was Subdued"—became the site of his meditative practice aimed at thwarting the attacks by the Tsang Desi. Notably, 1618 was considered astrologically unfavorable for Zhabdrung, making it an opportune time for him to enter a meditation retreat. The following wall mural of Zhabdrung with his two close attendants is located in the Gyalse Zimchung on the upper level of Tango Monastery—the seventeenth-century former private quarters of Gyalse Tenzin Rabgye.

One incident demonstrating Zhabdrung's spiritual strength as a bodhisattva occurred during a night of meditation in Dudul Phug. The cliff above his cave suddenly collapsed, sealing off the entrance with boulders and thick mud, trapping him inside. Despite this perilous situation, Zhabdrung remained remarkably composed. Through deep meditative concentration, he discerned that the disturbance was the result of black magic employed by the Tsang Desi to harm him. Undeterred, Zhabdrung proceeded to subdue the malevolent spirits involved through prayers to Mahakala.

The local followers, understandably concerned for his well-being and anticipating serious injury or worse, hurried to the scene. To their amazement, they found Zhabdrung unharmed and deeply absorbed in meditation. Above him, a massive boulder, the size of a yak, hung suspended by nothing more than a cloth canopy. He effortlessly brought it down with his bare hands in a magnificent display of supernatural strength before tossing it aside.

Despite his followers' pleas for him to leave the cave and end his meditation, Zhabdrung refused. Instead, he used this incident as a teaching opportunity. He emphasized that his response to challenges serves as an example of perseverance and confidence in one's innate spiritual abilities, highlighting the importance of unwavering focus despite distractions. Throughout this ordeal, Zhabdrung embodied the qualities of a bodhisattva: fearless, determined, wise, optimistic, and steadfast, with unshakable clarity of mind.

As word of Zhabdrung's miraculous escape spread like wildfire, his stature as a revered spiritual master became firmly imprinted in the hearts and minds of the people. Rooftops burst with colorful flags, and the air was laden with the scent of fragrant smoke offerings—a jubilant tribute to this miraculous event.

As he continued his meditation, numerous supernatural signs manifested, indicating the summoning of the Tsang Desi's spirit. Mysterious animal footprints appeared in the flour used for creating ritual sculptures, the Tsang Desi's effigy occasionally moved and emitted sounds of distress, and fireballs shot upward from Zhabdrung's cave in the direction of the Tsang Desi's residence in Shigatse. During these rituals, Zhabdrung underwent a profound transformation, assuming a fierce and wrathful appearance amid the scent of burning flesh.

Those who witnessed this display noted that, despite his menacing appearance, Zhabdrung emitted a radiant aura that instilled both fear and transformative experiences in those nearby. These actions exemplify the tantric abilities possessed by high-level bodhisattvas, all undertaken for a higher purpose.

It must be emphasized that Zhabdrung conducted sacred Mahakala practices during his retreat to subdue the Tsang Desi and safeguard the Drukpa Kargyu teachings and its adherents. His actions were aligned with a bodhisattva's commitment to benefiting others. While some have labeled these rituals as black magic, their understanding of high-level spiritual practices and their intent is limited and the accusations incorrect. Black magic in occult practices stems from selfish motives, a characteristic not applicable to Zhabdrung's actions. Instead, his rituals epitomize the wrathful

Seventeenth-century wall mural at Tango Monastery of Zhabdrung Ngawang Namgyal (Photo © Zhung Dratshang)

activities in a bodhisattva's toolbox. From a Buddhist perspective, his actions could be seen as aiding the Tsang Desi rather than causing harm, by preventing the accumulation of negative karma in his future lives.

As Zhabdrung repelled the wrongdoings of the Tsang Desi, evidenced by the appearance of scorching fireballs and powerful gusts of wind directed toward Tibet, the Tsang Desi's downfall became inevitable. Meanwhile, the Tsang Desi attempted to overthrow the Gelug hegemony in Lhasa and encountered numerous ill omens, attributing them to Zhabdrung's spiritual powers.

In response, the Tsang Desi assembled a group of sorcerers to perform black magic aimed at harming Zhabdrung. Around the same time, a smallpox epidemic swept through the region, leading to the deaths of the Tsang Desi and his family. To maintain the prevailing status quo, however, the Tsang government concealed their deaths for a period of three years, a customary practice of the time. Nevertheless, due to Zhabdrung's prophetic foresight, he had anticipated the Tsang Desi's death during his retreat in 1618.

The famous phrase "Don't compete with the Drikungpas for wealth, don't compete with the Sakyapas for power, and don't compete with the Drukpas for tantric sorcery" originated in Tibet when the Tsang Desi's rapid downfall at the hands of Zhabdrung became evident. Subsequently, Zhabdrung gained a reputation throughout central Tibet as a powerful spiritual practitioner.

Let's revisit Zhabdrung's response to the Tsang Desi's threatening letter prior to the invasion. In that response, he declared, "If I cannot eliminate you, it will be clear evidence that not only the Drukpa Kargyu order has no spiritual guardians but that I am not the true incarnation of Pema Karpo." This statement became a reality when the Tsang Desi met his demise. This prophecy significantly bolstered Zhabdrung's followers' belief in his status as a true incarnation of Pema Karpo. Following the public announcement of the Tsang Desi's death a few years later, this belief greatly assisted him in his quest to unify the Southern Land.

Triumphant and elated in the knowledge that he had eliminated the principal threat to his mission in Bhutan, Zhabdrung penned a sixteen-line victory declaration, known as the *Nga Chudrugma* (the Sixteen I's, or the Seal of the Sixteen Acclaims). As far as can be determined, this declaration was composed during or shortly after his meditation retreat in 1618. It was also crafted as a physical seal and used as a national symbol on important documents. Beyond commemorating the victory over the Tsang Desi, the *Nga*

Chudrugma proclaims Zhabdrung as the prophesied incarnation, establishing his position as a bodhisattva king.

Below is the full text of the *Nga Chudrugma*:

> I am he who turns the wheel of the dual system,
> I grant refuge to all;
> I am the holder of the precious teachings of Palden Drukpa,
> I am the conqueror of all who pretend to be Drukpas;
> I am the one accomplished in poetry,
> I am the source of moral aphorisms;
> I am the master whose views are free from extremes,
> I refute those who hold wrong views;
> I am the master of power and strength in debate,
> I am him before whom everyone trembles;
> I am the hero who conquers the host of demons,
> I am him whose powers cannot be obstructed by any sorcerer;
> I am the powerful lord of speech in expounding religion,
> I am the one who excels in all sciences;
> I am the incarnation prophesied by predecessors,
> I am the one who eliminates deviant incarnations.

At first glance, the frequent use of the pronoun "I" may seem self-centered. However, considering that he had just overcome a significant adversary of the Dharma, we can grasp the depth of his emotions. As a highly realized master, he likely experienced a profound sense of achievement, knowing that he had cleared the path for his mission to benefit others. In fact, he demonstrated mastery in the third activity of a bodhisattva—the magnetizing activity—adeptly leveraging the admiration and respect of his followers to lead them on the righteous path. The *Nga Chudrugma* perfectly epitomizes this approach.

Examining this verse provides insight into his character. Zhabdrung personified confidence, straightforwardness, and decisive leadership—qualities crucial for consolidating his authority and building a nation for the welfare of all. Furthermore, his actions and beliefs indicate that he saw himself as the genuine reincarnation of Pema Karpo and an emanation of Chenrezig, as prophesied by the great masters of the past.

From a sacred perspective, the *Nga Chudrugma* holds hidden significance. Recognizing the wild and untamed nature of the land, where certain nature spirits were revered, Zhabdrung strategically placed the victory seal in areas inhabited by these unseen beings to mitigate their potentially disruptive influences. This act also served as a gesture of goodwill toward those who worshipped these spirits. Today, the seal serves as a protective amulet, warding off negative

Nga Chudrugma seal (Photo © Zhung Dratshang)

energies when displayed in cars, homes, or worn around one's neck. From a sacred standpoint, the seal symbolizes Zhabdrung's enlightened qualities and realizations, signifying his triumph over extreme views and his attainment of ultimate selflessness. Therefore, it is erroneous to view the declaration seal as an egotistical display; its purpose is quite the opposite.

Parallels can be drawn from the *Lalitavistara Sutra*, where Shakyamuni Buddha similarly reflects on his achievements and realizations:

I am a worthy one of the world,
I am the unsurpassed teacher.
Among the gods, demigods, and divine spirits,
There is no rival to me.

From this point onward, support for Zhabdrung surged. His display of miraculous feats not only cemented his followers' admiration but also earned him the respect and devotion of a substantial cross section of the populace. It became increasingly noticeable that he was steering this once lawless and directionless land into a sovereign state anchored in peace under his compassionate guidance. Each passing day marked a step closer to this ultimate goal. These events aligned with the spiritual prophecies of centuries past, hinting at the auspicious coincidences soon to arise that would greatly assist him in unifying the Southern Land.

CHAPTER 8

Auspicious Coincidences

Could there be another possibility—a greater plan for all of us,
governed by the law of karma?

This question has often lingered in my thoughts. After the Tsang
Desi's demise, events unfolded in a way that solidified the foundation of the Drukpa Kargyu teachings in Bhutan—suggesting a
larger destiny at work.

When we examine the events that influenced Zhabdrung's life
purpose in Bhutan, they might initially appear as a series of random, unrelated occurrences, arising by mere coincidence. But are
they truly random? In our own lives, seemingly unrelated circumstances often lead to positive outcomes, though we may not fully
understand the deeper, interconnected reasons that have brought
us to this point.

This lack of spiritual awareness is a prevalent issue, particularly
in modern times. We often cling to the past and focus on future
goals, rarely pausing to contemplate the bigger picture. The inter-
play of events in Zhabdrung's life, which I prefer to call "auspicious
coincidences," seems to have played a mystical role in guiding him
toward his destined future.

The Death of Zhabdrung's Father

In the year 1619, not long after Zhabdrung's meditation retreat in
the cave at Tango, he received word that his father, Tenpai Nyima,
had passed away at the age of fifty-two. Many suspected that his
death was at the hands of the Tsang Desi's followers.

Zhabdrung's heart weighed heavy with regret for not having seen his father in his final years and missing the chance to hear his parting words. Yet Zhabdrung was no ordinary person, and his grief took on a different form. As a bodhisattva, he was consumed by a powerful surge of devotion and compassion when he recalled his father's kind deeds and holy teachings. To Zhabdrung, his father was more than a parent; he was his root guru—his spiritual guide on the path to enlightenment. Despite feeling the sorrow of his loss, Zhabdrung found solace in the knowledge that his father had left behind a legacy of wisdom and virtue that would endure. In this way, Zhabdrung honored his father's memory, recognizing that his teachings would continue to inspire and guide him on his own spiritual journey.

At first glance, the passing of Zhabdrung's father might not seem an auspicious coincidence. Yet this event soon proved to be the catalyst for a series of developments that propelled Zhabdrung toward his destiny—the unification of the Southern Land.

According to ancient prayers and texts, Zhabdrung's father was a bodhisattva—a being of great spiritual power and wisdom. Some even speculated that his father may have had the ability to control the timing of his own death, a characteristic of bodhisattvas of high spiritual realizations. Whatever the case may be, Zhabdrung could not ignore the fact that his father's passing had indirectly paved the way for him to achieve his predestined path. It was a turning point in his life, a moment that would shape his destiny and that of Bhutan.

His father's body was smuggled across the border and brought to Dudul Phug at Tango—the very cave where Zhabdrung had meditated a year earlier to put an end to the Tsang Desi's tyranny. Deep within the inner recesses of the cave, the body was carefully placed on a rock platform adorned with precious gems and vibrantly colored silk fabric in the traditional five Buddha colors—red, white, blue, yellow, and green. Each day, devotees laid flowers, offered incense and scented water, and lit butter lamps where Zhabdrung would come to prostrate himself before the body. He performed this ritual hundreds of times a day, recalling his father's deep compassion and wisdom.

As part of the funeral rites, Zhabdrung arranged for tea and meals to be offered across the monasteries of the U-Tsang region, as well as to the lineage holders. Not surprisingly, in Bhutan, offerings continued for many months in monasteries of all traditions—reflecting his deep respect for diverse religious traditions.

At the time of the body's cremation, Zhabdrung and his devotees created a funeral pyre using sandalwood, scented oils, various grains, and flowers, along with blessed, individually handwritten prayers. As the body was consumed by flames, favorable signs graced the sky: rainbows arched across the horizon, raindrops turned to milk, and fragrant petals floated gently down from above. These phenomena were interpreted as blessed signs that a highly realized master had passed away.

As the ashes simmered, numerous pearl-like relics were discovered, each one a tangible reminder of his father's spiritual realizations. These precious relics were gathered and temporarily stored in a small silver container, to be interred inside holy statues and stupas at a later date. Even as the final embers dimmed, the skull bone lay intact, embraced by the residual warmth of the once-raging flames. Adorned with intricate Buddhist symbols, it stood as further evidence of his father's exceptional spiritual achievements.

I would have had a hard time believing the presence of these relics if not for my own experience many years earlier in Nepal. On a hill overlooking the sprawling Kathmandu Valley, at a monastery called Kopan, I had the rare opportunity to view the sacred relics retrieved from the ashes of an elderly monk who had passed away there in 2001. Geshe Konchog, as he was respectfully known, had spent over twenty-five years in solitary retreat in the remote mountains of Nepal, surviving on little more than wild nettle and other forest foods.

I distinctly recall the anticipation I felt as the tall, slender caretaker monk carefully inserted the key into the ancient lock of the holy shrine room. With each precise turn, the aged mechanism produced a faint metallic click that echoed softly down the hushed corridor.

Guiding me forward with a motion both gentle and deliberate—one that I had grown accustomed to during my time at the monastery—I stepped into the shrine room. A deathly silence fell over the space. I can still feel the warmth of the sun's rays as he drew back the heavy velvet maroon curtains to reveal a simple window. It is remarkable how the mind retains even the most trivial details from such significant moments in one's life.

My eyes widened with astonishment as I beheld the relics before me. While I had heard stories of such things, never had I imagined witnessing them firsthand. Lama Konchog's crystallized eyeball and heart, impeccably preserved, lay before me. His tongue bore the unmistakable imprint of the goddess Tara, a symbol of feminine energy and wisdom, while pearl-like relics in the five Buddha colors shimmered in the gentle morning light. It was a surreal experience, defying any rational explanation. As someone trained in the scientific approach, I struggled to reconcile this encounter with my understanding of reality. Yet there was no denying the profound impact of what I witnessed—it caused me to recalibrate my view of reality. I later learned that extraordinary signs often accompany the passing of an accomplished spiritual master, including the discovery of relics from cremated ashes—a phenomenon that persists to this day.

In the wake of his father's cremation, Zhabdrung took on a laborious responsibility. He spent countless hours mixing his father's ashes with clay and painstakingly crafting thousands of Buddha and deity figures, along with miniature stupas known as *tsa tsa*.

With the final cremation rites and rituals completed, he began to envision something grander: a *kudung chorten* (stupa). This sacred structure, shaped like an inverted cup used for interring cremated ashes of a highly realized Buddhist master, would house many of the molded statues and tsa tsa. The remaining ones would be placed at sacred sites around the country.

As mentioned earlier, Zhabdrung foresaw the death of the Tsang Desi during his meditation retreat in 1618. This provided him with the confidence to continue with his plans of spreading the Dharma and unifying the land as foretold by the prophecies.

While he mourned the loss of his father, he also felt a strong sense of responsibility to preserve the precious Drukpa Kargyu teachings in honor of his memory. And in his ear was Tshewang Tenzin of Tango, who was urging him to establish a formal monastic seat for the Drukpa Kargyu order to secure and propagate these sacred Dharma teachings.

A Groundswell of Support

Despite the relentless attacks from the Tsang Desi over the years, Zhabdrung's following continued to grow. Remarkably, these challenges only strengthened his support as his displays of spiritual prowess and exceptional leadership during the counterattacks captivated many, transforming adversity into powerful proof of his spiritual strength and vision.

After his father's passing, Zhabdrung connected with a wealthy man in Chapcha, south of Thimphu, who had been a loyal devotee of his father. Through him, Zhabdrung met others in the region, including a prosperous trader from the Indian state of Bihar. Together they became Zhabdrung's financial patrons, providing crucial support to establish a monastic seat for the Drukpa Kargyu order. With their assistance, Zhabdrung solidified his position and paved the way for his future accomplishments.

The death of his father proved to be a catalyst for significant developments in Zhabdrung's life. One notable breakthrough was his enhanced ability to rally a group of individuals who ultimately aided in the construction of his monastic seat at Cheri. Random coincidence? Maybe not.

Establishment of the Drukpa Kargyu Seat in Bhutan

After his meeting with the Chapcha crew, Zhabdrung returned to Tango and reflected on the significant support he had managed to attract. Recognizing the importance of solidifying the Drukpa Kargyu order in Bhutan, he embraced Tshewang Tenzin's suggestion to establish a dedicated monastic teaching center. Not only did he seek a sacred site to enshrine the kudung chorten containing the molded statues and relics from his father's cremation but he also recognized that constructing a monastic center would effectively serve both purposes.

Entering a deep state of meditation before the Rangjung Kharsapani, Zhabdrung prayed for guidance to identify the perfect location for the center. During his meditation, the relic turned to face a spot across the valley from Tango. Ancient prophecies from the Mahakala texts and Guru Rinpoche seemed to confirm this choice, describing a center perched on the side of a cliff resembling a raven's beak. This location, situated between two rivers on a mountain shaped like an inverted heart, was foreseen as the life force of the Drukpas.

Indeed, the mountain possessed the prophesied triangular shape, reinforcing Zhabdrung's belief in its suitability. He named the site Chagri Dorjiden (commonly known as Cheri) drawing inspiration from a similar-looking hill in Lhasa known as Chagpori. Zhabdrung may have also perceived parallels between Cheri and Dorjiden in India, the sacred site where Buddha attained enlightenment. To further affirm this choice, Zhabdrung recalled his faithful yak, Nyima Senge, who had accompanied him on the arduous journey to Bhutan, bleating from the rocky outcrop at Cheri—a favorable sign in his eyes.

In 1620, the Year of the Monkey, the foundation stone of Cheri Monastery was laid. That same year, on Guru Rinpoche's birthday, bodhisattvas, yogis, and devotees gathered to begin its construction. Situated on the northern outskirts of Thimphu, this monastery would become the first Buddhist institute from which the Drukpa Kargyu teachings would spread across Bhutan.

Zhabdrung's vision for a grand monastic center at Cheri swiftly materialized into a reality, with Tshewang Tenzin of Tango eagerly assuming the responsibility for overseeing the construction.

Expert craftsmen and sculptors from Nepal crossed the border to lend their skills, while goldsmiths from U and Tsang shared their

Aerial photo of the triangular hill where Cheri Monastery sits, nestled between two rivers (Photo © 2024 Tshering Wangdi)

expertise. Devotees from nearby Kabesa, along with Zhabdrung's students, worked tirelessly from dawn until dusk, often continuing late into the night with the support of local meditators. This effort was a collective one, driven by a shared dedication to Zhabdrung's vision. Gratefully, the entire construction was fully sponsored by the generosity of their newfound friends from Chapcha and Tshewang Tenzin.

According to Tsang Khenchen's biography, Pema Karpo constructed a small stupa to enshrine the Rangjung Kharsapani. Interestingly, he intentionally left it half unpainted, believing that it would be completed by his reincarnation. During the construction of Cheri Monastery, Zhabdrung instructed highly skilled Nepalese artisans to finish painting the stupa with the finest gold paint and adorn it with multicolored gemstones. This act could be seen as further confirmation of Zhabdrung's status as a true reincarnation of Pema Karpo.

Accounts of the construction of Cheri Monastery describe a smooth and largely obstacle-free process. In 1621, thirty novice

monks were enrolled at Cheri Monastery, marking the formal establishment of the monastic body known as the Zhung Dratshang and
representing the first steps toward unifying a lawless land into a
state under the Drukpa Kargyu leadership.

The Arrival of His Teacher

Zhabdrung's former teacher, Lhawang Lodro, was invited to Bhutan
by Zhabdrung to assist in the precise construction of the kudung
chorten, which would house the remains of Zhabdrung's father.
During his time in Bhutan, Lhawang Lodro also bestowed sacred
empowerments upon Zhabdrung, received directly from Pema
Karpo himself.

At the time of Zhabdrung's father's death, Lhawang Lodro resided
near Mount Kailash in Tibet, a sacred mountain to the west of the
Yarlung Tsangpo River—the mother river of the Tibetan people. His
journey, undertaken with his trusted attendant Pekar Tashi, retraced
the same path Zhabdrung had traveled years earlier. Despite the
extreme risks posed by the terrain and his advanced age, he arrived
safely around 1620-1621.

The joy surrounding their reunion after so long, and the reverence
and affection they held for one another, were palpable for everyone to see. According to Tsang Khenchen, Lhawang Lodro was a
bodhisattva, and his contributions to the flourishing of the Drukpa
Kargyu order in Bhutan were immeasurable.

As we examine the circumstances surrounding his arrival, we
find them to be both unusual and timely—interconnected in several ways. This particular type of *chorten*, essential for interring
the ashes of a holy being, was originally designed by Pema Karpo.
Lhawang Lodro, a close disciple of Pema Karpo and intimately
familiar with its precise dimensions, was summoned from Tibet
by Zhabdrung when he sought assistance to ensure the accuracy
of the measurements.

However, Lhawang Lodro's timely arrival in Bhutan proved significant in establishing the Drukpa Kargyu order, fulfilling several

critical purposes. Most notably, he provided clear confirmation of Zhabdrung's status as a true reincarnation of Pema Karpo, a validation crucial for legitimizing Zhabdrung's authority among the Bhutanese people.

The first incident supporting Zhabdrung's status as a genuine reincarnation of Pema Karpo occurred when he tentatively recorded what he believed were the measurements of the kudung chorten. Upon review, his teacher discovered that they precisely matched those originally designed by Pema Karpo.

The second incident arose when Lhawang Lodro questioned whether Zhabdrung fully embodied the mind, body, and speech of Pema Karpo, even suggesting he share the title with the rival candidate, Pagsam Wangpo—a proposal Zhabdrung firmly rejected, likely due to the confusion this would create for his unification efforts.

The following day, Lhawang Lodro recounted a vivid meditative vision from the previous night. In it, he received a book on Buddhist astrology based on the Kalachakra, authored by Pema Karpo himself. Unaware of this vision, Zhabdrung independently requested Lhawang Lodro to compose a similar text on the Kalachakra astrological system for the newly established monastic center.

This remarkable alignment of events convinced Lhawang Lodro of Zhabdrung's legitimacy as a true reincarnation of Pema Karpo. Supporting this endeavor, Tenzin Drukgyal—a devoted follower of Zhabdrung and his father, Tenpai Nyima—offered to publish the astrological text. With this confirmation, Zhabdrung's teacher was unequivocally convinced of his reincarnation status as Pema Karpo.

Lhawang Lodro's presence served another crucial purpose: providing stability and academic guidance to the newly established monastic institution at Cheri. The institution followed the procedural and constitutional framework Zhabdrung had devised during his adolescence for Ralung's first Buddhist lay community. Lhawang Lodro served as a teacher at Cheri Monastery for fourteen years, while Zhabdrung, despite his growing commitments elsewhere, remained its overseer.

Last, Lhawang Lodro ensured Zhabdrung received all the Drukpa

Kargyu teachings, transmissions, and empowerments, fully equipping him to carry forth the lineage with confidence in its purest, unbroken form.

It seemed that karmic forces were at play, converging to establish the Drukpa Kargyu order in Bhutan and aid in the nation's unification. Lhawang Lodro's sojourn in Bhutan became a lifelong stay, during which he diligently assisted Zhabdrung in propagating the Drukpa Kargyu teachings. He was undeniably a significant and auspiciously arising figure in the order's establishment in Bhutan.

Cheri Monastery and its intricate kudung chorten were completed in 1622, followed by an elaborate consecration ceremony presided over by Zhabdrung and Lhawang Lodro, and conducted by the monastic community of thirty novice monks. The ceremony was attended by many of Zhabdrung's loyal and trusted supporters, including Pekar Tashi, Tenzin Drukgyal, and Pekar Jungne. The establishment of Cheri Monastery marked a new chapter in the history of the Drukpa Kargyu order and the country's religious and cultural heritage, signifying the founding of the Lhodruk branch— the southern Drukpa Kargyu order—led by Zhabdrung.

The establishment of Bhutan's first formal Drukpa Kargyu seat at Cheri Monastery reveals a remarkable alignment of purpose. His father's passing served as the catalyst, prompting Zhabdrung to construct a monastery to house the kudung chorten and engage with the people of Chapcha. Summoning his aged teacher, Lhawang Lodro, from Tibet was an important step. Together with the people of Chapcha, they played vital roles in realizing Zhabdrung's vision and disseminating the teachings of the Drukpa Kargyu order.

These events seem to transcend mere coincidence, hinting at a greater guiding force at work. When one embarks on a spiritual journey with a higher purpose, it's as if the universe conspires to bring about the desired outcome. Such was the case with the establishment of Cheri Monastery and the fulfillment of Zhabdrung's prophesied destiny in Bhutan.

Cheri Monastery holds a special place in my heart, symbolizing the starting point of my own spiritual journey in Bhutan. What began as a random tourist visit in 2006 became a profound encounter, setting off a chain of events that ultimately led to the opportunity to write this book about Zhabdrung.

During that initial visit, I had the privilege of viewing—and even holding—Zhabdrung's walking stick, which was housed in a chapel near Cheri's main temple. At the time, it seemed like just an old stick—a weathered relic devoid of significance. The name Zhabdrung meant nothing to me, let alone the honor and blessing of being offered such an opportunity. Little did I know that this seemingly mundane moment would later become a treasured connection to the rich legacy of Zhabdrung.

Then another unusual incident occurred—a year before I even knew I would be tasked with writing this book. One day, a highly revered tulku visited my home in Thimphu to join me and a few Bhutanese friends for lunch. In preparation for his visit, I went all out with the spread: imported smoked salmon, a fresh garden salad, homemade lasagna, and the pièce de résistance—a pineapple cheesecake made from a recipe passed down from Miss California 1956, a friend of my mother-in-law's.

The doorbell rang. The air was charged with anticipation as the guests rose from their seats. As I opened the door, I was taken aback by a large rectangular object with two legs—my mind immediately conjured an image of SpongeBob SquarePants from the animation of the same name. It's amazing how the mind can play tricks.

"Hi, it's me," came the tulku's voice as he popped his head out from the side of the rectangle. "This is for you," he said, handing me the large object as I tried to conceal my bewildered expression. It was a massive portrait of Zhabdrung. "Wow, amazing!" I exclaimed, quickly scanning my small apartment to figure out where on earth it would go.

My Bhutanese guests marveled at the portrait, oohing and aahing and showering praise on this noble-looking, bearded lama. How did the tulku know? No one, least of all me, had any idea that I would be given the responsibility to write a book on Zhabdrung the following year.

As I came closer to writing the book, and even throughout the writing process, I noticed an increasing number of unusual incidents occurring in and around me. However, at the time I was oblivious to any pattern and unable to connect the dots.

Today, Zhabdrung's portrait holds pride of place in my apartment. I take great care to ensure not even a speck of dust settles on it, convinced that his eyes follow me around the room—either overseeing my dedication to his legacy or guiding my spiritual journey. I suspect both.

Reflecting on these experiences, I believe we all encounter auspicious coincidences in our lives; we simply need to recognize them. Keeping an open mind and relaxing into the flow of life is key to fulfilling and becoming aware of our karmic destiny—a passage shaped by our past choices and actions. And as a high-level bodhisattva, Zhabdrung inherently knew his destined path—a path made all the brighter and deeper by his unique qualities.

CHAPTER 9

Unique Qualities

Up until this point, we have explored Zhabdrung's abilities and achievements. But who was he as a person and how did he leave his mark on those around him? Firsthand accounts from individuals who knew him paint a compelling portrait of a man with a magnetizing presence and a generous, compassionate nature. These accounts not only shed light on his physical presence but also how he conducted himself across diverse situations, providing deeper insights into his character.

The most defining and endearing characteristic of Zhabdrung's physical appearance was his long, neatly groomed beard that reached down to his chest, curling to the right at its tip. Ask any Bhutanese, and they will say the same thing. Described as resembling long golden threads, his beard's shape and length were a display to the outside world of his mastery of the Vajrayana practices. He also sported thick, prominent eyebrows that framed a broad forehead, radiating a complexion of remarkable clarity, with skin as smooth as silk. His head, likened to a ceremonial parasol, often inclined skyward, hinting at a heightened spiritual awareness.

Interestingly, one of his teeth bore the image of Buddha, while another featured a right-turning conch shell—a symbol also imprinted on his right thumb. Within the Buddhist community, these markings were considered sure signs of his highly evolved spiritual nature.

Tsang Khenchen vividly portrays him as possessing a towering presence that inspired deep feelings of devotion and reverence in all who crossed his path. Zhabdrung was known for his kindness, welcoming demeanor, and frequent warm smile, and close interactions with him brought immense comfort to his devotees. His gaze, sharpened by years of meditation, radiated a profound awareness, while his clear, melodious voice uplifted all who heard it. His teachings—delivered with effectiveness, honesty, and tireless dedication—left a lasting impact on his listeners. Despite his remarkable qualities, perhaps his most impressive trait was his humility. He seldom claimed to be a bodhisattva, doing so only when absolutely necessary, despite his powerful spiritual insights.

Three-Year Meditation Retreat

In 1623, at the age of twenty-nine, following the construction of Cheri Monastery, the establishment of a community of thirty monks and teaching staff, and the receipt of the remaining Drukpa Kargyu teachings from Lhawang Lodro, Zhabdrung embarked on a rigorous three-year meditation retreat in a cave above the monastery.

During and after this retreat, Zhabdrung displayed remarkable mental discipline and physical endurance, evident in both his behavior and appearance. Emulating the famed yogi Milarepa, he subsisted on the nectar from flowers. For three years, he immersed himself in intensive spiritual practice, spending long stretches of time in a cave scarcely larger than his one-meter-square mat. He rested only briefly at midnight, for the time it took an incense stick to burn all the way through. His tenacious dedication set an exceptional example of self-control and commitment, inspiring others to follow suit.

Zhabdrung firmly believed in the power of discipline. He inscribed the words "Be mindful, Ngawang Namgyal" on his cave wall to maintain alertness during meditation. Performing an astonishing six thousand prostrations[47] each day, he endured weeping sores on his forehead, hands, and knees. Yet he remained resolute in his devotion to the Drukpa Kargyu teachings, showcasing his staunch discipline and physical stamina.

During his retreat, Zhabdrung recited meaningful phrases to himself, which he later expanded upon and shared with his disciples. Emphasizing the importance of discipline and mental strength, he articulated the following:

> Once you start an activity, even if bolts of lightning fall from the sky, the entire earth jolts, the sky and earth clash like cymbals, your head catches fire, snakes crawl on your lap, and you are suffering from cold and hunger, you should never leave it incomplete. Leaving unfinished business will only cause embarrassment in front of your friends and grave disappointment for your parents, relatives, and teachers. By any means, you should complete any task until the end.

Similarly, Shakyamuni Buddha also emphasized the importance of diligence, advising seekers of enlightenment to be energetic and persevering.

Zhabdrung also offered the following advice to his disciples:

> It is futile to be careless, inattentive, unruly, distracted, and mindlessly gossiping. Bearing in mind the need for determination to learn more and become a better person, always remind yourself to tame yourself and look at your own faults. After doing so for many months, assess your own progress in tasks like memorizing texts, praying, and other activities. If you see any improvement, be happy about your achievements. If not, reprimand yourself for being vulnerable to failures in both spiritual and worldly activities, and make even stronger commitments to advance thereafter, as a nonpersevering person's work yields no fruit.

Adding,

> A pampered child will never learn. Learning only takes place when one seizes the opportunity and endures hardship.

This quote prompted me to reflect on our modern society and its tendency to indulge children with an excess of choices. Could this indulgence be depriving them of the valuable opportunity to develop resilience and become mentally mature future citizens? Perhaps Zhabdrung was advocating what we now call "tough love"— sage advice that resonates even more today than it did four centuries ago. This example holds relevance for each of us. Excessive pampering, whether from family or society, has the potential to hinder our mental and spiritual growth, causing us to embrace a diminished, inauthentic version of ourselves.

Buddha's father tried to shield his son from the world's suffering by confining him within the palace grounds, attempting to impose his own views on the young Prince Siddhartha and prevent him from forming independent opinions. This effort to mold him into a dependent and weaker version of himself, akin to "babying him," could have had tragic consequences if the prince had not broken free from the restrictions of palace life. Had he remained confined, he would never have attained enlightenment in that lifetime, nor illuminated the path for others.

Zhabdrung not only preached but lived by example. Enduring long, arduous hours remaining motionless on his cushion with minimal sleep and nourishment, he showed no signs of exhaustion. Instead, he radiated a magnificent aura and brilliance. While subsisting primarily on a diet of flower nectar, milk, and juice from a white plant, he never fell ill. His heightened sense of awareness allowed him to perceive his surroundings even during deep sleep, and his eyesight became exceptionally sharp. Furthermore, his meditative accomplishments enabled him to encounter beings in unseen realms, such as deities and spiritual guardians.

After completing his three-year retreat, a grand offering ceremony was held in front of the Rangjung Kharsapani to seek divinations for his future. Many attendees were astonished by his displays of superhuman strength and noted remarkable changes in his appearance: he had grown taller, his skin had become fairer, his eyes and nose larger, and his hair had grown to over a meter in length. Those who encountered him claimed that merely laying eyes upon him opened their minds to the teachings of the Dharma.

During this period, Zhabdrung decided to build a *gonkhang*, a special shrine for the spiritual guardians, at Cheri Monastery. He carved intricate statues of these guardians from white sandalwood and adorned them with exquisitely colored silks. A collection of sacred relics was also installed, with Zhabdrung personally painting the wall murals depicting these spiritual guardians. As a result of these efforts, Cheri Monastery continues to be a sacred site of worship for the Bhutanese people.

Based on these accounts, Zhabdrung emerges as a dedicated practitioner deeply immersed in the teachings of Buddha. His imposing physical presence, coupled with remarkable mental stamina and a powerful spiritual aura, served as an inspiration to all those around him.

Arrival of the First Foreigners

In 1627, shortly after completing his three-year retreat, Zhabdrung had a chance encounter with two Portuguese Jesuit priests who were traveling through Bhutan en route to Tibet with the mission of spreading Christianity. Apart from being the first recorded Westerners to enter Bhutan, this encounter is particularly significant to our story because it offers an objective firsthand account of Zhabdrung.

Father Estevao Cacella and Father Joao Cabral became guests of Zhabdrung for an unexpectedly extended stay of almost eight months after first entering Bhutan in late February. According to the original report archived at the Society of Jesus in Rome by Father Estevao Cacella, they appear to have dedicated nearly their entire stay to Zhabdrung, splitting their time between Paro and Cheri Monastery.

At their initial meeting with Zhabdrung on the tenth of April, they presented him with firearms and ammunition, even offering military support from their homeland if needed—a gesture Zhabdrung graciously declined. They also gifted him a telescope, most likely sparking his curiosity.

At the time of their encounter, Zhabdrung was thirty-three years old by Western count, and the priests often referred to him as "the King." This title likely stemmed from his commanding spiritual presence, impressive leadership, and the ceremonial reverence with which the local people received him. They described Zhabdrung inside a silk-lined tent, seated on a lofty throne adorned with red Chinese brocade and gold trim.

Due to a lack of proficient interpreters, verbal communication with Zhabdrung was limited, forcing them to rely on visual and intuitive cues to understand his character. Described as generous, charismatic, and hospitable, Zhabdrung showed a keen interest in the visitors from a distant land, attempting to communicate with them through gestures and basic use of the local language.

Expressing regret over the language barrier, Zhabdrung took the initiative to bridge the gap by providing the priests with a tutor to learn the local dialect. Despite these linguistic challenges, the priests managed to grasp enough of the language to engage in simple conversations.

Recognizing the significance of the priests' presence in Bhutan and the serendipitous nature of their encounter, Zhabdrung displayed a genuine willingness to learn about their Christian teachings. This openness could be seen as an indication that he perceived a larger karmic destiny underlying their visit—a moment in history that would carry forward his legacy.

As described by Tsang Khenchen, the priests also depicted Zhabdrung as an imposing figure with an impressively long beard, which he kept under wraps in fine silk, except during religious festivals when it would be on display in all its glory. His long hair, symbolizing spiritual accomplishment, was said to be equivalent to one and a half meters in length.

During their casual conversations, Zhabdrung revealed his intention to shave his head after producing an heir to the Drukpa hereditary lineage. This remark reflected not only his plan to seek a consort and later take full monastic ordination but also his deep concern for preserving the Drukpa bloodline. He regarded its continuation as vital, given its unbroken ancient lineage and the importance ascribed to bloodlines in that era. In time, his focus would shift to broader governance concerns, culminating in the implementation of the dual system to establish administrative order.

The monks were described as each wearing a short tunic that left their arms exposed, paired with a large cloth that draped over their legs to their feet. Each also wore a cape loosely thrown over their body, closely resembling the attire of modern monks. Despite not yet being fully ordained, Zhabdrung likely adopted a similar style of dress. The priests also observed that the monks did not wear anything else, nor did they go about naked, a detail perhaps influenced by the priests' exposure to diverse cultures during their travels. The report also mentioned the presence of approximately one hundred monks, reflecting the growing prominence of the Drukpa Kargyu order.

Tsang Khenchen describes Zhabdrung as stately, while the visiting priests emphasized his kindness. They documented an incident involving a relative of Zhabdrung, a lama who had committed a serious offense against him. Although the specifics of the misdemeanor remain unclear, the priests highlighted Zhabdrung's exceptional compassion and tolerance. Despite the severity of the offense, Zhabdrung imposed a remarkably lenient punishment and ultimately chose to forgive his relative.

Zhabdrung's compassion extended not only to humans but also to animals, as evidenced in part by his strict adherence to a vegetarian diet consisting mainly of milk and fruit. His deep aversion to harming living beings was further accentuated by his staunch opposition to cattle sacrifice in pagan temples. Interestingly, he abstained from consuming rice, perhaps for health reasons, though the exact motive is not documented. The priests were particularly struck by Zhabdrung's ability to spend three years in seclusion within a small meditation cave, sustaining himself on minimal food and engaging in continuous prayer without human contact.

The priests were deeply impressed by Zhabdrung's diverse talents, particularly his creative and intellectual abilities. He graciously shared his artistic creations, presenting them with numerous religious paintings and intricately carved miniature sculptures of Buddha crafted from white sandalwood. Among these masterpieces was a stunning depiction of a sky-colored deity, possibly Vajradhara Buddha, the revered source of the Kagyu teachings. Another piece depicted a square house with a deity at its core, likely representing the mandala of Zangdopelri, the sacred abode of Guru Rinpoche. The collection also included various images of deities, including representations of Shakyamuni Buddha. Zhabdrung was not only acclaimed as a skilled artist but also recognized as a scholarly figure, celebrated for his Buddhist teachings that extended across kingdoms far and wide.

Zhabdrung led a lifestyle akin to that of a nomad, dwelling in a tent and actively engaging with the people alongside his disciplined retinue of monks. Rather than waiting for the populace to seek him out, he ventured forth to offer blessings and teachings. Refraining from imposing taxes, he relied on voluntary contributions from devotees, a practice that underscored his growing popularity among the people of western Bhutan.

During their interactions, Zhabdrung discussed the political turmoil he left behind, explaining how the Tsang Desi, "a king who lives some eight days' distance from here," relentlessly pursued him for a bone relic of his lineage's founder. He shared his decision to flee Tibet for Bhutan due to an unresolved dispute over the reincarnation of the leader of the Drukpa Kargyu order, and how he found solace in the sanctuary of Cheri Monastery, nestled in a secluded cliff face.

Insights gleaned by the visiting priests shed light on the relative freedom enjoyed by the Bhutanese people, attributed to Zhabdrung's unique leadership style. They observed a willingness among the populace to embrace his rule, facilitated by his avoidance of stringent controls. Zhabdrung's governance, characterized by a predominantly democratic approach, stood in stark contrast to authoritarianism. The priests noted his singular aspiration: the happiness and safety of the Bhutanese people. Their accounts painted a picture of a utopian paradise, governed by a bodhisattva king—Zhabdrung epitomized this ideal with unmatched grace.

Ecumenical Approach

One striking observation made by the Jesuit priests was Zhabdrung's openness and respect for differing belief systems. He listened attentively to their Christian preaching while remaining steadfast in his Buddhist faith. Zhabdrung not only encouraged the priests to stay in Bhutan but also offered to build them a church and residence in Paro. His genuine support for their mission was evident in his offer to send a few of his own monks to help establish their congregation. His interest in Christianity likely stemmed from genuine curiosity rather than a sense of threat, given his strong conviction in the enduring influence of Buddhism in Bhutan.

From a broader perspective, Zhabdrung's actions reflect his freedom from notions of superiority or inferiority based on creed, race, sex, or color. He understood inherently that all religions contained valuable truths. The choice of which path to follow was up to the individual, but for those who sought the Buddhist path, he was determined to show the way.

As a true spiritual master, he skillfully integrated his deep knowledge of the Dharma with his personal realizations. Through his actions it is evident that he held a profound belief that all sentient beings were part of an interconnected universal fellowship. This high level of acceptance earned him widespread respect both within the nation and beyond. His approach, mirroring that of the Buddha, addressed the diverse needs of individuals, further solidifying Zhabdrung's recognition as a genuine emanation of bodhisattva Chenrezig.

This ecumenical approach extended to his interactions with other Buddhist orders in Bhutan, as demonstrated by several incidents that highlight his character in this regard. After his father's passing, Zhabdrung adhered to the customary practice of sending tea and meal offerings to various monasteries throughout Bhutan. These offerings were not confined to the Drukpa Kargyu temples but were also extended to temples belonging to the Sakya, Gelug, Nyingma, and other Kagyu orders, potentially signaling his commitment to governing in a nonsectarian manner.

When he later introduced the dual system of governance, Zhabdrung ensured the impartial treatment of all major Buddhist monastic establishments, viewing freedom of religion as a fundamental right granted to the people. He honored and respected the pious of every belief system but remained uncompromising when it came to those who caused disharmony.

This approach fostered positive relations between these sects and the Drukpa Kargyu order in Bhutan, a legacy that endures to this day. While holding the supreme position in this monastic community, Zhabdrung emphasized the autonomy of other traditions, thus reducing potential conflicts. This inclusive strategy played a crucial role in his unification efforts.

Further Insights

Zhabdrung was anything but ordinary. As noted by the Jesuit priests, he possessed the mastery of an artist, often spending hours sculpting and painting religious murals, imbuing each stroke with spiritual significance. According to Buddhist texts, his ability to directly command and collaborate with spiritual guardians was unrivaled, a trait typically reserved for individuals of exceptional spiritual realizations.

While Zhabdrung was renowned for his kindness and compassion, there were moments when he displayed a wrathful demeanor for the greater good. One such occasion occurred during a tumultuous encounter with the Tsang Desi. Clad in robes resembling a wrathful deity, Zhabdrung exuded an aura of controlled fury, his words resonating with power as he confronted the injustices of his adversary. Witnessing this awe-inspiring spectacle, his attendants were struck by a mix of fear and astonishment, mesmerized by the intensity of Zhabdrung's gaze. This remarkable scene unfolded deep inside Dudul Phug, his meditation cave at Tango, driven by a noble objective: protecting the precious Dharma from potential obliteration.

Despite occasional displays of wrath, Zhabdrung's life story portrays a remarkable individual of noble birth, enriched with wisdom, mental strength, and boundless compassion. Upon personal reflection, what truly distinguishes Zhabdrung is his unwavering commitment to restraint. Despite possessing the ability to unleash havoc at will, thanks to his mastery over the wrathful powers of a bodhisattva, he rarely resorted to their use. This capacity for self-restraint underscores his nobility and signifies a person who has achieved mastery over his own mind. In the rare instances when he did unleash his wrathful side, it was always with the aim of benefiting the situation. Many would have succumbed to uncontrollable rage or, at the very least, simmering resentment when faced with the animosity and harassment of the Tsang Desi. Yet Zhabdrung displayed no signs of vengeance.

His actions could be likened to those of a pacifist. He fled from all attacks directed at him by the Tsang Desi and later, the Gelug-Mongol alliance.[48] When resolving conflicts, he turned to meditation, manifesting visions of superhuman armies that unsettled his opponents and ultimately caused them to retreat—never once brandishing a sword in defense. He was a real-life Buddhist warrior in the truest sense of the word. Even when dissenting lamas in Bhutan attempted in vain to undermine his growing support, he remained unperturbed by their jealousy. He was a man of conviction, steadfast in his vision of a unified Bhutan and confident in his ability to realize it.

A closer examination of the vicious attacks directed at Zhabdrung sheds light on his remarkable nature. At no point did Zhabdrung label the Tsang Desi, Phuntsok Namgyal, as inherently bad or evil. When faced with the Tsang Desi's aggression, which proved unbearable, Zhabdrung simply chose to walk away when diplomatic reasoning failed.

In contrast, the Tsang Desi exhibited an insatiable appetite for power, relentlessly pursuing the precious Rangjung Kharsapani to legitimize his rule, leaving little room for negotiation. Despite enduring countless attacks, Zhabdrung never engaged in direct retaliation. It was his supporters who ultimately decided to confront the forces from Tibet. During such times, Zhabdrung, ever mindful, was often found in prayer. When necessary for the greater good, such as the unification of Bhutan and the spreading of the Dharma, he would employ his magical spiritual powers.

The way Zhabdrung faced and overcame obstacles and frustrations in his life serves as a profound inspiration as we navigate our own daily challenges. It is inevitable that we will encounter individuals who seem cantankerous or problematic. However, it is within our power to choose how we perceive and respond to difficult people and situations. In our pursuit of happiness, we may be tempted to put others down—whether openly or in our thoughts—as a feeble attempt to elevate ourselves and create a fleeting illusion of superiority. The ways in which we demean others, labeling them as horrible, nasty, or cruel, may seem endless. Yet such reactions, while they may appear justified, lack spiritual sensibility. In truth, we are merely feeding our egos and indulging our sense of self-worth by engaging in such behavior.

Zhabdrung displayed no such aversion toward the Tsang Desi, despite the persistent provocation. While others might have been consumed by negative emotions, he remained resolute in the present moment. He had an unwavering conviction to establish a Dharma state where the teachings of Buddha could flourish. This unwavering commitment reflects the true nature of a bodhisattva. For Zhabdrung, the Dharma was the real treasure; he considered it his only protection. Such was his unshakable faith in Buddha's teachings. He had offered everything of himself to the point where there was no ego left, allowing the mirror of his innate wisdom to shine through and liberate all from suffering. This remains his priceless gift—his magnanimity knew no bounds.

While the jealousy and animosity directed toward him by the Tsang Desi and his followers must have caused him discomfort and disappointment, and at times even homesickness for Ralung, Zhabdrung handled each situation with grace. He possessed a determined focus and a calm mind, never overreacting and always keeping his overarching goal in sight: to serve others and the Dharma.

Reflecting on Zhabdrung's response to Tsang Desi Phuntsok Namgyal's relentless aggression, I'm reminded of the mandala practice in Vajrayana Buddhism, which I completed years ago and found immensely beneficial. This practice involves cultivating generosity of mind and letting go of all attachments. Zhabdrung's unwavering resilience in the face of adversity stemmed from his profound understanding of impermanence and detachment. As the saying goes, "The deepest fetter of attachment is found in both intense aversion and attraction." Zhabdrung exhibited neither, which explains his capacity to remain compassionate in any circumstance.

Buddhism teaches us that no matter how dire the circumstances, we must seek the silver lining and focus on it. We should never succumb to negative emotions such as anger, jealousy, or ignorance. Instead, we should view our adversaries as precious teachers. While easier said than done, observing how Zhabdrung handled conflicts can certainly teach us a thing or two—he was a true exemplar. He taught that negative situations can be blessings, providing opportunities to shape our minds for the better and further our own purpose. However, this doesn't mean we should passively accept wrongdoing. As we've seen, he also stood up against moral injustices to protect the greater good.

Once again, Zhabdrung's story and the qualities he displayed hold particular significance in our modern era of transformation and upheaval, where regions are often marred by conflict and distressing images of inhumanity regularly flash across our screens. In a world increasingly focused on materialism, many struggle to find true meaning in their lives, resulting in a sense of emptiness and a loss of spiritual connection. This disconnect has led to a lack of unity, purpose, and direction, with some fearing the emergence of a new global power structure devoid of core human values such as compassion and spiritual wisdom.

In this regard, we can enrich our lives by learning from Zhabdrung's outstanding qualities. As a spiritual master who maintained total awareness, he deliberately directed every action toward a spiritual goal, free from attachment or any notion of personal gain. We too can take small steps to increase our awareness in every situation life throws at us. As sentient beings, our natural inclination is to seek happiness rather than suffering, making it illogical to react without thoughtful consideration. By deepening our awareness, we can understand that putting others down to elevate ourselves only causes further suffering and is never a permanent solution.

Zhabdrung also possessed an emotional and gentle side. His humanity became evident in poignant moments, such as when he experienced homesickness after the initial attack from the Tsang Desi. Longing to see his father and his homeland of Ralung, he yearned to enter long-term retreat, despite knowing his destined mission. These feelings of sadness and yearning likely lingered within him, shedding light on his human qualities.

Finally, at different points in his life, Zhabdrung had to project a courageous facade. Some may have perceived it as arrogance or egotism, but a more fitting description would be fearlessness coupled with strong leadership skills. This was evident when he authored the *Nga Chudrugma* shortly after proclaiming victory over the Tsang Desi. In an era devoid of email or social media, Zhabdrung's approach involved declaring his triumph and asserting his presence through a proclamation that marked the introduction of the dual system of governance. It portrayed him as a self-assured and straightforward individual with an unwavering commitment to the Dharma.

Having explored the various qualities and descriptions of Zhabdrung, a vivid image emerges. He epitomized the qualities of a bodhisattva—unparalleled spiritual power, compassion, and wisdom—while excelling as a gifted leader and statesman. Any inadvertent harm he caused was invariably rooted in a solid commitment to a higher purpose. Guided by the Dharma, every action and decision reflected his deep spiritual understanding. Beyond his physical stature, Zhabdrung exuded remarkable benevolence, generously sharing his time and possessions, all while maintaining the boundless curiosity of a child.

By recognizing the depth of his compassion and wisdom, we can aspire to emulate these qualities in our own lives. After all, one of the main purposes of studying the historical accounts of great spiritual masters is to learn by their example and influence successive generations.

Zhabdrung's narrative, though firmly anchored in the distant past, continues to resonate with fundamental human emotions and desires. His gentleness, equanimity, impartiality, and unwavering determination transcend both time and cultural boundaries, playing a crucial role in the monumental steps he was about to undertake.

CHAPTER 10

Ascent of the Thunder Dragon

Just before the arrival of the Jesuit priests in 1627, a series of significant signs emerged illuminating Zhabdrung's path to unifying the land into a prosperous Dharma state. These signs appeared toward the end of his three-year retreat, as he grappled with the choice between returning to meditative seclusion or fulfilling the ancient prophecies that foretold his destined path.

As Zhabdrung approached the end of his retreat, a deep desire enveloped him—a longing to remain in meditation and follow the path of great yogis such as Milarepa. At this crossroads, he experienced a vivid vision of his father, who reminded him of a centuries-old prophecy by Tsangpa Gyare. It foretold the establishment of a distinctive dual system where governance would be shared between a spiritual and a civil leader. In the vision, his father urged him to embrace his predestined path, knowing full well that he was the reincarnation of Tsangpa Gyare. This was one of several profound signs that deepened Zhabdrung's resolve to fulfill his karmic destiny. During this time, he also dreamed of the three spiritual guardians of the Drukpa lineage, who made desperate pleas for him to unify the land and vowed their unwavering support.

In his quest for added reassurance, Zhabdrung turned to his trusted teacher, Lhawang Lodro, and sought solace from the Rangjung Kharsapani. Both sources offered resolute and comforting advice, leaving no room for doubt. It became unequivocally clear to him that he must establish a unified state based on the dual system to foster the growth of the Drukpa Kargyu teachings in the south and bring peace to the land.

Lhawang Lodro advised Zhabdrung to begin his mission by appeasing the unseen forces of the land: the Lord of Death, female protectors, demons, mountain-dwelling spirits, local gods, serpents, and other harmful entities. To accomplish this, he instructed Zhabdrung to undergo a brief meditation on Bhairava, a powerful Dharma protector. Through this practice, he would subjugate these ethereal beings and foster harmony among them, ensuring they would not obstruct his path.

He ascended the steep, moss-covered stone steps leading to the cave above Cheri Monastery where he had completed his three-year retreat. Once again, he would shut out the distractions of the outside world as he prepared to immerse himself in the practice.

Unbeknownst to him, sinister forces were at play. Karma Tenchong Wangpo, the Tsang Desi at the time, harbored a vengeful plot to avenge his father's death through the dark arts of black magic. His nefarious scheme nearly succeeded but for the timely intervention of the spiritual guardian Palden Lhamo, who sensed the danger. Acting swiftly, she prevented Zhabdrung from unwittingly straying out of his sanctuary, averting a fatal misstep over the cliff's edge during a sleepwalking episode.

This miraculous intervention marked a turning point. From that moment, Zhabdrung entrusted the welfare of his monastic community entirely to Palden Lhamo, who assumed the role of protector for Bhutan's monastic community—a duty she continues to fulfill to this day.

Following his teacher's guidance, Zhabdrung continued his meditation inside the cave until all the unseen spirits unanimously pledged their support to safeguard the sacred teachings of the Drukpa Kargyu order.

During this period, Zhabdrung took another significant step toward unification. He issued a far-reaching edict, bearing the emblem of the *Nga Chudrugma*, which was distributed across valley floors and icy mountain peaks, directed at all sites believed to be inhabited by revered nature spirits. Mountains, rivers, boulders, and trees were seen as possessing their own unique consciousness, reflecting the deep connection between the land's inhabitants and the natural world. Zhabdrung sought to ensure that the nature spirits understood his intentions in governing the land of Lhomon Khazhi, the "Southern Kingdom of Darkness of the Four Approaches," an ancient name for Bhutan. This acknowledgment of all beings, across every dimension of existence, became a key element of his unification strategy, a belief he steadfastly upheld throughout his life.

The edict stated,

> The gods, demons, and spirits residing in Thimphu, Paro, and all regions of Lhomon Khazhi must adhere to the vajra holder's order. They must take care of the beings residing within their jurisdiction. If they fail to follow these orders or disobey the command, they will be dealt with.

Flags were unfurled alongside the edict atop every prominent hilltop, along riverbanks, and within deep forested valleys, accompanied by sacred blessed pills. These actions evoked both fear and admiration among the people, symbolizing Zhabdrung's emergence as the sovereign ruler of the land. The edict marked one of his first steps in solidifying his role as both the temporal and spiritual leader, formalizing his intention to unify the Southern Land under a dual system of governance.

By the end of 1626, Zhabdrung's vision of a unified land had gained strong support. His leadership was characterized by fairness, respect, and impartiality, extending even to other major Buddhist sects. By offering religious freedom in exchange for loyalty, he earned widespread acceptance among many lamas who were drawn to his magnanimous approach. Any troublesome sects were swiftly expelled.

These early unification efforts received substantial backing from the established patron families of the Drukpa Kargyu lineage in Bhutan. Descendants of Phajo Drukgom Zhigpo's lineage, spread across the Thimphu, Paro, Punakha, and Wangdue Phodrang districts, rallied behind him. Also supporting him were the Obtsho family in Gasa, as well as the Zarchen and Hungral families, both of which belonged to Phajo's lineage in Paro, the Tshamdrag family in Chukha, and the lineage of Drukpa Kunle in Thimphu.

Zhabdrung dedicated himself to perfecting the arts and sciences under the guidance of Lhawang Lodro. He also composed numerous prayers and eulogies dedicated to the masters of the Drukpa Kargyu lineage, enriching the religious corpus of his growing spiritual community. Additionally, he maintained an extensive teaching schedule to strengthen and fortify the principles of the Drukpa Kargyu order.

In the spirit of a bodhisattva, he embarked on a regional tour, showcasing sacred relics, disseminating teachings, bestowing blessings, and inspiring as many people as possible to follow the path of Dharma. The response was overwhelmingly positive, with people captivated by his presence. With each stop his following grew exponentially, attracting patrons and devotees from all walks of life. It was during his stay in Paro, hosted by the descendants of the Hungral and Zarchen families, that he first encountered the Jesuit priests. Throughout this journey, the devotion shown by the people in every region seemed to fulfill the ancient prophecies before their very eyes.

Despite the promising growth in followers, Zhabdrung's closest disciples harbored a pressing concern: securing the continuity of the Drukpa hereditary lineage amid the expanding congregation. In those days, hereditary bloodline succession was customary among the Tibetan Buddhist traditions. Under pressure from Tshewang Tenzin and other trusted disciples, Zhabdrung agreed to marry Damcho Tenzin, a nineteen-year-old disciple and descendant of Nyima, the son of Phajo Drukgom Zhigpo. This union resulted in the birth of a daughter, though not the successor they had hoped for.

After the Jesuit priests' departure in late 1627, Zhabdrung turned his attention to constructing fortresses known as *dzongs*. Envisioning these structures as both symbols of his spiritual authority and practical institutions for implementing the dual system of governance, he embarked on a significant undertaking. Beyond their fortification purposes, these regional dzongs served as courts where the clergy and administrators presided, ensuring the enforcement of various rules and regulations.

During an era marked by the unchecked power of rulers, Zhabdrung recognized the need for a formal legal framework to ensure fairness and hold those in authority accountable. In 1629, while preparing to construct his first dzong, he began formulating a code of law. Building on earlier laws he had composed in Ralung for his lay community of practitioners, and guided by the principles set out in the edict, he created what became known as the *Chayig Chenmo*—a comprehensive code of law for his envisioned unified nation. Founded on religious precepts, this code governed both administration and moral conduct, reflecting his dedication to righteous and compassionate governance.

With the introduction of this early legal framework, the foundation for a cohesive nation began to solidify, perfectly aligning with Zhabdrung's vision of an enlightened society. These laws served as guiding principles that would steer the nation toward progress and harmony.

In 1629, another milestone was reached with the laying of the foundation for the first dzong at Simtokha, in the Thimphu district. Known as Sangag Zabdoen Phodrang (the Palace of the Sacred Profound Mantra), this dzong was built on sacred land generously donated to Zhabdrung by a devoted lama. Its strategic location at the convergence of three footpaths from Thimphu, Paro, and Wangdue Phodrang further underscored its importance.

The architectural design of the dzong was inspired by a monastery constructed by Pema Karpo in the Tsang area, characterized by a central tower and twelve corners. Interestingly, in the twelfth century, a lama named Zhang Yudragpa prophesied the arrival of a reincarnation of Naropa who would govern Simtokha and establish a seat in the district of Wangdue Phodrang, strongly hinting at Zhabdrung's predestined role in Bhutan.

During this period, while many Buddhist sects acknowledged Zhabdrung's authority as outlined in the edict, the Lama Khag Nga and their followers adamantly refused to submit. Their defiance became evident during the construction of Simtokha Dzong, where jealousy drove relentless attempts to disrupt the work overseen by Tshewang Tenzin and Zhabdrung's devoted followers. Despite resorting to arrows, fireballs, stones, and sticks, and spreading baseless rumors, their efforts were in vain. Undeterred, Zhabdrung continued to oversee construction by day while imparting secret tantric teachings, known as the Six Yogas of Naropa, in the sacred solitude of the night.

Amid the turmoil at Simtokha Dzong, Zhabdrung's consort, Damcho Tenzin, fled to western Tibet for reasons that remained undisclosed and was not seen for the next decade. Despite her absence, the need to secure a male heir remained a pressing concern. During this tumultuous time, Lhawang Lodro reportedly had a dream in which Zhabdrung's father, Tenpai Nyima, presented a walking stick to Gokar Drolma, a woman known to Zhabdrung. This dream was interpreted as a sign that Zhabdrung's father would be reborn through her. By 1630, as the construction of Simtokha Dzong neared completion, Zhabdrung took Gokar Drolma, a twenty-nine-year-old devotee, as his consort.

By all accounts, 1631 was a peaceful and joyous year. Despite his advanced age, Lhawang Lodro made the journey from Cheri Monastery to Simtokha Dzong to preside over the consecration ceremony. During the same year, Gokar Drolma gave birth to the long-awaited Drukpa successor—a son named Jampel Dorji. Under the guidance of his primary tutor, Damcho Gyaltshen, the boy would go on to receive rigorous training in Buddhist philosophy, arts, and sciences, while his father bestowed upon him the essential empowerments and instructions of the Drukpa Kargyu tradition.

The following year, Sakya Dagchen, the head of the Phuntsok Phodrang branch of the Sakya school, arrived in Bhutan from Tibet at the invitation of the Sakya representative. His visit solidified the deep trust and reverence between him and Zhabdrung, ultimately leading to the entrustment of all Sakya monasteries in Bhutan under Zhabdrung's care. This growing support for Zhabdrung intensified the resentment and concern of the Lama Khag Nga and Tsang Desi, Karma Tenchong Wangpo.

At the age of eighty-four, Lhawang Lodro, who had served as a teacher at Cheri Monastery for nearly fourteen years, sensed his time on Earth was drawing to a close. He approached Zhabdrung, who had already secured an heir for the Drukpa hereditary lineage, and urged him to take the final ordination vows, known as the *bhikshu* vows. Zhabdrung, then thirty-nine, personally received these vows from Lhawang Lodro. Shortly thereafter, in 1634, Lhawang Lodro passed away, having fulfilled his karmic destiny.

The Second Conflict

As Zhabdrung tirelessly pursued his mission, his efforts gained momentum, earning the admiration and support of many for his just and compassionate leadership. However, his growing influence incited jealousy and resentment within the Lama Khag Nga faction. Seeking to counter his rise, they aligned themselves with Karma Tenchong Wangpo, the Tsang Desi, and proposed a plan to seize Simtokha Dzong. The Lama Khag Nga misinterpreted the construction of Simtokha Dzong as a bid for political control, failing to recognize Zhabdrung's broader vision founded on compassion. His inclusive approach extended not only to the welfare of the people but also to the natural world and unseen spirits, as exemplified in the edict.

In 1634, Simtokha Dzong came under siege from four directions— Gasa, Paro, Bumthang, and Punakha. The attack was led by an army loyal to the Lama Khag Nga.

Anticipating the impending battle, Zhabdrung charged Tenzin Drukgyal, one of his closest disciples and allies who had protected him when he crossed the border into Bhutan nearly two decades earlier, with prioritizing preparedness and seeking peace if possible. Zhabdrung's directive was clear: "Do not put me or Yeshe Gonpo in the middle. As for everything else, do as you wish."

Shortly after giving these instructions, Zhabdrung ventured eastward into the wilderness, eventually arriving at Wachen Dzong in the Shar region of Wangdue Phodrang. This fortress, believed to have been built by the descendants of Sangdhag Garton, the son of Phajo Drukgom Zhigpo, became the site where Zhabdrung left certain relics for safekeeping, while carrying with him a few precious items likely intended for blessing purposes.

As the invading forces overran Simtokha Dzong and plundered its treasures, a miraculous event unfolded inside its walls. Just before chaos could consume the situation, boxes of explosives unexpectedly detonated, catching the invaders off guard. Widely believed to be the work of the spiritual guardians, the explosion caused mayhem, resulting in the deaths of generals and soldiers from the Tibetan camp. Amid the ensuing confusion, both sides resorted to taking hostages.

During these turbulent happenings, Zhabdrung sought refuge in a village nestled on a hillock in the Wangdue Phodrang district. As he quietly contemplated by a nearby stream whether he should retreat to India if the war persisted, the spiritual guardian Legon Jarog Dongchen materialized before him. The guardian prophesied Zhabdrung's victory over the invading forces and his successful unification efforts. The village then became known as Jarogang[49] as news of Zhabdrung's mysterious encounter spread.

Upon his departure that morning, Zhabdrung left gifts for his host family: a pair of cymbals, a bell, a conch shell, a miniature image he personally sculpted of himself, and another of the Rangjung Kharsapani. He also made a humble request to his hostess for a piece of jackfruit. After planting its seeds, he requested that a jackfruit be brought to him whenever it bore fruit, no matter where he resided.

I visited the village of Jarogang one autumn as winter began to settle in. Despite the cooling season, the weather remained remarkably hot, owing to its close proximity to the southern district of Tsirang, bordering Wangdue Phodrang. After a forty-kilometer drive from Punakha, I reached a cantilevered bridge. Following the instructions I had found online, I crossed it, veered right onto a winding road, and soon spotted a sign for Jarogang Monastery. Along the way, a sizable black snake slithered across my path before disappearing into the underbrush. I was told it was a deity—a good omen signifying that obstacles had been cleared from my path.

Jarogang village, Wangdue Phodrang (Photo © 2024 Sasha Wakefield)

The steep, narrow, and rocky road to the village seemed precarious, twisting through numerous hairpin bends. I held my breath, prayed for Zhabdrung's protection, then cast aside my fear, hoping to reach the village without a puncture or any other mishap.

After a hair-raising fifteen-minute drive, I arrived at Jarogang, perched on a gentle knoll. It was rice-harvesting season, and the surrounding fields glowed with a warm golden hue as villagers tirelessly threshed the rice on large woven mats. It was the most beautiful village I had ever seen—a paradise tucked away in the middle of nowhere. As I stepped out of my car, a smiling monk greeted me and offered to show me around.

A larger monastery was being constructed in honor of Zhabdrung, so the statues and relics from the original monastery were temporarily stored in a separate building. After paying my respects to the statues of Zhabdrung and the buddhas, I noticed a set of three divination dice—a common feature in Bhutanese monasteries, where each number holds either a positive or negative meaning. I focused on a thought and threw. "Ah, good, very good, madam," the monk exclaimed excitedly. "Ten is Zhabdrung's number."

A large metal safe held the village's most precious relics. I was given the chance to hold Zhabdrung's cymbals, bell, and conch shell, and I also received blessings from his miniature image, sculpted from cooked rice by Zhabdrung himself, as well as the revered image of the Rangjung Kharsapani, which he had also sculpted. Afterward, the monk led me on a tour of the fields, where we came across the famous jackfruit tree. It was colossal—its girth three times the size of a typical mature tree. He invited me to return in July when the tree would bear fruit and offered to give me one—a blessing I couldn't refuse!

Despite the extensive damage inflicted upon Simtokha Dzong, Zhabdrung regarded it as a spiritual victory, reflecting the strong support he received from the spiritual guardians and reinforcing his resolve to unify the land. However, the significant destruction left the dzong in ruins for an extended period, with its reconstruction only taking place much later, in 1671, under the reign of the third Druk Desi, Minjur Tenpa.

Upon returning to Cheri Monastery, Zhabdrung conducted prayers for those who had lost their lives in the battle. Despite the ruin of Simtokha Dzong and the many hardships he faced, his determination to construct a new, larger, and more impressive dzong elsewhere remained at the forefront of his mind. This new dzong would serve as the central hub for the Drukpa Kargyu order in Bhutan.

During this time, Zhabdrung's first consort, Damcho Tenzin, returned to Bhutan from western Tibet at the age of around twenty-nine. As Zhabdrung had already taken full ordination as a monk, he arranged for her marriage to Tshewang Tenzin of Tango. This union was significant for the Drukpa hereditary lineage, leading to the birth of their son, Gyalse Tenzin Rabgye, a few years later in 1638. Gyalse Tenzin Rabgye carried a collateral bloodline from the Drukpa hereditary lineage, as illustrated in the diagram on page 25.

By now it had become apparent that Zhabdrung's son, Jampel Dorji, born to his second consort Gokar Drolma, faced a debility that prevented him from ascending to the throne. Consequently, the responsibility of upholding Zhabdrung's legacy and succession fell upon Gyalse Tenzin Rabgye.

As we will come to see, Gyalse Tenzin Rabgye emerged as a key figure in both the Drukpa Kargyu order and the Drukpa hereditary lineage after Zhabdrung's death. He was later unanimously enthroned as the fourth Druk Desi and assumed the role of overseeing the state's responsibilities. During his reign from 1680 to 1694, he actively advanced Zhabdrung's vision of a unified sovereign land and played an important role in shaping Bhutan's national identity.

By this time, the search for the ideal location for the main center of the Drukpa Kargyu order in the southern region was well underway, prompting Zhabdrung to scout the regions of Punakha and Wangdue Phodrang. During his stay at Dzongchung, a small temple situated at the confluence of the Mo Chu and Pho Chu (mother and father rivers) in Punakha, he experienced a profound connection to the place. This temple, originally built in the fourteenth century by Drubthob Ngagi Rinchen, the root guru of Kunga Peljor (whom Zhabdrung was believed to be the reincarnation of), held deep spiritual significance for him. As a result, Zhabdrung settled on Punakha as the center of his administration.

The choice of Punakha was no mere stroke of luck. Ancient prophecies by Guru Rinpoche had foretold the emergence of a great being named Namgyal at the base of a mountain resembling an elephant's trunk, at the confluence of two rivers, where he would strengthen the buddhadharma. These prophecies aligned perfectly with Zhabdrung's instincts, making Punakha the ideal resting place for the holy Rangjung Kharsapani, the spiritual guardians, and a magnificent site for his monastic community. It served as the nucleus of his dual system of governance. Rising like a phoenix, Punakha became the capital of his burgeoning nation, with the majestic Punakha Dzong erected on the banks of the confluence, paying homage to his spiritual homeland of Ralung.

In 1637, the foundation stone was laid at the confluence in Punakha, adjacent to Dzongchung. Before long, cocooned by the deliciously cool shade of milky turquoise waters, a dzong like no other would rise from its banks. However, creating such a palatial structure required the expertise of a master carpenter.

For this important assignment, Zo Bhalip, a highly acclaimed carpenter from the nearby village of Bhalingkha, was summoned. Upon meeting Zhabdrung, Zo Bhalip presented offerings: an overflowing wooden pail of milk and a basket brimming with ripe red berries. Zhabdrung, skilled in discerning auspicious signs, immediately recognized that he had found the right man to construct the dzong. He interpreted the milk as a favorable omen, indicating that the Drukpa Kargyu order would flourish far and wide, while the abundance of red berries symbolized the growth of his red-robed monastic community.

Without hesitation, Zhabdrung invited Zo Bhalip to be his guest for three nights at his residence. On the first night, Zhabdrung bestowed blessings upon him and, through a telepathic connection, transmitted the design of the dzong.

On the second night, Zo Bhalip experienced a vivid dream where he found himself in Ralung, guided there by the spiritual guardians on Zhabdrung's command. Upon awakening, he retained a clear vision of the monastery's precise design and accurate dimensions.

On the last night, Zo Bhalip journeyed to the realm of Zangdopelri, the copper-colored mountain paradise of Guru Rinpoche. Once again, he clearly recalled this sacred place. Under Zhabdrung's guidance, he built a miniature Tashi Gomang temple[50] of Zangdopelri to be kept at Punakha Dzong.

Many believed that Zo Bhalip embodied the essence of Vishvakarma, revered as the principal architect of the universe in Hindu mythology. Given the grandeur of the final product, it is understandable why such beliefs arose.

Delighted by these revelations, Zhabdrung instructed Zo Bhalip to commence the construction of Punakha Dzong, modeled on Ralung Monastery and inspired by the visions of the past three nights. The oversight of the dzong's construction was assigned to Pekar Rabgye, who would later serve as its first governor (dzongpon). Demonstrating his forward-thinking and ambitious nation-

Punakha Dzong, Pungthang Dewachenpoi Phodrang (Photo © 2024 Tshering Jamtsho)

building strategy, Zhabdrung made the bold decision to build a main assembly hall capable of accommodating six hundred monks, far surpassing the previous count of one hundred.

In a heartwarming display of unity, devotees from Punakha, Paro, and Thimphu joined hands to construct the dzong. This collective effort received mystical assistance from supernatural beings and local deities, believed to have contributed by supplying essential building materials. For instance, the protective deity of the neighboring village of Tsachuphu generously contributed logs by floating them down the Pho Chu, which flowed past the dzong's location. However, the tale goes that a mischievous mermaid upstream intercepted most of the logs, leaving only a few to reach their final destination.

Another instance of supernatural intervention during the construction is attributed to a serpent deity known locally as Dori Choom, the "Lady with All the Wealth of Rocks and Minerals." Residing above the construction site, she granted permission for the necessary stones to be used in building the dzong. With the combined efforts of many individuals and divine assistance, the dzong was completed in just a year and a half, by the end of 1638.

These spellbinding tales of nature spirits, deities, mermaids, and serpents form an integral part of the enchanting allure that makes Bhutan so magical. One summer, yearning for respite from the confines of Thimphu life, I embarked on a journey to Punakha. I chose to stay at a charming resort offering a magnificent panorama overlooking Punakha Dzong, hoping that the sight of this historically rich and intriguing landmark would inspire my writing.

To my surprise, during my stay, I learned that Mr. Sangay, the resort owner, came from the family who owned the land where Dori Choom resided. Graciously, he led me to the overgrown quarry adjacent to the resort, where stones for the dzong were sourced. There, he shared the enchanting stories passed down through generations of his family.

The seamless integration of these popular animistic beliefs into Bhutan's Buddhist cultural landscape can be attributed, in part, to Zhabdrung's visionary foresight. His recognition of the significance of these nature spirits to the local people helped realize his vision for a unified and peaceful nation.

About a year into writing this book, I had my own unusual encounter with the world of nature spirits. At the crack of dawn, as I began my brief meditation in the sitting room of my apartment in Thimphu, I noticed something peculiar. Despite the tightly drawn curtains, I could make out some movement in the dim light. Perplexed, I wondered, *What could this be?* None of the windows or doors leading to the veranda had been opened the previous day, and I always kept the veranda doors secured with fly screens when I opened them for fresh air.

After my eyes adjusted to the darkness, I made out two pigeons in front of my altar, as if they had always belonged there. Startled by their presence—especially given my intense fear of birds—I sprang into action. I tore apart the curtains, flung open all the windows, and did my best to keep the pigeons as far away as possible. Then I grabbed the broom and attempted to shoo them out, throwing in a few high-pitched squeals for good measure.

Dori Choom (Line drawing © T. Sangay Wangchuk)

Once the mission was accomplished, I slumped onto the couch, my heart pounding like a lead weight against my chest as a wave of disbelief washed over me. It was yet another incident that defied logical explanation. Once again, I failed to snap a photo—this time, due to sheer panic. Fortunately the birds left behind two white feathers, providing tangible proof that I wasn't losing my mind!

The next day, seeking an explanation, I turned to my teacher. His response, delivered with an air of nonchalance, sent shivers down my spine—the pigeons were dakinis, celestial beings, drawn to the altar to make offerings. Whatever the case may have been, I clung to this otherworldly interpretation, as there seemed to be no rational way of explaining their appearance.

In the days that followed, I couldn't shake the feeling that this encounter held significance beyond its mysterious appearance. Perhaps it was an affirmation from the universe, a silent reassurance that I was indeed on the right path in my writing. Yet beneath the surface, a lingering sense of awe and confusion left me grappling with what had clearly unfolded before my eyes. I came to accept that there is more out there than meets the eye, a reality that Zhabdrung knew all too well.

In 1638, during the construction of Punakha Dzong, Zhabdrung initiated the building of another dzong in the Wangdue Phodrang area. He personally oversaw the design and dimensions, crafting images of protective guardians for the gonkhang. Nyama Kuked, a local man from the village of Jarogang, was entrusted with overseeing the construction under Zhabdrung's guidance. The dzong was completed within a year and a half, and in recognition of his contributions, Nyama Kuked was appointed as its governor.

Wangdue Phodrang Dzong's history unfolded in a mysterious manner. During the twelfth century, a lama named Zhang Yudragpa prophesied that a future incarnation of Naropa would establish a significant presence at the very location where Wangdue Phodrang Dzong stands today.

As fate would have it, during a period when Zhabdrung was contemplating the unification of the Southern Land, he sought refuge in meditation at Chimi Lhakhang, a temple situated in the Punakha district. There he sought guidance from Yeshe Gonpo (Mahakala), one of the primary spiritual guardians of the Drukpa Kargyu order. In a moment of deep reflection, a distinctive figure believed to be Yeshe Gonpo himself appeared before Zhabdrung. This swarthy, enigmatic man conveyed to him that by meditating on a specific ridge, distinctly revealed to Zhabdrung in a vision, he could bring about national unity.

Intrigued by this mystical encounter, Zhabdrung directed his attendants to locate the exact ridge described in his vision. Astonishingly, upon arriving at a specific spot in Wangdue Phodrang, they were greeted by a captivating sight: four ravens gracefully circling above before soaring off in four different directions. This unusual occurrence reinforced Zhabdrung's belief that they had indeed discovered the site he had envisioned during meditation. Interpreting the presence of the four ravens as a divine sign, he believed it to be an affirmation from his protective deities, assuring him that his teachings would flourish in all four corners of the nation.

Convinced that this spot was the exact location from his vision, Zhabdrung traveled there to meditate. Soon after, the local landlord, deeply impressed by Zhabdrung's qualities, generously gifted him all his landholdings. The seamless alignment of these events reinforced Zhabdrung's sense of destiny to unite the country under the state of Palden Drukpa.

Meanwhile, as the construction of Wangdue Phodrang Dzong progressed, another momentous event unfolded: the birth of Gyalse Tenzin Rabgye. This birth held profound significance, as Gyalse Tenzin Rabgye would later emerge as a key figure, entrusted with the noble responsibility of safeguarding and furthering Zhabdrung's enduring legacy following his eventual passing.

The State of Palden Drukpa Is Founded

After establishing the teachings of the Drukpa Kargyu order and completing Punakha Dzong around 1638, a magnificent consecration celebration unfolded. Devotees and patrons from every corner of Bhutan converged for this momentous occasion, bringing with them elaborate offerings as tokens of their profound respect and unwavering devotion.

The gifts presented during this grand ceremony formed an impressive mound, creating a breathtaking spectacle near Punakha Dzong. Inspired by this sight, Zhabdrung named the area Pungthangkha, meaning "ground of heaps." This, in turn, led to the dzong being called Pungthang Dewachenpoi Phodrang, or "the Celestial Palace of Great Bliss Resting on the Ground of Heaps."

This significant event, which gave rise to the *zhugdrel* ceremony—a cherished tradition symbolizing Bhutanese generosity—is of great cultural significance and will be further explored in chapter 13.

Following the consecration, the establishment of the state of Palden Drukpa gained rapid momentum. Inspired by a vision of his father during his three-year retreat at Cheri Monastery, Zhabdrung introduced the dual system of governance as prophesied. In this system, the Drukpa Kargyu lineage became the main religion, with the monks assuming roles in both religious and secular spheres. Sacred relics were ceremonially installed, and the monastic community from Cheri Monastery, including his son Jampel Dorji, resettled in Punakha Dzong.

While formal appointments for key positions came later, several individuals played crucial roles in establishing and managing the dual system. Pekar Jungne, who would later become the first Je Khenpo, managed monastic affairs. Damcho Gyaltshen, a close attendant of Zhabdrung, oversaw ecclesiastical matters but was not appointed as Je Khenpo due to his responsibilities to Zhabdrung. Tenzin Drukgyal took charge of civil affairs and eventually became the first Druk Desi. Pekar Rabgye, instrumental in overseeing the construction of Punakha Dzong, later became its inaugural governor.

Zhabdrung assumed supreme leadership over both civil and spiritual matters, skillfully guiding the nation. He formally declared Punakha Dzong as the radiant centerpiece and main seat of the

Drukpa Kargyu order in Bhutan, known as the Lhodruk, or southern Drukpa branch. Although exiled from his homeland, he remained connected to his spiritual community, with Punakha Dzong recreated in the likeness of his beloved Ralung Monastery.

The state of Palden Drukpa began to take shape as prophesied. Its people became known as Drukpas, and the nation itself as Drukyul, after the Drukpa Kargyu order—the predominant faith.[51] For Zhabdrung, the welfare and happiness of the people, along with the preservation of the sacred Buddhist teachings, were paramount; everything else was secondary. He was no longer just the head of a Buddhist order—he was now the Dharma king of a new nation.

The Third Conflict

In 1639, the Year of the Earth Hare, a troubling undercurrent of envy and resentment surged among the ranks of the Lama Khag Nga. The tangible evidence of Zhabdrung's growing reputation—evident in the magnificent dzongs at Punakha and Wangdue Phodrang—served as a constant reminder of his rising popularity and authority across the land.

As Zhabdrung's influence grew, tensions among the Lama Khag Nga escalated, leading them to seek military support from Tsang Desi Karma Tenchong Wangpo to dismantle the two dzongs. Although initially hesitant, the Tsang Desi agreed to dispatch troops, stressing the importance of pursuing a peaceful resolution if possible. He remained keenly aware of Zhabdrung's spiritual authority and the formidable protection of his spiritual guardians.

In contrast to his father, Tsang Desi Karma Tenchong Wangpo did not exhibit an aggressive demeanor. Instead, he inherited the ongoing conflict with Zhabdrung and sought to resolve it through alternative means. Tsang Khenchen described him as a deeply devout individual who found great fulfillment in supporting various Buddhist sects within the Tsang region.

As the abbot of the nonsectarian Buddhist center in Shigatse, established under Karma Tenchong Wangpo's patronage, Tsang

Khenchen witnessed his generosity and inclusive outlook firsthand. The center welcomed scholars from diverse Buddhist traditions, including Kadam, Sakya, Nyingma, Kagyu, and Jonang, exemplifying Karma Tenchong Wangpo's magnanimity. Even the Jesuit priests, who encountered him in Tibet after traveling through Bhutan, portrayed him as a compassionate and handsome young man, renowned for his philanthropic efforts to aid the impoverished.

Against this backdrop, it became clear that the Tsang Desi was reluctant to confront Zhabdrung, acting primarily under pressure from the Lama Khag Nga. At the same time, he faced more pressing concerns. The Mongolian faction, led by Gushri Khan—a descendant of Ghengis Khan and aligned with the Gelug school—posed a far greater threat than Zhabdrung, who remained focused on his efforts in the south.

The conflict unfolded with Tibetan troops launching attacks from two fronts: from the ridge overlooking Paro and from the northern slopes near Gasa. As in past confrontations, Zhabdrung sought refuge inside the secure confines of Cheri Monastery. Legend has it that from the sacred gonkhang he urged the spiritual guardians to intervene in the battle. That night, witnesses reported a remarkable event: a massive fireball shot forth from Jela Dzong above Paro town, striking the opposing camp on the ridge. Amid the ensuing chaos, a heavy snowstorm claimed many lives. Upon learning of the incident, Zhabdrung, moved by profound compassion, implored the deities of the local mountain, Jomolhari, to calm the storm and minimize further loss of life.

During the battle, the other reincarnate candidate, Pagsam Wangpo, experienced extreme bodily weakness, as if bound by heavy lead chains—a sensation many attributed to Zhabdrung's superior spiritual powers. Confronted with his own deterioration and the undeniable influence of Zhabdrung's spiritual prowess, he resolved to initiate a peace agreement to end the persistent tensions between Tibet and Bhutan. These tensions, he believed, stemmed largely from the rival claims to the reincarnation of Pema Karpo—a role in which he unwillingly found himself.

He enlisted the assistance of the then Sakya Dagchen, Ngawang Kunga Sonam, to negotiate. Ngawang Kunga Sonam subsequently sent two emissaries to Zhabdrung with a letter seeking negotiations. He also instructed the Tsang Desi to send a letter to his general, who was leading the attack and stationed in Paro, ordering him to halt all hostilities with the aim of reaching a mutual agreement. The Tsang Desi, now fully convinced of Zhabdrung's superior spiritual powers and the negative consequences of refusing mediation, requested a high Sakya master, Thutob Wangpo, to resolve the issues on his behalf.

By this stage, Zhabdrung had moved from Cheri Monastery and taken refuge inside the imposing walls of Wangdue Phodrang Dzong, where he distributed protective amulets to those present. These amulets were not only given to the prince of Ladakh, who was studying in Bhutan and attending to Zhabdrung at the time, but also to the Bhutanese forces preparing to confront the Tibetan army stationed in Gasa's rugged terrain.

As the Bhutanese forces charged toward the Tibetan camp, onlookers witnessed a sight that transcended the ordinary. Despite the relatively small number of Bhutanese soldiers, the Tibetan warriors saw an army so vast that the terrain seemed to shimmer with a sea of armor. The sight struck terror into their hearts, and overwhelmed by the illusion, they surrendered and scattered like ants before a storm.

Behind the scenes, negotiations continued through an exchange of letters, with Zhabdrung outlining specific demands to reach a resolution. First, he insisted that Pagsam Wangpo renounce any claim to being the reincarnation of Pema Karpo and forfeit associated privileges. Second, he demanded the return of the Drukpa Kargyu monasteries in central and southern Tibet, asserting the authority to make all appointments from Bhutan. Third, Zhabdrung requested the complete return of all Pema Karpo's manuscripts. Last, Zhabdrung required the submission of the two most assertive lamas from the Lama Khag Nga, belonging to the Lhapa and Nenyingpa sects, along with their followers. He believed that the only way to bring peace was either to make them acknowledge his authority or to banish them altogether.

After a series of negotiations, the Tsang Desi and Pagsam Wangpo yielded to most of these demands, resulting in a peaceful resolution, although the issue of Pema Karpo's reincarnation was never truly settled. The Tsang Desi dispatched a letter of submission, its words finely etched in gold—a clear sign of his growing apprehension and respect for Zhabdrung.

Both the Tsang Desi and Pagsam Wangpo came to deeply appreciate Zhabdrung's spiritual power. The Tsang Desi openly admitted to feeling weakened and burdened, attributing his rapid decline in overall well-being to Zhabdrung's command over the spiritual guardians and his imposing spiritual powers. A deep sense of regret washed over him as he recognized that his father's past animosity toward Zhabdrung was the root cause of long-standing misunderstandings. The weight of history had finally borne down upon him, illuminating the path for genuine reconciliation, understanding, and cooperation. Similarly, Pagsam Wangpo found himself humbled by Zhabdrung's diplomacy and spiritual strength and willingly embraced the path to peace.

In 1640, a formal peace agreement marked a momentous turning point, signifying a new era of amicable relations between Bhutan and Tibet. The Tsang government officially recognized Zhabdrung as the sovereign ruler of Bhutan. As a gesture of goodwill, the Tsang Desi made offerings to Zhabdrung and extended an invitation for him to visit Tibet. However, Zhabdrung graciously declined, guided by an inauspicious sign from the spiritual guardian Legon Jarog Dongchen. This premonition would later foreshadow the impending downfall of the Tsang government.

After the peace accord, Pagsam Wangpo took up residence at Druk Sangag Choling Monastery, located in the Jayul province of southeastern Tibet. This monastery, one of the thirteen *lings*, or sacred places, originally established by Pema Karpo, is believed to be the site of Pagsam Wangpo's passing. At the same time, Zhabdrung reclaimed the principal Drukpa seats including Longdel, a small monastery established by Tsangpa Gyare. As neighboring nations conveyed their felicitations and offered tributes, peace seemed to take root. It appeared that the ancient prophecies about Zhabdrung were gradually coming to fruition.

As the nation's unification efforts progressed smoothly, Zhabdrung shifted his focus to expanding the monastic community. Embarking on extensive journeys across the land, he encouraged each family to offer one son to the monastic community. Over time, the number of monks grew from a mere one hundred to a substantial 360. Zhabdrung also established an institute dedicated to promoting the teachings of Pema Karpo, where he continued to bestow empowerments and teachings. Through these concerted efforts, the state of Palden Drukpa gradually solidified under the Lhodruk branch of the Drukpa Kargyu order.

The Lama Khag Nga disbanded, with the most contentious sects—particularly the Lhapa and Nenyingpa sects—choosing to depart for Tibet rather than submit to Zhabdrung's authority. Over the following months, their monasteries in Bhutan gradually fell under the administration of the Drukpa Kargyu order. In contrast, the remaining sects—including the Ganden Shingtapa, Barawa, Chagzampa, Nyingma, and Sakya—chose to remain in Bhutan, continuing to impart their teachings to their followers.

In the following year, Zhabdrung took control of the Lama Lhapa monastery in Thimphu, then known as Do Ngon Dzong. He later renamed it Tashicho Dzong. This magnificent structure served as the summer residence for the monastic community, which moved to its present-day location during the reign of the thirteenth Je Khenpo, Yonten Thaye (1771-1775). The previous site was later renamed Dechen Phodrang Monastery.

With the establishment of the summer residence in Thimphu, the biannual migration of the monastic body between Thimphu and Punakha, their respective summer and winter seats, began. This migration, marked by a ceremonial procession of men on horseback known as chibdrel (meaning "ride [chib] in a uniform line [drel]"), is believed to have originated as early as the fifth century at Nalanda

University in India. It was later observed during the reign of Tibetan King Trisong Detsen in the eighth century and was refined by Zhabdrung with distinctive flair upon his arrival in Bhutan.

Wangdue Phodrang Dzong, completed shortly after Punakha Dzong, also became a significant monastic seat and played a crucial role in fortifying the southern regions of the nation.

As the state of Palden Drukpa buzzed with optimistic activity, a foreboding shadow loomed on the northern horizon, hinting at trouble yet to unfold.

CHAPTER 11

Political Shifts and Triumphs

Amid escalating political tensions in Tibet, the Gelugpas—members of the Gelug school of Tibetan Buddhism—sought both religious supremacy and political control. Aligning with the Mongols under Gushri Khan's leadership, they launched a campaign to unify the Tibetan Plateau and diminish the influence of the Tsang Desis, a ruling dynasty known for their patronage of the Karma Kagyu sect. This power struggle destabilized the region, ultimately validating Zhabdrung's efforts to unify the South under the Drukpa leadership.

These political shifts to the north led to two additional conflicts for Zhabdrung during his lifetime that further served to highlight his compassionate leadership. During this turbulent period, Pagsam Wangpo was caught in a dispute between a lama and his attendant, which tragically led to his death at age forty-eight. His passing in 1641 had profound implications for Zhabdrung's followers, who had placed their faith in an earlier remark by Zhabdrung—made during a heated debate—that the true reincarnation of Pema Karpo would outlive the other.

In 1642, the Gelug-Mongol forces launched a military campaign into the Tsang region, resulting in the deaths of Tsang Desi Karma Tenchong Wangpo and his ministers, along with the defeat of their Karma Kagyu allies. After their victory, Gushri Khan granted religious authority over U, Tsang, and Kham to the Fifth Dalai Lama, the spiritual leader of the Gelug school. Seizing this opportunity, the Fifth Dalai Lama established the Ganden Phodrang government, consolidating both political and spiritual authority under the leadership of the Dalai Lamas. Gushri Khan pledged his support as the defender of the Ganden Phodrang government, ensuring its stability.

Driven by these harrowing conditions, Tsang Khenchen, a key figure in Zhabdrung's life story, decided to escape Tibet for Bhutan. He described Tibet as a land engulfed by war, haunted by spirits, and plagued by death. As Tsang Khenchen descended the towering mountain passes alongside his sister and a small retinue, he marveled at the land before him. Bhutan appeared to him as a sacred paradise, blessed by Guru Rinpoche, with lush hills adorned with an astounding variety of medicinal plants—a world away from the desolate, war-torn landscape of his homeland.

In anticipation of Tsang Khenchen's arrival, emissaries were dispatched to notify Zhabdrung. This joyful news held special significance for Zhabdrung, as Tsang Khenchen's father, Gawa Zangpo, had been a devout follower and generous patron of both Zhabdrung and the Drukpa Kargyu order during Zhabdrung's time in Ralung. With genuine respect, humility, and warm hospitality, Zhabdrung personally welcomed Tsang Khenchen to his winter residence in Punakha Dzong.

At the time, the largely cordial relations between the Drukpas and Gelugpas in Bhutan had fostered a false sense of security among Zhabdrung's advisers regarding the intentions of senior Gelug officials in Tibet. Though Zhabdrung hesitantly approved the decision—anticipating potential trouble on the horizon—his senior officials resolved to send a congratulatory message. In response, a delegation led by Zhabdrung's half brother, Tenzin Drukdra, was dispatched to Tibet, bearing gifts for the newly established Ganden Phodrang government.

Upon receiving the formal letter promoting friendly relations, Sonam Chopel, the secretary to the Fifth Dalai Lama and later Desi of the Ganden Phodrang government, reportedly made an unexpected demand: the return of all monastic estates in Bhutan belonging to the exiled Lama Khag Nga, as well as Zhabdrung's return to Ralung in submission to the Gelug-Mongol hegemony.

This demand, most likely largely influenced by the Lama Khag Nga and their followers, greatly infuriated Zhabdrung. In response, he promptly sent a messenger instructing the delegation from Bhutan to reverse their course and return with all the gifts intact.

The brief period of friendly relations between the two nations began to fracture when they failed to reach a mutually agreeable solution. The Ganden Phodrang government persisted in their demands, while Zhabdrung staunchly refused to yield. Tensions intensified, resulting in the Ganden Phodrang government banishing Drukpa Kargyu monks from all monasteries in Tibet. In retaliation, Zhabdrung expelled the Tibetan monks from the few Gelug monasteries in Bhutan.

In 1643, with an imminent invasion by the Gelug-Mongol forces on the horizon, Zhabdrung gathered his followers as they prepared for the attack. True to his usual passive modus operandi, he blessed them and invoked supernatural forces for protection, then fled.

As the Gelug-Mongol faction amassed north of Punakha along the ridge at the Tibet-Bhutan border, Zhabdrung turned to a customary practice in times of critical decision-making: consulting an oracle. Oracles, acting as conduits for communication with the spirit world, provide guidance during vital moments. This consultation was likely intended to provide reassurance and direction to his army of supporters rather than for his own benefit. A positive prediction would undoubtedly boost their confidence. To this end, Zhabdrung prayed to Guru Rinpoche for guidance and sought the expertise of Karma Rigzin Nyingpo from the Konpo region of Tibet, a distinguished lineage holder of the Nyingma terton tradition.

One of Karma Rigzin Nyingpo's attendants was chosen to invoke and become possessed by a deity from this lineage, effectively serving as the oracle. While in a trance and performing a ritual dance with a sword, his fierce and erratic movements startled most of those present, prompting them to hastily leave the room. However, the oracle suddenly halted before Zhabdrung, prostrated three times, and delivered a prophecy: "Bhutan would emerge triumphant, and the teachings of the Drukpa Kargyu order would flourish."

The Fourth Conflict: The First Gelug-Mongol Invasion

In the autumn of 1644, bolstered by the oracle's prediction, a small but dedicated army, blessed by Zhabdrung, gathered in Paro in preparation for an attack. For reasons unknown, the conflict with the Gelug-Mongol forces did not commence until the weather turned warmer. It is possible that Zhabdrung influenced the timing of the Gelug-Mongol invasion through supernatural means to ensure a successful outcome.

As foretold, the invading army was defeated. Historical records reveal that at some point during the invasion, the Gelug-Mongol forces attempted to overrun Kawang Dzong in Thimphu—likely a manor used for fortification purposes in central Thimphu. However, the Tibetan soldiers faltered against the superior strength of the Bhutanese, whose triumph was assured under Zhabdrung's spiritual protection.

Among the captured Tibetan soldiers were a group of generals, one of whom was the senior general, Nangso Ngedub. Stripped of their weapons, the remaining soldiers were promptly sent back to Tibet. However, the generals faced a different fate. In the presence of Zhabdrung, deep within the confines of Punakha Dzong, the generals were forced to surrender their weapons to the spiritual guardian Yeshe Gonpo—a humiliating experience designed to impart a lasting lesson. Detained for a few years, they were eventually released and sent home with gifts in the hope that they had learned from their experience and would refrain from causing further harm to innocent lives.

When reflecting on the outcome of this war, and considering the violent atmosphere of this historic period, most victorious parties would have condemned their captives to miserable, untimely deaths. However, this was not the case with Zhabdrung. He managed the hostile situation with great leadership and conspicuous acts of compassion, displaying no hint of resentment, anger, or violence. As a result of his diplomatic approach, an agreement was signed with Tibet, requiring respect for specific territorial boundaries between the two nations.

Tsang Khenchen described several powerful spiritual experiences while Zhabdrung was in residence in Punakha Dzong. He recounted seeing the shape of Chenrezig in the clouds and hearing the six-syllable mantra of Chenrezig—OM MANI PADME HUM—in the sound of the two rivers flowing nearby, which deepened his devotion to him. On another occasion, Tsang Khenchen dreamed of a temple filled with large, magnificent ravens. The following morning, upon visiting Zhabdrung's chamber, he saw numerous tormas of the raven-headed deity Legon Jarog Dongchen—an emanation of Mahakala—displayed before him. In yet another dream, he saw Zhabdrung Rinpoche with four hands, playing a drum before a clay statue of the four-armed Mahakala. These extraordinary experiences strengthened Tsang Khenchen's belief that Zhabdrung held spiritual authority over Yeshe Gonpo, the Mahakala deity, and deepened his conviction that Zhabdrung was a genuine emanation of Chenrezig.

Around this time, Zhabdrung bestowed the empowerment of Chakrasamvara—one of the principal deities in Tibetan Buddhism, known for dispelling obstacles on the path to enlightenment—accompanied by explanations of the guru sadhana practice of Mahamudra, to Tsang Khenchen and a gathering of monastics. He also conferred the reading transmissions of the *Lalitavistara Sutra*, recounting the life story of Buddha, and the four sections of the *Vinaya Sutra*, providing key clarifications. Additionally, he granted the empowerment of White Sitatapatra, a female emanation of Chenrezig revered for averting evil and cleansing impurities. To ensure the Dharma's continued flourishing, he also committed to teaching each spring for one month, mirroring the footsteps of the Buddha.

Following the victory over the Gelug-Mongol forces, Zhabdrung was inspired to build a new gonkhang dedicated to Mahakala at Punakha Dzong and to place a statue of Mahakala in the gonkhang at Druk Phodrangding Lhakhang. Tsang Khenchen even gifted Zhabdrung a special knife for the gonkhang at Druk Phodrangding Lhakhang, a symbol believed to ensure favorable conditions for the successful completion of wrathful activities. Notably, essential materials for worship in these gonkhangs seemed to manifest spontaneously.

Following Tsang Khenchen's advice, Zhabdrung extended a formal invitation to Tulku Zing, a well-known Karma Kagyu master sculptor from Tibet who was believed by many to be an emanation of the future Buddha, Maitreya. Tulku Zing skillfully crafted sacred images for the gonkhang at Punakha, establishing it as the grandest gonkhang within Bhutan and beyond. It is believed that he also created exquisite sculptures for the gonkhang at Druk Phodrangding Lhakhang.

Zhabdrung wasted no time in identifying a strategic location in Paro to establish a dzong, a crucial step in his nation-building and fortification efforts. Due to Paro's proximity to the Tibetan border, it was deemed an ideal site for this purpose. Among various options, the Hungral family, descendants of Phajo Drukgom Zhigpo, insisted that Zhabdrung accept their ancestral temple in Paro, along with the surrounding land.

Interestingly, even before this generous offer was made, a local deity named Hungral Gonpo appeared before Zhabdrung, presenting him with the Hungral temple and the entire Paro Valley as a sacred offering. Paro Dzong, also known as Rinpung Dzong, was subsequently constructed on the grounds of the former Hungral temple and is believed to have been completed around 1645-1646.

Tenzin Drukdra, later appointed as the second Druk Desi, assumed the role of overseer of the dzong and held the position of Paro Ponlop, the feudal governor of the region. Concurrent with the dzong's completion, Zhabdrung reportedly had a visionary experience where he encountered a swarthy figure believed to be Yeshe Gonpo. During this encounter, Yeshe Gonpo offered Zhabdrung the sacred meditation site of Guru Rinpoche known as Taktsang (Tiger's Nest). Nestled amid the mountains overlooking the enchanting Paro Valley, Taktsang is adorned with cascading waterfalls and lush woodlands. Zhabdrung had a premonition that a physical person would eventually present him with this sacred location, so he instructed his attendant not to hinder anyone from meeting him.

During this period, the caretaker of the Taktsang area developed an unusually intense devotion to Zhabdrung. Overwhelmed by this intense sensation, he hurried down to Paro Dzong, offering the only item he could afford—a humble head of garlic, reflecting his impoverishment. When Zhabdrung met him, he was deeply moved, interpreting the encounter as the favorable sign he had awaited. In response, he gave the caretaker a white flag and instructed it to be raised at the Taktsang site. This act served as an official proclamation, declaring the area under his authority.

In the weeks that followed, Zhabdrung and the monastic community conducted grand offerings at Taktsang. During these rituals, miraculous signs were witnessed, such as holy water bubbling up and emerging from rock crevasses and sacred statues. Zhabdrung also experienced visions of Buddha Amitayus and Guru Rinpoche, who is believed to have flown from Tibet to Taktsang on the back of a tigress and meditated at this very site. The air was perfumed with a sweet aroma during the ceremonies, as vivid rainbows painted the sky.

Following these rituals, Zhabdrung visited numerous holy sites in and around the Paro Valley. Upon returning to his ancestral temple of Druk Choding in Paro's main town, he was warmly received by his devotees and patrons, who celebrated his successful accomplishments.

Meanwhile, back in Tibet, a political storm was brewing. The Ganden Phodrang government sought to exercise greater authority over neighboring lands. To win the favor of kingdoms such as Ladakh, who were supporters of the Drukpa Kargyu order, the Ganden Phodrang government pressured the Fifth Dalai Lama to recognize a young boy named Mipham Wangpo (1641-1717) as the reincarnation of Pagsam Wangpo. The selection was purely politically motivated and bypassed the traditional tulku recognition process. Under duress, the Dalai Lama finally agreed to the request, conferring upon him the title Gyalwa Drukchen Thamche Khyenpa, a title famously associated with Pema Karpo.

In retaliation for their recent defeat in the war against Bhutan, the Tibetan general Nangso Ngedub, who had previously been held captive in Bhutan for two years, was dispatched by the Tibetan government to seize Ralung and other Drukpa monastic estates in the U-Tsang region. This marked the end of centuries of hereditary lineage history. With the Ganden Phodrang government now in control of all Drukpa Kargyu monasteries in Tibet, Ralung Monastery was handed over to Pagsam Wangpo's reincarnation, Mipham Wangpo.

In response to these developments and recognizing the risks posed to the Drukpa Kargyu followers in Tibet, Druk Namgyal, a disciple tasked with the care of Ralung following the peace deal of 1640, chose to flee back to Bhutan. Upon his return, he received a warm welcome from Zhabdrung and was appointed to the senior position of *zhung dronyer*, or chief of protocol. Druk Namgyal, known for his unwavering loyalty to Zhabdrung, played a key role in encouraging the eastern regions of Bhutan to participate in nation-building initiatives.

Despite the significant loss of the Drukpa Kargyu seats in Tibet, Zhabdrung remained resolute. He promptly took measures to consolidate the Drukpa Kargyu order in Bhutan. This setback actually served as a catalyst for him, spurring concerted efforts and firm determination to bring all the regions under a unified Drukpa state.

While Zhabdrung himself did not venture into the eastern regions, he delegated the mission of bringing the east under his leadership to a team of three competent and loyal supporters. Zhabdrung's confidence in their success stemmed from a distinct vision he had of the Dharma teachings spreading beyond the western regions and coming under the umbrella of the Drukpa state.

The trio charged with this endeavor consisted of Minjur Tenpa, who later assumed the position of Trongsa Ponlop and eventually became the third Druk Desi. Joining him were Druk Namgyal and Lama Namse, a learned scholar from Tshatsi in the southern district of present-day Pemagatsel and a distant relative of Zhabdrung's father.

Whether fortuitously or by design, the Drukpa forefathers, through long-standing patronages between Ralung and Bhutan since the twelfth century, had appointed head lamas in many monasteries in the east. This proved invaluable for Zhabdrung's ongoing unification efforts. Accompanied by numerous supporters from various regions, the three men slowly but surely brought the eastern regions into Zhabdrung's orbit.

While most people embraced this new rule, occasional resistance arose as expected. However, the underlying intention was for the greater good—stability, protection, and future prosperity for all—a vision that only Zhabdrung had the foresight to predict and the capability to realize.

The mission to incorporate the eastern regions into the Drukpa state began around 1647-48. It encompassed various areas within Bumthang, Trongsa, Lhuntse, Mongar, Tashiyangtse, Tashigang, Zhemgang, and Pemagatsel (see the map of Bhutan at the front of the book). These areas collectively came to be known as the eight spokes of the Dharma wheel of the East, or *sharchog khorlo tsibgyed* in the local language.

Tsang Khenchen's account unveils Zhabdrung's ameliorating influence over more than thirty thousand settlements within the newly formed state. Guided by compassion, Zhabdrung prioritized the welfare of the people. Regions previously deprived gained access to clean water, travel routes were cleared through challenging terrain, existing temples were improved, and bridges were constructed. These once-troubled areas transformed into havens of peace and abundance where various types of fruits and flowers flourished effortlessly.

Economically, Zhabdrung's reign brought much-needed prosperity by establishing trade routes with Tibet, Nepal, and India. These routes facilitated the importation of valuable commodities such as gold, silver, cotton, tea, and salt, thereby fostering international trade relationships. Furthermore, he implemented a legal framework that ensured a harmonious environment for the people of Bhutan, enabling them to go about their day-to-day activities without fear of robbery or violence. With stringent measures in place, individuals who disregarded the karmic consequences of their actions were held accountable, fostering a sense of security and acting as a deterrent against crime and corruption.

Zhabdrung's philosophy became increasingly evident: one that emphasized healing over conquest, and the distribution of wealth over its accumulation. He championed peace, unity, acceptance, and cooperation—a stark contrast with the divide-and-conquer mentality of his time and one that sadly continues in our world today.

After large sections submitted to the Drukpa hegemony, dzongs were constructed across the southern, central, and eastern regions, including Bumthang, Dagana, Zhemgang, Lhuntse, Mongar, Tashigang, Gasa, and Trongsa. Even the northern regions, such as Gasa and Lingzhi, came under Zhabdrung's control, and dzongs were eventually built there. This strategic expansion unfolded as foretold in ancient prophecies, and according to the ancient texts, much of the eastern regions came under the newly formed state by the mid-1650s.

This topic brings to mind a funny story from a road trip I made in September 2015 to visit the famous sacred sites in the east. At that time, my understanding of Zhabdrung and his significance to Bhutan was limited, and I was unaware of the challenges he faced in unifying the eastern regions. I mentioned to my traveling companions that I wanted to visit Lhuntse Dzong. Although it was slightly off our route, one of my friends serendipitously knew the senior lama there, who had the nickname "Zhabdrung," most likely due to his long beard during his student days. I have since learned that in Bhutan, most monks have nicknames, which has often placed me in the rather awkward situation of only knowing their monikers!

I remember every detail of that trip as though it were yesterday. The air was crisp and pure, filling our lungs with joy as we made our way toward our destination. Along the way, we stopped spontaneously by the side of the road, overlooking a gushing river. We unpacked our snacks and enjoyed them with a cup of tepid, milky tea graciously prepared by our kind host from the night before. With a sense of freedom and abandon, I flung off my shoes and stepped into the refreshing aqua-colored water, welcoming the smooth river pebbles as they gently massaged my weary feet. A sacred hush fell over our small group as we stood there, mesmerized by the breathtaking views of towering mountains and the vast expanse of the sky, brushed with wisps of clouds. Time seemed to stand still until we reluctantly tore our gaze away and hurried back to the car, eager to reach Lhuntse Dzong before the sun dipped below the horizon.

"Zhabdrung" greeted us with the same warm Bhutanese hospitality that we had encountered throughout our journey. I vividly recall sitting in the exquisitely adorned reception room, basking in the gentle afternoon sunlight, feeling as though I were someone important! The room, with its sun-kissed, centuries-old wooden floorboards and walls splashed in deep red, yolk yellow, and vibrant blue, immediately transported me to a bygone era. The melodious echoes of "Zhabdrung"'s infectious laughter resonated through the monastery, filling the corridors with joy as he shared his humorous anecdotes, much to the delight of my friends.

During our conversation, "Zhabdrung" shared his ambitious plan to place hundreds of Zhabdrung statues in a monastery in Mongar, a charming town in eastern Bhutan. He humorously recounted how he had ordered the statues from Kathmandu, but when the time came for the down payment, he confessed to the shop owner that he had no funds, eliciting a roar of laughter from deep inside his belly. I couldn't help but feel a twinge of sympathy for him. His unwavering motivation and belief that everything—including the funds—would miraculously fall into place, struck a chord with me. Without hesitation, I offered to contribute one Zhabdrung statue to support his noble endeavor. Although the individual statues carried a hefty price tag, something deep inside me assured me it was the right thing to do. Later I heard that "Zhabdrung" had realized his aspiration, and in retrospect, I can't help but think that some unseen force was guiding me to play a small role in preserving and perpetuating the extraordinary legacy of this celebrated figure—even back then.

The Fifth Conflict: The Second Gelug-Mongol Invasion

After securing victory in three consecutive wars against the Tsang Desis and repelling the Gelug-Mongol invasion in 1644, Zhabdrung's newly unified nation stood on the verge of long-term stability. However, in 1648, the Gelug-Mongol forces, seeking to reclaim lost prestige, launched another invasion. Despite their oracle's prediction of failure, they advanced through Gasa in the north and Phari in the west, posing threats to Punakha and Paro.

Undeterred by the threat, Zhabdrung responded with his characteristic wit. When concerns were raised about successive attacks, he remarked, "They can't be trusted, and will most probably attack again, but they are unable to harm us because we have seized enough of their weapons. Instead, they may come with the best silk and scarves."

Historical records describe the daunting challenges faced by the Tibetan army as they navigated the rugged terrain on the Phari side, just across the border in Tibet, directly in line with Paro. Despite their commanding presence, they faltered. Tsang Khenchen notes that even with fireballs and catapults they failed to dislodge a single wall painting. At some point during the invasion, they set fire to their own tents. With smoke obscuring their path, they lost their way—only to end up directly in front of the Bhutanese forces. In their haste to flee, they abandoned most of their weapons. Leading the Bhutanese charge from Paro was Tenzin Drukdra, the Paro Ponlop, under whose command the Drukpas successfully captured hundreds of Tibetan soldiers.

In a surprising turn of events, the Sakya Dagchen, known to both sides, intervened as a mediator. As a result, the Tibetan hostages were released, though their remaining weapons were seized. This development led to a victory celebrated by the people of Paro. To commemorate their triumph, a dzong was erected at the very site where victory was declared. Built in 1649—the Year of the Earth Ox—this imposing fortress was named Drukgyal Dzong, "the Fortress of the Victorious Drukpas."

After the Bhutanese victory in Paro, the invading army's relentless advance toward Punakha Dzong continued. It was here that Zhabdrung's supernatural prowess and strategic brilliance became evident. Legend has it that, tapping into his profound connection with the spiritual guardians, Zhabdrung conjured a mesmerizing illusion in the minds of the encroaching forces. Suddenly the tranquil fields of haystacks and scarecrows transformed into a phantom army, unnerving the invaders.

Despite their unease, the invading army descended upon the hill of Jiligang, aiming to secure its strategic high ground as a step toward seizing Punakha Dzong. However, their journey was fraught with unexpected challenges. The slippery pine needles underfoot caused numerous falls among their ranks, further complicating what was supposed to be a straightforward assault. Adding to their woes, news of their defeat in Paro reached them, delivering a significant blow to their morale.

Seizing the opportune moment, Zhabdrung swiftly mobilized his supporters, made up of mainly farmers and peasants. Without hesitation he directed them to open the entry and exit doors of the dzong, commanding them to march in and out repeatedly, creating the illusion of a formidable army far exceeding its actual size. Zhabdrung's strategy was never to inflict harm but to instill fear through tactical ingenuity, a method that proved highly effective.

Confronted with an unending procession of soldiers and hindered by difficult terrain, the Tibetan army, despite its intimidating numbers, found itself overwhelmed and gripped by panic. In their disarray, they hastily abandoned their supplies and weapons, fleeing from the scene in utter chaos.

After securing victory, Zhabdrung arranged a grand prayer gathering known as the first Punakha Dromcho as an expression of gratitude. *Dromcho*, a sacred Vajrayana practice and religious festival, includes prayers, rituals, visualizations, dance, and music aimed at elevating one's consciousness, receiving blessings, and dispelling negativity. The dances, meticulously choreographed to represent deities, were inspired by Zhabdrung's supernatural communications with Yeshe Gonpo. He himself even led a mask dance in the courtyard of Punakha Dzong, captivating hundreds of onlookers.

During the dromcho ceremony, colored sand symbolizing jewels and relics, including one representing the Rangjung Kharsapani, is traditionally thrown into the river. If this event did indeed take place during the invasion, it was likely a strategic ploy to mislead the attackers. The Rangjung Kharsapani relic remains closely guarded in Bhutan, while this practice—rooted in local folklore rather than historical record—continues as part of the ceremony to this day.

By the end of the decade, a pervasive sense of peace had settled over Bhutan, following the decisive victory. Meanwhile, Zhabdrung's influence had reached unprecedented levels. Through his strategic and spiritual wisdom, he not only subdued rival religious sects but also established a robust legal framework that ensured stability and order. Under his guidance, a vibrant community of 360 monks flourished, becoming a cornerstone of both spiritual and social cohesion. Looking back, it is undeniable that without Zhabdrung's adept leadership, Bhutan might have succumbed to conquest during those perilous times.

These devoted monks dedicated their days to rigorous studies, engaging in prayers that spanned from dawn until late evening on holy days. They also pursued Buddhist arts such as drawing, ritual dances, and various chants, even during their leisure time. Zhabdrung further ensured the spiritual well-being of the land and its people by introducing monthly recitations of important prayers in all the dzongs.

At the forefront of these spiritual endeavors, Zhabdrung periodically led the recitation of millions of sacred phrases known as mantras, including the recitation of the six-syllable mantra of Chenrezig. This mantra, which held special symbolic meaning for Zhabdrung, was recited millions of times.

Having weathered numerous storms, Zhabdrung now stood on the brink of fulfilling his mission, with only a few loose ends left to tie up. He had realized his karmic destiny, as foretold by ancient prophecies: a united nation founded on a dual system of governance guided by spiritual principles such as compassion, fairness, and respect for all living beings and the environment.

CHAPTER 12

Mission Accomplished

After uniting a land once marred by lawlessness, Zhabdrung sensed his earthly mission drawing to a close. As the jubilant echoes of victory celebrations gradually faded, he found solace in redirecting his focus toward spiritual pursuits. His thoughts turned introspective, pondering the deeper significance of his monumental achievements and considering how best to safeguard the nation for successive generations.

Man of Compassion

In his final years, Zhabdrung devoted himself to meticulously crafting miniature images depicting buddhas and deities, each measuring a mere one to three finger-widths in height. This labor of love stemmed from a profound sense of compassion for the lives lost—both human and other sentient beings—during five wars, conflicts with the Lama Khag Nga, and the construction of dzongs. These diminutive representations served a noble spiritual purpose: to guide departed souls toward liberation from the realms of suffering and to bring continued peace and prosperity to the people of Bhutan.

Zhabdrung's unyielding dedication was evident in the crafting of 115 unique molds, each depicting the likeness of a particular buddha or deity. Serving as prototypes, these molds underwent replication on a monumental scale—one hundred thousand times over—using a blend of sacred substances. The result? An astonishing array of

11.5 million images, each painstakingly adorned with layers of gilded gold and silver. These exquisite creations found their place inside intricately carved wooden boxes, carefully labeled and filled with mantras specific to the deity or Buddha they represented.

In a vast display of positive karma, many monks had gathered to assist Zhabdrung in this initiative. However, it was Zhabdrung himself who labored tirelessly into the night, undeterred by exhaustion, to ensure that each statue was crafted to perfection. Despite his fingertips becoming worn and his eyesight straining from the relentless effort, he soldiered on. The finished products were nothing short of exquisite, showcasing craftsmanship unrivaled by even the most skilled artisans. This achievement stood as a tangible testament to Zhabdrung's elevated status as a tenth-bhumi bodhisattva.

Approaching Death

As he felt the life force gradually draining from his now diminished frame, Zhabdrung summoned his two closest attendants, Tenzin Drukgyal and Damcho Gyaltshen, to his chambers. Damcho Gyaltshen, a former tutor to his son Jampel Dorji and a dear friend, was chosen alongside Tenzin Drukgyal to convey Zhabdrung's final instructions to the senior leaders of all monastic institutions, as Zhabdrung was too weak to address a large gathering. Zhabdrung also provided them with further guidance for the governance of the state, acknowledging that he wouldn't be there to physically oversee the nation.

Before entering permanent retreat, Zhabdrung took a significant step by formally appointing the heads of religious and civil affairs. Pekar Jungne was appointed as the first Je Khenpo, and Tenzin Drukgyal assumed the role of the first Druk Desi. Additionally, Zhabdrung tasked Damcho Gyaltshen with overseeing spiritual affairs, a role distinct from that of the Je Khenpo, and made him responsible for attending to him during his permanent retreat.

Zhabdrung's final task was to create a statue that would represent him in leading the monastic body's procession between its summer

ཞབས་དྲུང་ཁམས་གསུམ་ཟིལ་གནོན།

Zhabdrung Khamsum
Zilnon statue
(Photo © 2024
Zhung Dratshang)

and winter residences when he was no longer physically present. Just over a foot tall, the statue is believed to have been crafted by Tulku Zing and consecrated by Zhabdrung himself. Along with sacred items and substances, he molded a miniature statue in his likeness to be placed inside the larger one. According to legend, when he asked this statue to act as his representative, it nodded in agreement.

Known as the Zhabdrung Khamsum Zilnon, "Zhabdrung Who Overcame the Three Realms," it continues to lead the biannual procession of the monastic body between Thimphu and Punakha to this day.

After delegating all responsibilities, issuing specific instructions, and completing the final sacred rituals for the spiritual guardians, Zhabdrung was ready to retreat forever. He entrusted his two loyal attendants, Tenzin Drukgyal and Damcho Gyaltshen, with strict orders: to ensure his meals were served promptly and rituals performed without fail, whether he was alive or dead. Additionally, he extracted a promise from them to keep the news of his passing a secret for as long as possible—at least for the next twelve years—indicating his intention to remain in thukdam, a post-death meditative state, for a prolonged period.

In the presence of his two attendants, Zhabdrung invoked Guru Rinpoche's prophecy from the *Kulu Khari* text. The prophecy foretold that if he meditated for one, three, or six years, the nation would be free from conflict and the teachings of the Drukpa Kargyu order would flourish for the benefit of all. By committing to retreat for at least the next twelve years, he ensured lasting peace for the nation and the continued strength of the Drukpa Kargyu lineage.

He then declared, "The end date of my retreat will be determined solely by my own discernment and confidence in Guru Rinpoche's prophecy." With these parting words, driven by his deep desire to safeguard the nation's peace and prosperity, he entered permanent retreat deep within Punakha Dzong at the age of fifty-seven, by Western count, in the year 1651. The exact date and time of his physical death during the retreat remain unknown. However, it is widely believed that he clinically passed away and entered thukdam on the very day he began his retreat—the tenth day of the third month in the Bhutanese calendar during the Year of the Iron Rabbit.

Surpassing the prophecy's expectations, Zhabdrung remained in thukdam for over fifty years, for reasons known only to him. Nevertheless, he had laid such a solid foundation for the nation that it remained relatively peaceful during this period, with power struggles kept at bay and the general populace unaware of his entry into thukdam.

Great spiritual masters are known to remain in this extended meditative state following clinical death. During this period, their bodies maintain warmth and posture, stay upright without any signs of decay, and emit pleasant aromas. Buddhists believe that during thukdam, the master's mind merges with the true nature of mind, a state of profound awareness and clarity known as luminosity. This state is regarded as a clear indication of the practitioner's advanced level of realization and spiritual achievement.

The news of Zhabdrung's clinical death was kept from the general public for nearly fifty-five years, disguised as his strict meditation. This concealment served a strategic purpose: With no capable hereditary heir to oversee the newly formed state, Bhutan faced imminent instability in the short to medium term. Zhabdrung's son, Jampel Dorji, was unable to govern due to his lifelong debility, and he passed away in 1681, well before the public announcement of his father's death, thus ending centuries of direct Drukpa bloodline lineage.

Another potential, though distant, heir to the Drukpa hereditary lineage was Gyalse Tenzin Rabgye, the son of Zhabdrung's first consort, Damcho Tenzin, and Tshewang Tenzin of Tango. However, his young age at the time of Zhabdrung's permanent retreat disqualified him from stepping forward to oversee the nation.

Concealing Zhabdrung's death during this interim period proved to be a wise decision. Premature news of his passing could have created a significant power vacuum, potentially allowing Bhutan to fall under the control of its northern neighbor, resulting in the permanent loss of sovereignty. Had this happened, the Bhutan we know today might never have existed.

Around 1667, during Zhabdrung's retreat, the broader monastic community learned of his entry into thukdam through the efforts of the third Druk Desi, Minjur Tenpa. Shortly after assuming office, Minjur Tenpa swiftly made his way to the sacred chamber where Zhabdrung was believed to be in deep meditation. His suspicions were confirmed when he found Zhabdrung upright in the post-death meditative state.

In 1680, Minjur Tenpa was ousted from office due to public discontent over his mandatory labor taxes and other grievances. Gyalse

Tenzin Rabgye, who enjoyed widespread support from both the public and the monastic communities, was unanimously appointed as the fourth Druk Desi. Despite pressure from Minjur Tenpa to produce an heir, Gyalse Tenzin Rabgye was unable to fulfill this expectation.

During Gyalse Tenzin Rabgye's reign from 1680 to 1694, he upheld Zhabdrung's vision of a unified state, ensuring a period of relative stability. In 1695, shortly before his death, as the last surviving bloodline heir from Ralung, Gyalse Tenzin Rabgye initiated the system of reincarnate successors to oversee the state.

Following Gyalse Tenzin Rabgye's death in 1696, Kunga Gyaltshen, the reincarnation of Zhabdrung's son Jampel Dorji, was appointed as his successor as the nation's overseer. As he contemplated his responsibilities, he felt a deep and inexplicable devotion toward Zhabdrung, stirring a strong sense of familiarity within him. Intrigued, Kunga Gyaltshen resolved to visit the meditating Zhabdrung.

Inside the dimly lit room, his eyes fixated on the meditating figure—radiant and upright, with an uncanny warmth that belied the stillness of death and a gaze that seemed to pierce through the shadows with an unsettling intensity. Over seven nights, Kunga Gyaltshen prostrated himself before Zhabdrung, earnestly pleading for his retreat to end or for him to reincarnate.

After Kunga Gyaltshen's devout prayers, a remarkable event unfolded: three rays of light emanated from Zhabdrung's body, extending upward. Simultaneously, his physical form crumbled, his eyes closing gently for the last time. Some interpreted these rays as a sign that Zhabdrung would reincarnate in three aspects: body, speech, and mind. His body was believed to be born as the prince of Sikkim; his speech as Chogle Namgyal in Dagana, Bhutan; and his mind as Jigme Dragpa in Tibet in 1724.

The revelation of a possible reincarnation in Bhutan led to the public announcement of Zhabdrung's death around 1708, which was crucial for maintaining stability within the state of Palden Drukpa. Despite Zhabdrung's failed attempts to produce a hereditary heir and his involvement in the reincarnation controversy over Pema Karpo, he never provided specific details of his reincarnation. Some texts, however, indicate that he mentioned he would be succeeded by reincarnations rather than hereditary heirs. Therefore, while the story of the three rays is remarkable and may have occurred, it should not be considered conclusive evidence of his reincarnation. As a tenth-bhumi bodhisattva, Zhabdrung had the ability to manifest as countless emanations, embodying divine qualities such as compassion, wisdom, patience, and generosity. It is highly probable that this is what he did and continues to do.

At the heart of Zhabdrung's story lies his focus on preserving the dual system as a stabilizing and unifying framework of governance. This arrangement allowed the Drukpa Kargyu tradition to flourish, benefiting the people while maintaining a democratic form of governance that prevented any single entity from seizing absolute control.

For all those years, meals were served on time, and the rhythmic tolling of bells and drums continued as if he remained in meditation. Whether in life or in death, the blessings of Zhabdrung's meditation shielded the nation from further threats. The secrecy surrounding his passing had now revealed its crucial role in fortifying the newly formed state. As a bodhisattva, Zhabdrung's singular aim was to benefit all sentient beings, a goal he undoubtedly achieved. Without his boundless compassion and visionary leadership, Bhutan's history could have been vastly different.

PART THREE

The Legacy

CHAPTER 13

Outer Activities

Zhabdrung left an indelible mark on Bhutan, particularly in shaping its distinctive culture and democratic governance. The formation of this ancient Buddhist nation, foretold by revered spiritual figures such as Guru Rinpoche, Tsangpa Gyare, his father Tenpai Nyima, and the three eminent spiritual guardians of the Drukpa Kargyu order, was not merely significant but destined.

The issuance of an edict around 1626 to expand its scope to encompass nonhuman life-forms and unseen beings serves as a testament to Zhabdrung's remarkable foresight. His acknowledgment of all beings across all dimensions reflects a deep spiritual and ecological awareness that was well ahead of his time. While symbolizing a decisive advancement in the unification process, the edict also highlights the importance he placed on broader environmental awareness—an aspect that we've only just begun to earnestly consider in the past fifty years. From 1626 onward, Zhabdrung's single-minded determination for the well-being of all became increasingly apparent as he meticulously implemented a thoughtful and strategic framework to realize his vision for the emerging state.

To recap, the process of unifying the land commenced with the proclamation of the founding seal, known as the Sixteen I's, or the *Nga Chudrugma*, following Zhabdrung's completion of his retreat in a cave in Tango around the end of 1618—an inauspicious year according to Buddhist beliefs. Subsequent stages unfolded with the establishment of the Zhung Dratshang, the southern branch of the Drukpa Kargyu order, at Cheri Monastery around 1621. This was followed by the issuance of the edict around 1626, the codification of the *Chayig Chenmo* monastic legal code in 1629, and the completion of Punakha Dzong as the primary administrative center of governance in 1638, closely followed by Wangdue Phodrang Dzong.

Formal recognition of the state by neighboring countries occurred in 1640 after a peace agreement with the Tsang government, and incorporation of the eastern regions into the state occurred sometime later. By the end of the fourth decade and into the fifth, the state was largely unified, with Zhabdrung's capable aides ensuring stability as he quietly slipped into his permanent retreat in 1651.

These historical events highlight the gradual evolution of the state, underscoring Zhabdrung's visionary leadership and the collective support of the majority. Before examining the tangible transformations Zhabdrung brought to the nation, it is essential to consider cultural beliefs through a spiritual lens, distinct from regional cultural norms. This exploration will offer deeper insight into Zhabdrung's motivations and overarching objectives.

Buddhist Spiritual Beliefs versus Traditional Cultural Beliefs

The Buddhist spiritual path aims to awaken individuals to the pure perception of reality, transcending cultural influences, personal conditioning, and fleeting impulses. Buddha taught that understanding the true nature of reality requires us to move beyond our fixed, conditioned sense of self—the ego.

Zhabdrung's unshakable dedication to shaping Bhutan's cultural identity might seem at odds with this spiritual goal. Yet without this distinct identity, the sacred land—blessed by countless spiritual masters—would have been vulnerable to colonization, endangering the teachings preserved through his unbroken transmission lineage. By fostering a strong cultural foundation grounded in Buddhist principles, Zhabdrung ensured Bhutan's autonomy and its status as a beacon of spirituality and resilience in an ever-changing world. This remarkable achievement is reflected in Bhutan's global recognition for its rich cultural heritage.

The vibrant Buddhist culture also serves as a unifying force. Timeless rituals, such as the annual religious ceremonies performed in every Buddhist household and many other cherished traditions introduced by Zhabdrung, remind the Bhutanese to stay focused on the spiritual path. Through these distinctive cultural practices, the people can gradually deepen their understanding of spirituality, a dimension often absent in the Western world. Just as Buddha compassionately imparted eighty-four thousand different teachings to cater to individual preferences and levels of awareness, Zhabdrung provided Bhutan with its distinct cultural identity, knowing that it would someday inspire and unite its people—a masterful example of the use of *skillful means* to achieve a higher purpose.

However, societal norms and traditional cultural expectations have deeply influenced the mindset of many in Bhutan, fostering the perception that life must adhere to certain unchanging, predictable, and conformist patterns dictated by society and one's elders. As a proud nation, Bhutan has understandably followed these long-held traditional thought patterns for generations.

Yet it's worth considering whether this truly aligns with Zhabdrung's spiritual vision. As an outsider unbound by rigid cultural expectations, I believe these entrenched patterns may not reflect what Zhabdrung envisioned when he nurtured Bhutan's renowned cultural vibrancy. The colorful rituals and traditional culture serve as a bridge to Dharmic teachings, not as a trap of superstition and obligation. He wanted people to be free to discover their true selves and life purpose. Isn't that what following the spiritual path is all about—growing wiser rather than falling into mindlessness, becoming more compassionate rather than thoughtless?

Buddha's teachings center on impermanence, fluidity, and understanding the true nature of the mind, emphasizing flexibility over rigid adherence to societal expectations and family obligations. Social norms, however, often reinforce the illusion of permanence and fixity. Mindful cultural change is not only possible but essential for growth, enabling us to release the conditioned negative aspects of culture while embracing its positive elements. This transformation not only leads to a more liberated spiritual existence and a healthier society but also embodies the vision Zhabdrung held for his people from the very beginning.

As Shakyamuni Buddha taught, one should not blindly accept his words out of reverence but instead investigate them, just as a goldsmith tests gold by burning, cutting, and rubbing. This teaching is well known in Buddhist scriptures, including those preserved in the Kangyur. It is likely that Zhabdrung held a similar view.

Hence, it is valuable to look at how he led by example and shaped Bhutan's unique identity. What lessons can we glean from Zhabdrung's life story, and how did his actions and legacy bring us closer to living a more spiritual life for the benefit of all? Throughout this book, it is clear that his primary intention was to illuminate the spiritual path—a path focused on liberation rather than entrapment.

In summary, I believe that Zhabdrung came to Bhutan for two distinct and destined reasons:

1. To preserve the Dharma teachings, particularly the unbroken teaching lineage of the Drukpa Kargyu order founded by Tsangpa Gyare by unifying a lawless land.
2. To inspire and guide future generations on the spiritual path, using Bhutan as inspiration and guidance in an increasingly materialistic and perilous world.

Upon reflection, Zhabdrung could have gone anywhere. Yet guided by a powerful karmic pull and ancient prophecies foretelling the unification of the Southern Land, his destiny led him to Bhutan. His presence and the dissemination of the Dharma created unparalleled conditions for benefiting sentient beings in Bhutan— conditions unmatched by any other master. While many great spiritual figures were born in or visited Bhutan, their accomplishments did not parallel his, as it was not their prophesied destiny.

With great foresight and compassion, Zhabdrung established the following rules, regulations, and cultural points of difference to unite and safeguard the nation of Palden Drukpa, with the underlying intention of guiding sentient beings on the spiritual path. I cannot imagine him intending to ensnare and bind its people within a societal structure where one must conform because it is expected, as opposed to doing what one feels is intuitively and morally correct. Engaging in critical thinking, listening to one's intuition, and acting according to spiritual values are behaviors I am certain that Zhabdrung would have wholeheartedly endorsed.

Now, armed with this perspective, we can turn our attention to the tangible elements intentionally introduced and refined by Zhabdrung. These elements not only shaped Bhutan's distinct cultural identity but also played a crucial role in founding a new state.

Dual System of Governance

Before Zhabdrung's arrival in Bhutan, religious and civil powers were not clearly delineated. Each valley was ruled by its own feudal leader, with distinct religious affiliations and governing practices. This decentralized system fueled ongoing conflicts and instability throughout the region. Zhabdrung's emergence marked a turning point as he unified disparate factions under a singular, cohesive authority, effectively ending discord.

One of the primary ways he unified the land was by introducing the dual system known as *chosi nyiden*, which translates to "Dharma and secular." This system, prophesied to be introduced to Bhutan centuries earlier by Guru Rinpoche, established a political framework where spiritual authority coexisted harmoniously with a civil ruler. The post of Je Khenpo was created to oversee spiritual affairs, while the post of Druk Desi managed civil affairs, both under the authority of a compassionate, spiritually minded leader. Zhabdrung initially took on the role of Dharma king, serving as the supreme overseer or head of state.

As of today, there have been seventy Je Khenpos and around fifty-nine Druk Desis. In 1907, the hereditary monarchy replaced the previous system, bringing stability to a nation plagued by power struggles in the wake of the public announcement of Zhabdrung's death—a transition that will be discussed in the next chapter.

The dual system remains a cornerstone of Bhutan's governance, embodying a just and effective framework. At its core, the head of state serves as both overseer and protector, offering sage counsel when needed. What sets this system apart is its break from traditional succession based solely on bloodline or reincarnation, as was the case in Tibet. Instead, Zhabdrung ingeniously designed a merit-based structure that rewarded loyalty and diligence. This approach not only reduced the risk of manipulation but also distinguished Bhutan from its northern neighbor.

However, Zhabdrung continued to uphold the bloodline not as a governance strategy but out of profound respect for the ancient hereditary Drukpa lineage. This sentiment deeply resonated with the people, nurturing a sense of continuity and legitimacy.

The concept of meritocracy was a core principle of Bhutan's dual system of governance, designed to address the inherent inequalities stemming from the lottery of birth, race, and other arbitrary factors. While meritocracy is a fundamental aspect of democracy, its practical implementation varies globally, contingent on the integrity of those in power. As Bhutan navigates the twenty-first century, it stands poised for further advancements in gender equality, diversity, and racial justice. Zhabdrung's visionary governance structure has laid a robust foundation for these developments, promising continued stability for the nation.

In Bhutan, a popular saying immortalizes Zhabdrung's achievement in unifying a lawless land: "Zhabdrung introduced laws where there had been none and affixed handles where pots had none." Before his arrival, Bhutan existed in a legal vacuum, with local rulers acting as mediators in disputes. However, Zhabdrung's transformative vision changed this landscape. Before his passing, he announced Bhutan's inaugural set of written laws, drawing inspiration from Buddhist canonical scriptures. This marked a monumental shift toward a centralized legal system anchored in principles of equity and communication, in contrast to the previous ad hoc rulings of tribal chieftains. The culmination of this effort came in 1652, during the reign of the first Druk Desi, Tenzin Drukgyal, with the codification of these laws etched on slate at the entrance to Punakha Dzong.

As we now know, the task faced by Zhabdrung wasn't easy. Disputes and hostilities were rife, with peace deals between warring parties rarely lasting. The scholar John Ardussi mentions that Zhabdrung faced the enormous challenge of articulating a vision of common purpose and establishing a governing structure that could outweigh the forces of localism.[52] The fact that he managed to unite people with a history reminiscent of the Wild West under the banner of the Drukpa Kargyu order is an accomplishment that should not be underestimated.

The tangible manifestation of Zhabdrung's efforts to establish the dual system of governance was the construction of Punakha Dzong, envisioned as the central administrative seat of his government and a symbolic replacement for his lost seat of Ralung. Following the formal establishment of the seat of Palden Drukpa, Zhabdrung became extremely active, traveling throughout the western regions of Bhutan to deliver teachings and initiations, fostering connections with inhabitants of the various valleys, and solidifying the Drukpa Kargyu teachings. As a testament to his tireless efforts to unify the land, the principles of the dual system of governance remain in place in Bhutan to this day.

The Institution of the Je Khenpos

Zhabdrung's genius lay in founding the enduring institution of the Je Khenpos—the supreme spiritual leaders of Bhutan's Central Monastic Body, the governing body of the Drukpa Kargyu order in Bhutan. The post of Je Khenpo has remained unbroken ever since and is currently held by the seventieth Je Khenpo. Unlike most Tibetan Buddhist traditions reliant on the reincarnation of spiritual heirs, Zhabdrung boldly departed from this norm. Instead, he instituted a merit-based selection process—a transformative approach that safeguarded stability and ensured the unbroken transmission of Tsangpa Gyare's sacred teachings.

Chayig Chenmo (Great Code of Law)

Most organizations rely on written governing rules and regulations enforced through various measures. Similarly, Zhabdrung based his dual system of governance on the *Chayig Chenmo*, a legal framework closely connected to Buddhist canonical texts. The first indications of this legal framework and his intentions of implementing the dual system of governance emerged in his victory declaration, the *Nga Chudrugma*, when he states, "I am he who turns the wheel of the dual system."

The *Chayig Chenmo*, inspired by the rules and regulations from Ralung and Cheri monasteries and Zhabdrung's own regulations for lay practitioners, crafted when he was a teenager, was formally codified in 1629 and refined in 1652 by Tenzin Drukgyal, the first Druk Desi. These laws primarily served as guidelines for the monastics involved in the running of Zhabdrung's government, the governing body at the time.

The *Chayig Chenmo* served as the foundation of Bhutan's legal system until the late 1950s, when it was overhauled by the third king, Jigme Dorji Wangchuck. The third king introduced a series of progressive and comprehensive laws known as the *Thrimzhung Chenmo* (Great Government Law), which addressed key aspects of Bhutanese life such as landownership, livestock, marriage, inheritance, and property. These laws marked a significant shift in state focus from religious to secular concerns. Despite these modernizations, the new laws maintained strong ties to the earlier legal framework established by Zhabdrung, with the dzongs continuing to serve as centers of governance and the Drukpa Kargyu tradition firmly upheld.

Driglam Namzhag (Harmonious Way of Behaving)

In addition to the *Chayig Chenmo*, Bhutanese society adhered to a set of social norms known as *Driglam Namzhag*. These guidelines for proper etiquette, while not legally enforceable, were essential for social acceptance and deeply ingrained in Bhutanese culture. Rooted in Buddhist ethics promoting wholesome body, speech, and mind, *Driglam Namzhag* played a crucial role in shaping everyday interactions and maintaining societal harmony.

A form of *Driglam Namzhag* existed as early as the seventh century, dating back to the time of Guru Rinpoche's arrival in Bhutan. As a Buddhist nation, Bhutan appears to have also adopted these behavioral norms from the teachings of Buddha, particularly the vinaya code of behavior, which contains the rules and regulations for the monastic community. When the term itself is deconstructed— *drig* (harmonious), *lam* (path or way), *namzhag* (a method to maintain)—it signifies a method to maintain a harmonious way. This system was one of the tools used by Zhabdrung to support his vision of national unity and continues to be taught in schools to this day.

From Zhabdrung's arrival in Bhutan until his passing, he meticulously refined these social codes of conduct for both the monastic body and laypeople, formally naming them the *Palden Drukpai Driglam Namzhag*. This comprehensive social code covered various aspects of behavior, including general courtesy and respect for parents, elders, higher authorities, and spiritual teachers. It also included guidelines for giving and receiving; social etiquette such as dressing, eating, and speaking; and a fundamental concern for the well-being of others.

I grew up in Australia during a time when the multicultural debate was at its peak. Over the decades, various policies were implemented at all levels of government and public service. Australia became a melting pot of different cultures and cultural influences (*moi* being a classic example). This transformation led to greater acceptance of the different nationalities that made up the population, along with greater respect for the indigenous people who had experienced great marginalization. As a result, the nation underwent continued economic prosperity, fueled by the contributions of hardworking immigrants, both skilled and unskilled. Australians, both newcomers and long-established residents, pursued economic prosperity over any particular cultural identity.

Don't get me wrong—Australia is a great country, known for its diverse beauty, commitment to equality, and economic opportunities; arguably one of the best in the world. However, despite these strengths, there is a notable absence of the sense of togetherness and unity that permeates all aspects of life in Bhutan—a legacy cultivated by Zhabdrung. As a first-generation Aussie, I personally experienced this lack of belonging and unity prevalent in Australia, a sentiment shared quite possibly by many in other developed nations around the world.

As Bhutan realized many decades ago, thanks to the foresight and wisdom of His Majesty the fourth king of Bhutan, gross national happiness—a measure prioritizing broader well-being indicators over purely economic ones—is a more holistic indicator of prosperity than gross national product. Ironically, many Bhutanese long to leave for the glitzy allure of the West. Yet for those who venture abroad, the majority eventually return home, drawn by the cultural vibrancy, family closeness, and, above all, the profound sense of belonging and unity that exert a magnetic pull on their psyche. This deep loyalty courses through the veins of the Bhutanese—an unseen connection often missing in many industrialized nations and one that must be preserved for generations to come. *Driglam Namzhag* stands as a vital cultural tradition, refined and institutionalized by Zhabdrung, yet it sadly faces the risk of dilution from the rapid spread of Western cultural influences.

National Costume and Language

Turning to the national costume and language, Dzongkha, it is often claimed that Zhabdrung introduced these cultural aspects, particularly the national costume. While we cannot categorically attribute the national dress code to Zhabdrung due to limited historical information, it is plausible that he refined preexisting garb upon his arrival giving it a distinctly uniform touch, laying the groundwork for what is now recognized as the *gho* for men and *kira* for women.[53]

Regarding language, Bhutan—a geographically isolated land at the time of Zhabdrung's arrival, characterized by towering peaks and harsh terrain—was home to over twenty dialects. Ngalongkha, the language spoken in the western valleys, originated from the Sino-Tibetan family of languages and became the language used in administrative and monastic centers. Both Tibetan and Ngalongkha—later called Dzongkha, from the twentieth century on—were most likely the main languages used in the dzongs during the time of Zhabdrung's leadership. The term *Dzongkha* combines *dzong*, referring to administrative centers, and *kha*, meaning "language" or "mouth," reflecting its role as the language of governance in modern times.

During Zhabdrung's era, Ngalongkha existed solely as a spoken language, while the written language, Chokey, utilized the classical Tibetan script employed by monastics. It was not until the early 1960s that Dzongkha began its transition into a written language, formally adopted as the national language in 1971 by decree of Bhutan's third king, His Majesty Jigme Dorji Wangchuck.

Dzongs

Dzongs, or fortresses strategically located at sites of spiritual significance, were instrumental in Zhabdrung's efforts to unify Bhutan. These architectural marvels served as central hubs for Bhutanese cultural, religious, and political life.

Zhabdrung was celebrated nationwide for his extensive construction of dzongs. While these structures functioned as defensive fortifications, they also symbolized Bhutan's unique cultural identity and enhanced its stunning scenery. Their placement was strategic in terms of defense and also positioned according to the results of divination and at sites of spiritual significance. For example, the tradition of constructing dzongs at river confluences and atop hills was believed to foster conducive environments for the propagation of the Dharma.

These dzongs functioned as centers for both spiritual and civil administration, operating within the framework of the dual system of governance. During his lifetime, Zhabdrung personally over-saw the construction of four dzongs: Simtokha Dzong, Punakha Dzong, Wangdue Phodrang Dzong, and Paro Dzong. As Zhabdrung advanced the Drukpa Kargyu order eastward and southward, his loyal attendants constructed additional dzongs to strengthen his vision of a unified nation.

Trongsa Dzong, established by the third Druk Desi, Minjur Tenpa, governed the eastern regions, and Dagana Dzong, established by Druk Namgyal, governed the southern regions. Paro Dzong, built by Zhabdrung himself, governed the western regions. These three dzongs, under the leadership of regional governors known as pon-lops, wielded significant influence in their respective regions, with Punakha Dzong serving as the central seat of governance for the unified state.

The Zhugdrel Ceremony

The zhugdrel ceremony, officially titled the Zhugdrel Phunsum Tshogpa Tendrel, holds immense cultural significance and rever-ence in Bhutan. It serves as the inauguration for significant events, ranging from parliamentary sessions to social gatherings, such as weddings. This section explores the origins of this ceremonial prac-tice and showcases how Zhabdrung adeptly utilized it to promote unity within the Bhutanese state.

The term Zhugdrel Phunsum Tshogpa Tendrel translates to "an Auspicious Row of Seating to Invoke Good Omens."[54] While cere-monies involving offerings and hierarchical seating arrangements existed in both civil and monastic spheres prior to Zhabdrung's arrival in Bhutan, it was Zhabdrung who refined and formalized these rituals into the unique zhugdrel ceremony seen in Bhutan today. Alongside the *Driglam Namzhag*, this ceremonial practice, with origins drawn from tantric Buddhist practices, played a crucial role in establishing harmony and stability in Bhutan, where it had previously been lacking.

The formal idea of the Bhutanese zhugdrel ceremony appears

to have arisen during the consecration of Punakha Dzong. Patrons from around the nation came to pledge their allegiance to Zhabdrung, and in the process, many gifts were offered, accumulating into a huge heap. Deeply touched by the large gathering of people, Zhabdrung immediately recognized the auspiciousness of this event and named the area Pungthangkha, which translates literally to "the Ground of Heaps."

After arranging the guests in rows according to their status, Zhabdrung proceeded to offer back to the people the gifts that were given to him. He did this while reciting prayers in honor of the Drukpa Kargyu masters, the order that effectively became the predominant religion of Bhutan upon unification. Zhabdrung later formalized this gathering of people, the gift giving, and prayer recital into what became known as the zhugdrel ceremony. Since then, this uniquely Bhutanese ceremony has been performed before any important event as a means of creating the causes and conditions for auspiciousness.

The zhugdrel ceremony consists of two primary components. The first involves acts of generosity and the cultivation of prosperity. Participants are seated in rows based on their status, and offerings such as fruit, beverages, money, and blessed substances are presented. These offerings are first dedicated to beings like the buddhas, bodhisattvas, and spiritual guardians before being given to the chief guests and other participants. The second component centers on receiving blessings and merit through a prayer composed by Pema Karpo, invoking the Drukpa Kargyu lineage lamas for the well-being and prosperity of all present. This prayer is accompanied by additional prayers for auspiciousness and aspiration.

The "Zhabdrung Phunsum Tshogpa" prayer, chanted during the zhugdrel ceremony, praises the lineage of Drukpa Kargyu incarnations, from Chenrezig to Pema Karpo, and concludes with Zhabdrung himself. Its purpose is clear: to unite the people under the Drukpa Kargyu rule, affirm Zhabdrung's legitimacy as the reincarnation of both Tsangpa Gyare and Pema Karpo, and express wishes for the success of his enlightened activities for the benefit of all. These prayer recitals fostered unity between monastic (spiritual) and lay (civil) communities from diverse backgrounds, nurturing support for the dual system of governance in a harmonious atmosphere.

The zhugdrel ceremony played a crucial role in cultivating a Buddhist value system and establishing new behavioral norms rooted in the emerging Drukpa Kargyu ideology. By bringing together monastics and laypeople, it introduced a form of unified discipline and direction, which aided in the unification and organization of a previously disorderly society. As mentioned earlier, Bhutan was a diverse country with many warring factions within the various valleys. The zhugdrel ceremony introduced a hierarchical system to replace the existing anarchy. This innovative approach to managing diversity and discord served to unite the people under one ideology.

The ceremony also proved instrumental in unifying the land by reinforcing the teachings of the Drukpa Kargyu order and the dual system of governance, benefiting all involved. By integrating acts of generosity, such as offering fruits and food to participants, blessings, and the cultivation of auspiciousness into a single ceremony, people naturally felt more cooperative and compassionate toward one another, transcending geographical and ideological differences. Zhabdrung skillfully taught by example, mindfully cultivating the spiritual qualities of generosity and kindness among the people. Furthermore, Zhabdrung's practice of returning the gifts offered to him created a sense of obligation among the people, fostering greater loyalty and willingness to serve him and his newly established government.

What emerges is a ceremony that proves to be an ingenious tool in uniting the people around a collective goal to support the newly formed state. Zhabdrung openly involved the people in creating the causes and conditions for their own good fortune, deliberately reinforcing the dual system of governance through acts of generosity and goodwill.

Examining the zhugdrel ceremony from this perspective evokes a sense of gratitude for Zhabdrung's vision in preserving the Drukpa

Kargyu teachings and his genuine concern and compassion for the people of Bhutan. I now regard the ceremony with newfound and deeply appreciative insight. As I immersed myself in writing this book and the stories of Zhabdrung's compassion and diplomacy, I found myself overwhelmed by admiration and fondness for this larger-than-life figure. My understanding of Zhabdrung has evolved significantly; what was once embarrassingly superficial has transformed into a clear recognition of his compassion and brilliance in thought and action, leading me to believe that he was a bodhisattva of unparalleled stature.

Religious Festivals

In 1618, during Zhabdrung's meditation inside Dudul Phug, the cave at Tango, he assumed a wrathful appearance and used his exceptional spiritual abilities to quell the constant harassment by the Tsang Desi. This transformative experience inspired Zhabdrung to create a wrathful mask dance known as the *zorcham*. Drawing inspiration from supernatural communication with Yeshe Gonpo following the victory over the Gelug-Mongol forces, similar dances, including the zorcham, were incorporated into a religious festival and sacred Vajrayana practice called dromcho. This sacred Vajrayana festival involves prayers, artistic dance expressions, and visualizations, and has been observed annually in Bhutan's dzongs to bestow blessings and promote peace. While these religious festivals were significantly enriched during the reign of the fourth Druk Desi, Gyalse Tenzin Rabgye, it was Zhabdrung who originally introduced these performances to Bhutan.

Apart from their spiritual significance, these religious gatherings also served a social function, drawing devotees from far and wide to witness the performances and receive blessings. Its highly likely that these gathering were also seen as a social bonding strategy during Zhabdrung's quest for unification, guiding the populace to embrace the Dharma. To this day, these religious festivals continue to draw Bhutanese from across the country, dressed in their finest traditional silk attire—one of the visible testaments to Zhabdrung's enduring presence.

The Biannual Migration, the Procession, and the Sacred Statue

The colorful biannual migration of the monastic body between its winter residence in Punakha Dzong and its summer residence in Thimphu began in 1641 once Zhabdrung established the summer residence.

From 1641 until just before entering his permanent retreat in 1651, Zhabdrung personally led the migration of the monastic body between these two seats. Even after Zhabdrung entered permanent retreat, the biannual migration continued, with the Zhabdrung Khamsum Zilnon statue—declared by him to be no different from himself—leading the procession. This tradition remains unbroken among the monastic body to the present day.

One frosty November's morning, I had the honored privilege of joining the procession of the monastic body from Thimphu to Punakha, upon the invitation of one of the five high lamas. The journey began with the chibdrel ceremony at Tashicho Dzong—a dazzling fanfare rivaling that of any Broadway performance. Dancers in elaborately curated costumes led the procession, followed by the Zhabdrung Khamsum Zilnon statue, the Je Khenpo and five high lamas in full regalia, and monks playing horns and ritual drums.

As we set off in a convoy, following a lineup of flagged cars, the Zhabdrung Khamsun Zilnon statue—encased in a colorfully decorated box on the back of a pickup truck—led the way, permeating the crisp, pine-scented air with anticipation. What would ordinarily have been a few hours' drive stretched into a daylong adventure, taking us to the traditional, quaint village of Thinleygang, usually just an hour's drive from Punakha. This village, which hosted Zhabdrung during the biannual migration of the monastic body, felt frozen in time, except for the presence of cars and mobile phones.

I wonder what Zhabdrung would have thought of these modern intrusions. Would he have been fascinated by these new technologies, or delighted that the traditions he established have endured? I'd say a mix of both.

Along the entire route, villagers emerged from their homes, faces glowing with devotion. They offered tea and snacks while we all stood by our cars, engulfed by the fragrant smoke of burning juniper harvested from nearby forests. Despite being "tea-ed out," refusal was not an option. How could I turn down their gracious offerings, prepared with such meticulous attention to detail and devotion?

As the monastic body halted for the night in Thinleygang, I continued to a hotel in Punakha, preparing to reunite with the procession early the next morning at Punakha Dzong.

Inside the fortress's thick, ancient walls, I made my way to the main prayer hall. There I sat in reverence before an imposing golden statue of Shakyamuni Buddha, as the zhugdrel ceremony unfolded and the "Zhabdrung Phunsum Tshogpa" was chanted. The Je Khenpo then addressed the audience, his words of wisdom resonating throughout the hall in a sonorous, solemn tone.

As the ceremony concluded, I couldn't help but reflect on the profound sense of continuity and devotion that permeated the entire experience. This journey was more than just a physical passage from Thimphu to Punakha; it was a timeless voyage through Bhutan's rich cultural tapestry. The enduring traditions, the unwavering faith of the people toward the monastic body, and the serene beauty of the Himalayan landscape all combined to create a lasting impression. It was a poignant reminder that in Bhutan, the past and present coexist in a harmonious dance, each enriching the other in a continuous, vibrant flow of life.

As I reflect on the compassionate and extraordinary manner in which Zhabdrung united the nation, I find myself beginning to comprehend and deeply appreciate the subtle ties that bind the young and old, the monastic and lay communities, and the highlanders with the lowlanders. Zhabdrung skillfully wove an intricate web of unity that has endured for centuries, creating an unbreakable bond. This bond not only defined the nation but also safeguarded it from invasion—a remarkable sense of cohesion that is largely absent in many nations.

This unique blend of culture and spirituality requires constant nurturing, especially in a time when people the world over prioritize acquiring the latest smartphone or designer shoes over honoring age-old traditions. Upholding Zhabdrung's legacy is a powerful way of preserving Bhutan's unique heritage, as he is the source of Bhutan's independence and, along with the monarchs, defines Bhutan's identity. By sharing stories of Zhabdrung's selfless acts and noble intentions, which are deeply woven into Bhutan's heritage, his legacy will continue to inspire future generations. It is no wonder outsiders like Father Cacella and Father Cabral were drawn to the land, its people, and its rich traditions—all thanks to the hospitality of Zhabdrung Ngawang Namgyal and his vision for a peaceful and compassionate nation.

CHAPTER 14

Perpetuation of an Extraordinary Legacy

A day should not be judged just by the harvest you reap,

But by the seeds you plant.[55]

Zhabdrung is the national patriarch, and his contributions are deeply valued by the Bhutanese people. His forward-thinking and insightful leadership played a crucial role in shaping Bhutan's core identity and cultural traditions. His ideas, actions, and policies significantly influenced the nation's self-perception and cultural values, creating a lasting impact that continues to define Bhutanese society.

To truly understand Zhabdrung's legacy, one must recognize the challenges he faced as an outsider in a foreign land. Confronted by numerous obstacles, many would have given up or, at best, settled for building a single monastery to support their followers. However, Zhabdrung remained steadfast in his vision to create a unified and peaceful nation governed by Buddhist principles. His sheer determination to establish a society free from religious persecution, characterized by compassion and opportunities for all sentient beings to thrive, exemplifies his remarkable character and spiritual conviction. Through tireless effort, he ascended to the ranks of the most celebrated bodhisattvas, fulfilling the ancient prophecies.

Debates surrounding Zhabdrung's foreign origin pale in comparison to the profound impact of his achievements. During an era dominated by religious discord, his ability to unite a diverse populace for a collective purpose stands as a testament to his leadership.

Unlike his predecessors, Zhabdrung pursued a path of unification, shaping the nascent state of Drukyul and safeguarding the rich legacy of the Drukpa Kargyu lineage.

After unifying the land and establishing stability, Zhabdrung assumed the role of a bodhisattva king, becoming the ultimate overseer and protector of the land. As he approached the end of his life, he departed from the Tibetan Buddhist tradition practiced by high-ranking lamas, which typically involved providing a detailed written or verbal indication of the specifics of his reincarnation, thus his successor—details such as the parents' names and the direction of rebirth. We will never know for sure why this was the case; we can only speculate. The lack of clear direction regarding his reincarnation most likely stemmed from his acute awareness of the pitfalls inherent in the reincarnation system, informed by his own unpleasant experiences and the tumultuous history of power struggles within Tibetan Buddhist sects. Some texts, however, mention that he would be succeeded by reincarnations rather than hereditary heirs.

Recognizing the danger posed by power-hungry individuals if his reincarnation were to be revealed, Zhabdrung may have manifested in diverse roles over time—as a king, a doctor, a healer, or even a humble spiritual practitioner. One certainty remains: as a tenth-bhumi bodhisattva, he possessed the ability to multiply his essence for the eternal benefit of countless sentient beings.

Initially seeking a hereditary successor to continue the Drukpa lineage, Zhabdrung took on two consorts during his lifetime to appeal to the sentiments of the people. Regrettably, as mentioned earlier, his only son, Jampel Dorji, was unable to assume the throne. Consequently Zhabdrung's attention increasingly shifted toward Gyalse Tenzin Rabgye, who belonged to a collateral line of the Drukpa hereditary lineage through his father's side, as a potential successor.

In 1651, when Zhabdrung entered permanent retreat, Gyalse Tenzin Rabgye was too young to assume a leadership role. Therefore, Zhabdrung continued to serve as a figurehead for the nation, even while in retreat for over fifty years. By establishing the dual system of governance, he demonstrated foresight in ensuring the nation's stability. Even four hundred years ago, he possessed the wisdom to implement a stable, democratic system of governance that was both just and transparent.

Since the fourth king, His Majesty Jigme Singye Wangchuck, declared in 2005 that Bhutan would transition to a democracy, the dual system of governance has persisted unchallenged. The system consists of a hereditary monarch as the head of state, a prime minister overseeing civil affairs—a role previously fulfilled by the Druk Desi—and the Je Khenpo still guiding spiritual matters. This steadfast adherence to the dual system of governance continues to play a vital role in preserving Bhutan's unique identity and fostering progress in the modern era.

Centuries ago, Zhabdrung demonstrated an astute understanding by recognizing the important role of law in fostering a unified and just society. He understood that drafting laws alone was insufficient; effective enforcement was equally crucial. Throughout history, it has been evident that exploiting legal loopholes and operating beyond the boundaries of the law leads to inequality and discord. Zhabdrung's vision transcended his era, advocating for a society where thriving, not just surviving, was the norm—a principle that guided all his actions. Today, his legacy continues to inspire the pursuit of a fair and equitable society founded on the values he upheld.

Zhabdrung's remarkable achievements underscore his status as a figure of great significance in history. Unlike conventional leaders, he embodied the qualities of a bodhisattva, uniting a virgin territory amid seemingly insurmountable challenges. Zhabdrung came from modest beginnings, and with only a humble group of supporters, his approach contrasted sharply with that of a conquering general. Additionally, the fulfillment of prophecies foretold centuries earlier adds to the spiritual importance of his mission. Yet beyond these transcendent circumstances, it is important not to overlook the vastness and lasting influence of his contributions.

So, how has his legacy endured through the ages?

From the time the monastic body realized that Zhabdrung had passed away until the establishment of the monarchy in 1907, Bhutan, in theory, was overseen by reincarnate successors. Initiated by Gyalse Tenzin Rabgye in 1695, following his retirement as the fourth Druk Desi (r. 1680-1694), this system aimed to maintain continuity of leadership and stability. In practice, however, these overseers often played nominal roles due to their youth or lack of interest, allowing subordinate figures to wield substantial influence.

Over two centuries, a leadership void emerged, with authority shifting among the Druk Desis, Je Khenpos, ponlops, and *dzongpons* (governor of a dzong). This period was marked by frequent power struggles driven by greed, pride, and arrogance among the ruling class, fracturing the once cohesive nation and leading to internal discord and the gradual erosion of national unity.

During the latter half of the nineteenth century, tensions flared between Bhutan and British India due to border disputes and trade route issues. In response to the rapidly changing geopolitical environment, leaders of the time recognized the necessity of adopting a modern approach. Adaptability became crucial, reflecting the Buddhist principle of impermanence. Bhutan had to reassess its strategies and embrace change to safeguard its independence against external pressures.

Around 1904, amid British efforts to establish commercial trade routes and political ties with Tibet, Ugyen Wangchuck,[56] the Trongsa governor (also known as the Trongsa Ponlop), established a relationship with the British expedition leaders en route to Lhasa. Located in central Bhutan, the region of Trongsa was of strategic importance, serving as the sole passage between eastern and western Bhutan. Effective control of Trongsa equated to control over Bhutan itself, granting significant political and economic influence. Ugyen Wangchuck played a key role in the negotiations between the British expedition and the Tibetans, successfully brokering an agreement that earned him acclaim in Bhutan. This development led to closer ties between Bhutan and Britain.

In 1907, Bhutan transitioned from monastic rule to a hereditary monarchy. Ugyen Wangchuck, recognized for his adeptness in foreign affairs, was unanimously crowned as the first king of Bhutan, adopting the title of Druk Gyalpo (Dragon King). The grand coronation ceremony, attended by British officials, took place on December 17, 1907, at Punakha Dzong. Since that historic day, the Wangchuck dynasty has guided Bhutan into the twenty-first century, spearheading modernization efforts and moving the state beyond its feudal foundations.

The monarchy upholds strong connections to the past by honoring Zhabdrung's legacy in various ways. Alongside supporting the dual system of governance with the prime minister and Je Khenpo, one of the monarchy's key commitments is to honor the country's diverse spiritual traditions, maintaining an inclusive outlook. As devout Buddhists, the monarchs have also played a vital role in renovating and maintaining numerous Buddhist temples across the nation, as well as restoring and preserving precious artifacts, paintings, and manuscripts.

Throughout their reign, they have not only honored Zhabdrung's legacy but also served as a pillar of support in times of disaster, leading many Bhutanese to regard them as emanations of bodhisattvas—or even Zhabdrung himself. Through their actions, they have consistently striven to uphold his vision of a united nation governed by Buddhist principles.

To preserve the unity and sovereignty envisioned by Zhabdrung, the monarchs recognized the importance of adapting to the modern world. The second king, His Majesty Jigme Wangchuck, laid the groundwork for Bhutan's transition into a modern nation while safeguarding its cultural identity and values. He worked to consolidate the power of the monarchy and strengthen central authority, continuing the work of his father.

The third king, His Majesty Jigme Dorji Wangchuck, is celebrated for his farsighted vision and commitment to integrating Bhutan with the modern era. His efforts to introduce socioeconomic and political reforms earned him the title of Father of Modern Bhutan.

Following in his footsteps, the fourth king, His Majesty Jigme Singye Wangchuck, gained international recognition for prioritizing the well-being and happiness of his people over the nation's gross national product. During his reign, he paved the way for Bhutan's transition to a democratic constitutional monarchy, promoting greater public participation in decision-making—a move that reinforced the dual system of governance established by Zhabdrung centuries earlier.

The fifth and current king, His Majesty Jigme Khesar Namgyel Wangchuck, in collaboration with the government, continues to strengthen the nation by implementing innovative and forward-thinking initiatives aimed at accelerating Bhutan's development in preparation for the hurdles of the twenty-first century. Recognizing the opportunities and challenges posed by the ever-evolving digital landscape, Bhutan's leadership is spearheading upskilling programs, establishing specialized educational academies, and integrating cutting-edge solutions in business operations to ensure Bhutan's readiness for the transformative impact of emerging technologies on its economy and society.

A recent announcement unveils plans for a world-class, environmentally sustainable low-rise economic hub spanning 2,500 square kilometers in the southern Sarpang district, centered on Gelephu township and incorporating protected wildlife zones. Named the Gelephu Mindfulness City and designated as an independent special administrative region, this initiative reflects His Majesty's visionary leadership. It signals the nation's commitment to technological advancement while honoring Bhutan's rich cultural heritage and Buddhist mindfulness practices—a harmonious blend of tradition and modernity.

The monarchy's profound respect for Zhabdrung Ngawang Namgyal is visibly demonstrated through various practices. During the royal investiture ceremony, a significant ritual involves the offering and receiving of ceremonial scarves before the mummified body of Zhabdrung, referred to as the Zhabdrung Machen. This sacred relic is enshrined inside a stupa located in a lofty tower within Punakha Dzong—the act symbolizing the monarch's deep reverence for Zhabdrung and all that he had achieved.

I, too, had journeyed to Punakha Dzong to have the final draft of this book blessed by the Zhabdrung Machen. Access to the sacred space, where Zhabdrung's body rests, is restricted to only three individuals: the king, the Je Khenpo, and the lama tasked with its oversight—the *machen zimpon*. At the base of a majestic tower, with its soaring whitewashed walls adorned with intricately carved woodwork and vibrant paintings, I waited patiently while my teacher contacted the machen zimpon. After a few minutes, I caught a glimpse of a figure in red robes gracefully gliding down the steep wooden stairs. A monk had been instructed to take the final draft up to the machen zimpon for formal blessings from Zhabdrung. Fifteen minutes later, the draft was handed back, bound by a white *khadhar* (a long, thin, white ceremonial scarf) undoubtedly bearing Zhabdrung's blessings, alongside a blessed cord that I immediately tied around my neck. The job was done. The task was complete. My book was blessed, and so was I.

The king's crown also embodies Zhabdrung's history. At its pinnacle sits the figure of a raven's head, symbolizing Legon Jarog Dongchen, the spiritual guardian who mysteriously guided Zhabdrung to Bhutan. The raven's head, characterized by its intricate plumage and sharply protruding beak, rests upon a base of flowing red tassels. Fierce figures encircle the band of the crown, serving as protective symbols to safeguard the king and ensure the sanctity and auspiciousness of his reign.

The *Nga Chudrugma* seal holds special significance, prominently placed atop the Genja—the official agreement signed on December 17, 1907, marking Ugyen Wangchuck's ascension as the first king of Bhutan. This agreement effectively ended the era of monastic rule. Symbolically, the seal's position underscores that the monarchy did not replace Zhabdrung but would continue his enlightened vision through its own dynasty. The Genja was not merely a document but an oath of allegiance, symbolizing a formal pledge of loyalty from senior civic and monastic leaders, as well as regional representatives. It aimed to end the instability and chaos that had troubled Bhutan for over two centuries.

Ties to Zhabdrung

In Bhutan, there are various customs and practices that foster an important connection with Zhabdrung Ngawang Namgyal.

The Zhabdrung Dhag Nang Ma (Pure Vision)

One such practice is the Zhabdrung Dhag Nang Ma, a Buddhist visualization practice associated with Zhabdrung Ngawang Namgyal. This practice was initiated during the reign of the first king of Bhutan. As a devout Buddhist practitioner, he received teachings from a wide array of Buddhist masters belonging to the Drukpa Kargyu, Nyingma, Sakya, and Gelug orders. Among them was Shakya Shri, a revered Tibetan yogi and mystic.

A significant prophecy concerning the Wangchuck dynasty and Zhabdrung was revealed by Serkong Dorji Chang, a prominent Gelug master who had a close relationship with the first king and later became his root guru. According to His Eminence, the current Dorji Lopen and one of the most senior members of Bhutan's monastic body, Serkong Dorji Chang resided in the Bumthang region during his time in Bhutan, where the main royal palace was located. While Serkong Dorji Chang was meditating on Guru Rinpoche inside the sacred Kurje Lhakhang, named after Guru Rinpoche's body print inside the monastery, Zhabdrung appeared before him in a pure vision and instructed him to compose the Dhag Nang Ma, a practice aimed at invoking Zhabdrung through visualization and chanting (known as a sadhana).

He proceeded to compose the Dhag Nang Ma and advised King Ugyen Wangchuck that focusing on practicing this Zhabdrung sadhana would ensure peace and prosperity throughout Bhutan for him and his successors. This guidance is considered a mind treasure in Tibetan Buddhism, as it was revealed in a vision to a highly accomplished practitioner by a buddha or bodhisattva. What adds to its intrigue is that Serkong Dorji Chang, a Gelug master not aligned with the Drukpa Kargyu order seemed to have no underlying motivation or agenda to reveal such a prophecy.

As Tsang Khenchen notes in his biography of Zhabdrung, many great masters from various Tibetan Buddhist lineages held a deep interest in Nyingma practices. They also received visions of Guru Rinpoche and became primary lineage holders of numerous Nyingma lineage teachings. This illustrates that the boundaries of their own lineages did not restrict them from drawing wisdom from other traditions, and vice versa—a sentiment reflective of true Dharmic practice.

One must bear in mind that conflicts during Zhabdrung's time were commonplace and more a reflection of the era than any particular Tibetan Buddhist school. Wars and animosities aside, what stands out among the Tibetan Buddhist schools moving forward from this time period is their mutual respect for the inherent wisdom contained within their respective teachings.

Given these circumstances, it is not surprising that a Gelug master played an important role in perpetuating Zhabdrung's legacy through the Wangchuck dynasty. Additionally, it is essential to remember that Zhabdrung was believed to be an emanation of Guru Rinpoche, and it was through this connection that Serkong Dorji Chang received the significant prophecy. Can this be considered mere coincidence? Perhaps not.

Of further interest is the fact that Serkong Dorji Chang mentions the following in relation to the practice of the Zhabdrung sadhana ritual:

During the time of acute degeneration, it will become the practice and cause of the restoration of damage to the well-being of the buddhadharma and sentient beings. It will help avert foreign invasions and pacify internal conflict. It will clear away all sickness of men and domestic animals and expand the tradition of explaining and meditating on the buddhadharma.

As Serkong Dorji Chang was the root guru of King Ugyen Wangc-huck, His Majesty became deeply devoted to Zhabdrung and dili-gently practiced the sadhana. This commitment, exemplified by the first king and perpetuated by the Wangchuck dynasty, is believed to have significantly contributed to the peace and independence of the nation to this day. The Zhabdrung Dhag Nang Ma sadhana is also devoutly practiced by those seeking to strengthen and main-tain a connection with Zhabdrung, in pursuit of eternal blessings and longevity.

Zhabdrung Kucho

Zhabdrung Kucho, commemorating the death anniversary of Zhab-drung Ngawang Namgyal, is a revered tradition observed annually on the tenth day of the third month of the Bhutanese lunar calendar. This occasion holds deep significance, evoking immense devotion among the Bhutanese and symbolizing their reverence for Zhab-drung and gratitude for his enduring legacy. Initiated by the tenth Je Khenpo, Penchen Tenzin Chogyal, this cherished tradition has become a major event in Bhutan's religious calendar.

Jigten Wangchuk Prayer

The Jigten Wangchuk (Chenrezig) prayer[57] is a long-life prayer for Zhabdrung Ngawang Namgyal composed by his father, Ten-pai Nyima, at the time of Zhabdrung's enthronement at the age of thirteen (age twelve by Western count). It holds a special place in the hearts of the Bhutanese people. The prayer is regularly chanted throughout the kingdom, serving as a powerful invocation for pro-tection, prosperity, and all things auspicious.

Zhabdrung's influence extends far beyond mere traditional gov-ernance; he ushered his people into a larger cultural and spiritual realm where compassion, respect, and tolerance reigned supreme. His legacy transcends time, playing a potent archetypal role in a

Appliquéd Zhabdrung thongdrel, unfurled on the occasion of Zhabdrung Kucho at Punakha Dzong (Photo © 2024 Sasha Wakefield)

narrative that has resonated with generations and will continue to do so in the centuries ahead. Though he departed from his mortal body, the nation he established continues to endure, a testament to his lasting impact.

As a tenth-bhumi bodhisattva, Zhabdrung possessed the ability to manifest in countless forms for the benefit of sentient beings.

Therefore, it's highly likely that Zhabdrung's emanations are present among us, whether openly or in secret, working toward a more peaceful and harmonious world.

It is clear to me, as an outsider looking in, that Zhabdrung's influence extends far beyond what some claim it to be. He was not a warrior, a black magician, or a powerful colonizer propped up by a large army. To see him as such misses the point of his raison d'être. He was a bodhisattva of the highest standing whose focus was on uniting a lawless land and safeguarding the precious Buddhist teachings. It was for this reason he revealed his wrathful side. To most it may appear that he escaped his homeland due to the dispute over the reincarnation of Pema Karpo and the problems with the Tsang Desi, but these were merely the outer reasons or catalysts for the prophecies to ripen. He came to Bhutan because it was his prophesied destiny. His purpose was, and continues to be, far greater than our human minds could possibly perceive, and I sincerely hope that this book contributes to a deeper understanding and appreciation of the multifaceted aspects of this great being.

I trekked the forty-five-minute forest trail up to Cheri Monastery, reflecting on the final touches on the book. The trail led to the place where I had first held Zhabdrung's walking stick—to the place where it had all begun. I grasped it once again, this time with great reverence and a tighter grip. Perhaps I was seeking a sign to indicate that I had done justice to Zhabdrung's legacy, a reassurance. Then my teacher's words came flooding back to me: "No doubt, no ego, no expectation." I sat on the edge of a rocky outcrop, gazing out over the densely forested valley below, my mind at peace in the present moment.

Oddly, I had never seriously contemplated the logistics of my long stay in Bhutan to be close to my teacher for all these years. Prolonged stays in foreign lands are seldom straightforward, yet the years just seemed to roll on by. Obstacles presented themselves, but they didn't occupy too much of my thoughts. Could it be the blessings of the deities, my faith in the law of karma, or my devotion to my teacher? I'd say it's a combination of all three. My teacher stood as a steadfast anchor in this ancient Buddhist kingdom—never rusty, always sparkling like the most precious of jewels. His presence was a constant in both my thoughts and meditation practice. It truly felt like I had won the lottery.

The authentic story of Zhabdrung has now unfurled like prayers from fluttering prayer flags atop Bhutan's hilltops, bestowing blessings upon all. Looking ahead, my hope is that Bhutan continues to embody an archetype of a nation grounded in spiritual values, upholding fundamental principles such as respect for all sentient beings, diligence, and innovation—reflecting the very qualities that Zhabdrung held so dear.

May Zhabdrung's light shine bright for eons to come.

Acknowledgments

I am deeply thankful to all the individuals whose encouragement made this significant undertaking possible, even on what was often a lonely road fraught with many obstacles.

First and foremost, I extend my heartfelt gratitude to His Majesty Jigme Khesar Namgyel Wangchuck, for supporting my spiritual endeavors in Bhutan and for his unshakable commitment to the well-being of Bhutan and its people. I also offer my deepest appreciation to His Holiness Tulku Jigme Choedra, the seventieth Je Khenpo of Bhutan, for his lifelong selfless spiritual service to the nation.

I am profoundly grateful to my teacher, who entrusted me with the extraordinary opportunity to write this book—a task that would have been impossible without my unwavering devotion to him. Words cannot express how blessed I feel to have connected with him in this lifetime, and I hope our paths will cross in many lifetimes to come.

To a small circle of monastic scholars: thank you for having my back. This book could not have materialized without your invaluable assistance in deciphering ancient Chokey texts. Special thanks to Buddhist scholar Phub Namgay for always being there to clarify my doubts, and to Sonam Pelden, my assistant, for her help and companionship during the time we worked together. To everyone who offered a helping hand—both seen and unseen—throughout my writing journey: thank you.

I am deeply indebted to my family—Scott, Cooper, and Hunter—for their unwavering support, understanding, and enduring patience during my spiritual journey, which allowed my karmic connection with Bhutan to ripen. I am equally grateful to my parents, Toshiko Endo and Oliver Pazdernik, for never curbing my inquisitive mind.

Finally, I want to thank the team at Shambhala Publications for their support, professionalism, and dedication in bringing this book to life—especially my editor, Anna Wolcott-Johnson, for her invaluable insights and guidance, and to Nikko, who was the first to read and believe in the manuscript.

Zhabdrung's Lineages and Legacy

Tsang Khenchen (1610-1684)

Tsang Khenchen, an acclaimed scholar from the Tsang region, was born Norbu Zangpo in the upper Nyang valley of Tibet in 1610, the youngest of three siblings. Raised in a devout Buddhist family, he was deeply immersed in Dharmic activities and teachings from an early age, eventually becoming a great Buddhist scholar and master artist. His first formal teacher and most influential religious figure was the Sakya master Khenchen Lungrig Kunga Gyatsho, who ordained him into the Sakya order as Jamyang Palden Gyatsho at the age of thirteen.

Despite identifying with the Sakya tradition, he possessed a broad, nonsectarian perspective on Buddhism and was a great admirer of the tenth Karmapa, Choying Dorji (1604-1674), whom he encountered on his journey into Bhutan years later. This admiration led some scholars to consider him a prominent Karma Kagyu scholar, despite his Sakya background.

The foundation for a mutually respectful relationship between Tsang Khenchen, Zhabdrung, and the Drukpa Kargyu institution was laid years earlier, beginning with Tsang Khenchen's father, Genyen Gawa Zangpo. Genyen Gawa Zangpo held deep reverence for Zhabdrung and had been a patron of the Drukpa Kargyu tradition since the time of Pema Karpo. When Tsang Khenchen was around six years old, Zhabdrung stayed with his family on his way to Shigatse to meet with the Tsang Desi Phuntsok Namgyal, bestowing upon them the long-life and Tara empowerments. This encounter, as Zhabdrung later affirmed, proved fortuitous. Tsang Khenchen would go on to compose his biography, *The Melody of the Great Dharma Cloud*, completed in 1681—thirty years after Zhabdrung entered permanent retreat.

At the age of sixteen, Tsang Khenchen was enrolled in Serdogchen Monastery, studying under the famed Sakya polymath Pandita Sakya Tenzin. Upon completing his studies, he became the abbot of Pokhang Monastery in the Tsang region. Later, he was appointed by the Tsang Desi, Karma Tenchong Wangpo, as the abbot of a newly established nonsectarian religious center in Shigatse. Despite the prestige and affluence of these positions, Tsang Khenchen longed for a simpler, more peaceful life of retreat.

During this period, the Ganden Phodrang forces of the Fifth Dalai Lama, led by the Mongol warrior Gushri Khan, were advancing into the Tsang region. Aware of the potential challenges and dangers his followers could face due to his close ties with the Tsang Desi, Tsang Khenchen made the courageous decision to flee Tibet for Bhutan with a small entourage under the cover of darkness. It was during this southward journey in 1642 that he encountered the tenth Karmapa. Shortly afterward, the rule of the Tsang Desis collapsed, and the Ganden Phodrang government took control.

Passing through the northern gate of Gasa, the same route taken by Zhabdrung over twenty-five years earlier, Tsang Khenchen arrived at the steps of Punakha Dzong, Bhutan's seat of governance at the time. It was here that his bond with Zhabdrung was formed. Despite plans to venture to Sikkim, his connections with the Drukpa Kargyu hierarchy led him to spend the rest of his life in Bhutan.

Tsang Khenchen made significant contributions to the Drukpa Kargyu teachings by actively imparting sacred empowerments, teaching various forms of Buddhist practice, and penning Zhabdrung's biography. Notably, he introduced the Vajrakilaya Tibetan Buddhist practice, which focuses on removing negative influences and aiding spiritual realization.

Zhabdrung saw in him not only a man of substance and integrity but also someone with the capabilities needed to contribute to his state-building initiatives. Tsang Khenchen's familiarity with the Tsang governance style, along with his expertise in Buddhist logic and epistemology, were seen as both politically and spiritually advantageous. He eventually settled in Menchunang, a seat he established in the Paro Valley. There he spent many years in retreat, teaching arts such as embroidery, painting, woodworking, and sculpting, while also writing Buddhist commentaries. Menchunang was where he passed away, surrounded by many favorable signs.

Finally, despite their close spiritual connection, Tsang Khenchen emphasized the accuracy of his biography of Zhabdrung, citing his commitment to honesty and authenticity as a follower of Shakyamuni Buddha.

The Buddhist Lineages

In the story of Zhabdrung, two distinct lineages emerge: the Drukpa hereditary lineage (formerly known as the Gya lineage) and the Drukpa Kargyu reincarnation lineage (reincarnations of Tsangpa Gyare). During this time, these lineages were highly revered, and those recognized within them commanded considerable respect and influence.

Below, I provide a detailed explanation of these two Buddhist lineages. While there are instances of overlap between these lineages, since Drukpa masters may possess a combination of both, the list includes hereditary lineage masters who held the throne of Ralung from Tsangpa Gyare to Zhabdrung, as well as the reincarnations of Tsangpa Gyare.[58]

Drukpa Hereditary Lineage

Before listing the hereditary lineage masters who held the throne of Ralung, it is crucial to understand the origins of the Drukpa clan. This clan plays a significant role in the story of Zhabdrung, as both Tsangpa Gyare and Zhabdrung trace their ancestry to this ancient family lineage, initially known as Gya.

Succession among some of the Buddhist schools in Tibet during this period followed an uncle-nephew succession, known as *khu on*, which allowed religious thrones (*thri*) to retain both religious and secular powers within the family. Within the hereditary lineage of Ralung, however, consorts were accepted, leading to successors coming primarily from sons, with nephews and cousins only occasionally taking the throne. The close ties between Ralung and Bhutan led to several throne holders and heirs being born to women from Bhutan.

The origins of the Drukpa hereditary lineage can be traced back to the time of the Tibetan Dharma king, King Songtsen Gampo's rule (c. 617 to 650 C.E.). Historical records indicate that the famous statue of Jowo Shakyamuni, brought from China to Tibet after the king's marriage to a Chinese princess, was carried by two robust young men known as Lhaga and Luga, believed to be emanations of Chenrezig. In gratitude for Lhaga's service, King Songtsen Gampo granted him an estate in Ralung, Tibet. It was from him that the hereditary lineage of the Drukpa (Gya) clan began.

A descendant of Lhaga, Gya Jampel Sangwa, played a crucial role in solidifying this Buddhist hereditary lineage. From this lineage emerged many accomplished Dharma practitioners, including the eminent Tsangpa Gyare. During Tsangpa Gyare's time, the Gya hereditary lineage transitioned to become known as the Drukpa hereditary lineage.

In the early thirteenth century, Tsangpa Gyare established a subschool of the Kagyu tradition of Tibetan Buddhism, known as the Drukpa Kargyu order. Within this order, Zhabdrung was revered as a superior Dharmic holder owing to his possession of both the Drukpa (Gya) hereditary lineage and the reincarnation lineage, with Tsangpa Gyare being the source of this lineage.

At the time, many scholars and practitioners considered the Drukpa Kargyu order to be one of the finest Dharmic lineages due to its long history of producing numerous Drukpa hereditary lineage holders since the time of Tsangpa Gyare. This ancient reputation helped disseminate the teachings of the Drukpa Kargyu order across

Tibet, Bhutan, and eventually worldwide, garnering a large following and establishing it as one of the most prominent and authentic Mahayana teaching lineages today.

To provide a clear visual of the Drukpa hereditary lineage from Tsangpa Gyare, the successive Drukpa throne holders are listed below, along with their respective kinships. Notably, Tsangpa Gyare made a prophecy at Ralung before his passing, stating that he would be reborn following the birth of nine lineage holders bearing the name Senge and three bodhisattva emanations, known as the Rigsum Namtrul. True to his prediction, his reincarnation was born as Kunga Peljor in 1428 and became the thirteenth Ralung throne holder, inheriting both lineage lines.

Throne Holders of Ralung

1. Tsangpa Gyare (1161-1211): A Drukpa (Gya) hereditary lineage holder and the founder of the Drukpa Kargyu order of the Kagyu tradition. From Tsangpa Gyare onward, the Gya hereditary lineage became known as the Drukpa hereditary lineage.
2. Onre Dharma Senge (1177-1237): A nephew of (1).
3. Zhonu Senge (1200-1269): A nephew of (2).
4. Nyima Senge (1251-1287): A nephew of (3).
   Senge Sherab (1238-1280) was not a Ralung throne holder but was one of the nine Senges prophesied by Tsangpa Gyare.[59]
5. Senge Rinchen (1258-1313): The kinship is not clear, but it appears he was a cousin of sorts of (4).
6. Senge Gyalpo (1289-1326): A son of (5).
7. Jamyang Kunga Senge (1314-1347): A son of (5) who helped to establish the sacred Dechenphu Lhakhang in Thimphu.
8. Lodro Senge (1345-1390): A son of (7). His mother was Bhutanese and a descendant of Phajo Drukgom Zhigpo's relatives from the Gasa region.
9. Sherab Senge (1371-1392): A son of (8).

Nine Senges

10. Jamyang Yeshe Rinchen (1364-1413): A son of (8) and the first bodhisattva emanation (Manjushri).

11. Namkha Pelzang (1398-1425): A son of (10) and the second bodhisattva emanation (Vajrapani).

12. Sherab Zangpo (1400-1438): A son of (10) and the third bodhisattva emanation (Chenrezig).

13. **Kunga Peljor**[60] (1428-1476): A son of (12). He was the first reincarnation of Tsangpa Gyare.

14. Ngawang Chogyal (1465-1540): A nephew of (13) and the great-great-grandfather of Zhabdrung Ngawang Namgyal.

15. Ngagi Wangchuk (1517-1554): A son of (14) and the great-grandfather of Zhabdrung Ngawang Namgyal.

16. Mipham Chogyal (1543-1604): A son of (15) and the grandfather of Zhabdrung Ngawang Namgyal. He remained on the Ralung throne until his passing in 1604.[61]

17. **Zhabdrung Ngawang Namgyal** (1594-1651): A grandson of (16). He acceded the Ralung throne in 1606 at age twelve by Western count. (He was thirteen according to the Bhutanese calendar as they include the gestation period.)[62]

Reincarnation Lineage

In accordance with tradition, the recognition of a Drukpa reincarnation required approval from the main hereditary lineage holder of the seat at Ralung and/or a committee of Drukpa hierarchs. The process entailed rigorous examinations and the manifestation of favorable signs, irrespective of the candidate's origin or familial background. The recognition process became contentious during the identification of the reincarnation of Pema Karpo, as there were two candidates—Zhabdrung (1594-1651) and Pagsam Wangpo (1593-1641).

Reincarnations of Tsangpa Gyare, the founder of the Drukpa Kargyu order, in sequential order are as follows:

1. Second Palden Drukpa Rinpoche, Kunga Peljor (1428-1476, also from the Drukpa hereditary lineage)

2. Third Palden Drukpa Rinpoche, Jamyang Chokyi Dragpa (1478-1523)
3. Fourth Palden Drukpa Rinpoche, Pema Karpo (1527-1592)
4. Fifth Palden Drukpa Rinpoche, Zhabdrung Ngawang Namgyal (1594-1651, also from the Drukpa hereditary lineage)[63]

The Drukpa Kargyu Order

Founded by Tsangpa Gyare, the Drukpa Kargyu order encompassed a diverse group of practitioners, including members of the Drukpa bloodline, reincarnations of Tsangpa Gyare, and devoted practitioners. Today, its teachings have spread widely, driven by global interconnectedness and a growing interest in authentic Buddhist practice and philosophy.

After the passing of Tsangpa Gyare, his disciples carried forth his teachings, leading to the formation of three distinct branches:

1. Todruk (Upper Druk), founded by Gotsangpa
2. Bardruk (Middle Druk), founded by Onre Dharma Senge, with its main seat at Ralung
3. Medruk (Lower Druk), founded by Lorepa

Bardruk served as the principal branch, with Ralung Monastery as its stronghold, flourishing under Onre Dharma Senge, its founder and Drukpa hereditary lineage holder. Its popularity grew so vast that its followers were likened to dust particles in sunlight.

The Bardruk branch eventually split into two due to the unresolved dispute over the reincarnation of Pema Karpo:

1. Bodruk (northern branch), Drukpa Kargyu branch in Tibet.
2. Lhodruk (southern branch), Drukpa Kargyu branch in Bhutan. This offshoot became firmly institutionalized through Zhabdrung's unification efforts upon his arrival in 1616.

In the Drukpa Kargyu tradition, Tsangpa Gyare (1161-1211), Kunga Peljor (1428-1476), and Zhabdrung Ngawang Namgyal (1594-1651) were highly esteemed for possessing both hereditary and reincarnation lineages, underscoring their strong Dharmic pedigree.

Phajo and the Drukpa Kargyu Masters

Several influential Buddhist masters were instrumental in supporting Zhabdrung's unification efforts both before and during his leadership.

Phajo Drukgom Zhigpo's early presence in Bhutan laid a solid foundation for Zhabdrung's unification efforts, as did the contributions of Phajo's descendants. Zhabdrung's first consort, Damcho Tenzin, was from Phajo's lineage at Changangkha in Thimphu. Her marriage to "Tshewang Tenzin" of Tango, believed to be the reincarnation of "Phajo," resulted in the birth of Gyalse Tenzin Rabgye (1638-1696). Upon Zhabdrung's arrival in Bhutan, Tshewang Tenzin's gesture of offering the Tango area to him carried great significance, as it expanded the sacred sites under "Zhabdrung"—the reincarnation of "Tsangpa Gyare"—emphasizing their profound karmic connection.[64]

Gyalse Tenzin Rabgye was also a significant figure who greatly contributed to Zhabdrung's vision for a united nation. He eventually became the fourth Druk Desi and, following Zhabdrung's death, took the initiative to significantly expand Tango Monastery.

From Phajo's time in the thirteenth century until Zhabdrung's arrival in Bhutan in 1616, there existed a continuous exchange of Buddhist masters and students between Bhutan and the Drukpa Kargyu seat at Ralung. This interaction solidified a robust support network for Zhabdrung's arrival in Bhutan and subsequent unification efforts. Zhabdrung's ancestors—his great-great-grandfather Ngawang Chogyal, great-grandfather Ngagi Wangchuk, grandfather Mipham Chogyal, and father Tenpai Nyima—played indispensable roles in securing the Drukpa Kargyu teachings in western and central Bhutan during the fifteenth and sixteenth centuries.

Drukpa Kunle (1455-1529), a prominent lama from Tibet and the grandfather of Tshewang Tenzin of Tango, played an auxiliary role in Zhabdrung's narrative. As a member of a collateral line of the Drukpa hereditary lineage, Drukpa Kunle maintained close ties with the Drukpa family in Ralung. Renowned as the Divine Madman, he gained fame for his unconventional behaviors and played a role in spreading the Drukpa Kargyu teachings across western Bhutan. His son, Ngawang Tenzin, established a hermitage at Tango, where Gyalse Tenzin Rabgye later built Tango Monastery. Ngawang Tenzin's lineage continued with his son, Tshewang Tenzin, who famously offered the Tango area to Zhabdrung shortly after his arrival in Bhutan.

Drukpa Kunle had familial ties to Lhabum, the second-eldest brother of Tsangpa Gyare. Additionally, he was the nephew of Kunga Peljor (1428-1476), one of his primary teachers. Ngawang Chogyal (1465-1540), Zhabdrung's great-great-grandfather, was his second cousin, underscoring Drukpa Kunle's strong collateral ties to the Drukpa (Gya) hereditary lineage and his distinguished ancestry from Ralung.

The network of connections that facilitated the establishment of the Drukpa Kargyu order from Ralung within Bhutan was not only complex but also deeply rooted in blood ties. During that era, familial bonds were intricately woven, strengthened by connections with families originating from Phajo and Drukpa Kunle. These generational ties proved invaluable to Zhabdrung upon his arrival in Bhutan.

Gyalse Tenzin Rabgye, the fourth Druk Desi, was born to Damcho Tenzin (a descendant of Phajo and the first consort of Zhabdrung) and Tshewang Tenzin of Tango (the reincarnation of Phajo). As a member of the Drukpa hereditary lineage, Gyalse Tenzin Rabgye was seen as the natural successor to Zhabdrung's legacy, especially in light of his son's lifelong ailment. However, the lack of a capable direct heir to Zhabdrung's lineage caused concern and uncertainty among the Drukpas toward the end of his life.

Long-Life Prayer for Zhabdrung Ngawang Namgyal (Known as the Jigten Wangchuk [Two-Armed Chenrezig] Prayer)

At the center of Avalokiteshvara's (Chenrezig) wave of
  compassion,
Blossoms a thousand-petaled lotus of wisdom and
  compassion of all the buddhas,
You are the companion who radiates the sweet fragrances of
  life's temporal and ultimate benefits,
I supplicate at the feet of Ngawang Namgyal.

With your wisdom you dispel the widespread darkness of
  ignorance,
Through your compassion you never forsake to benefit others,
With power you subjugate the evil forces,
I supplicate at the feet of Ngawang Namgyal, lord of lords.

To liberate sentient beings from the three realms of cyclical
  existence,
You attain the supreme immortal vajra body,
Benefiting sentient beings through the four types of
  enlightened activities,
I pray that you live long.

I pray for your good health,
And for your supremely long life,
May your enlightened activities flourish,
Grant me your blessings so I may never be separated from
  you, my lama.

Through all my rebirths may I never be separated from the
  sublime lama,
May I be engaged in the enjoyment of the sacred Dharma
  teachings,

Achieving the realizations along the stages and paths,
May I swiftly attain the state of Vajradhara.

Composed by Zhabdrung's father, Tenpai Nyima, on the occasion of Zhabdrung's enthronement at the age of thirteen (age twelve by Western count).

Glossary of Names

Bodruk. Northern Drukpa Kargyu branch that remained in Tibet.

Changangkha Lhakhang. The fourteenth-century temple built by descendants of Phajo Drukgom Zhigpo in Thimphu.

Cheri Monastery. Buddhist monastery located near Dodena in northern Thimphu. Founded in 1620 by Zhabdrung Ngawang Namgyal. It became the site of Bhutan's first Drukpa Kargyu monastic body in Bhutan—the Zhung Dratshang. The monastery is built on one of two southward-facing hills deemed ideal for practicing the wrathful actions of Mahakala; the other being the site of Tango Monastery.

Chongye Depa (Ngawang Sonam Dragpa). Governor of the region of Chongye and close associate of the Tsang Desi. A key figure in the reincarnation drama advocating for Pagsam Wangpo as the legitimate reincarnation of Pema Karpo.

Damcho Gyaltshen. A close attendant of Zhabdrung who helped guide him to Bhutan. One of two attendants during Zhabdrung's permanent retreat. Main tutor to Zhabdrung's son, Jampel Dorji, and overseer of spiritual affairs in the monastic body.

Damcho Tenzin (1606-1660). First consort of Zhabdrung, descendant of Phajo Drukgom Zhigpo's son Nyima. Gave birth to Zhabdrung's daughter. Later gave birth to Gyalse Tenzin Rabgye with Tshewang Tenzin.

Drubthob Terkhungpa (Rinchen Dragpa Paldron). Thirteenth-century Drukpa Kargyu forebearer, disciple of Tsangpa Gyare, and ancestor of the Obtsho clan from Bhutan. Believed to have founded the Obtsho Dzong in the Gasa district.

Druk Choding Lhakhang. Drukpa Kargyu ancestral temple at the entrance to Paro town, built by Zhabdrung's great-great-grandfather, Ngawang Chogyal, around 1525. The ground floor houses a stupa containing sacred relics, a place where dakinis congregated and offerings naturally materialized.

Drukgyal Drung. A close attendant to Zhabdrung mentioned in the ancient texts. Believed to be Tenzin Drukgyal, the first Druk Desi.

Druk Namgyal. A close disciple of Zhabdrung, sent to oversee the Ralung estate after the 1640 peace deal with the Tsang Desi. Returned to Bhutan in 1646 after Ralung was seized and was appointed as the zhung dronyer (chief of protocol). One of three lamas tasked with bringing eastern Bhutan under Zhabdrung's rule.

Druk Phodrangding Lhakhang. Temple where Zhabdrung first sought shelter upon arriving in Bhutan. Built by Zhabdrung's great-great-grandfather, Ngawang Chogyal, around 1529. Located in northern Thimphu on the grounds of Pangri Zampa.

Druk Sewa Jangchubling Monastery (known also as Druk). A Drukpa Kargyu monastery founded in 1205 by Tsangpa Gyare at Namdruk—the site where he had a vision of dragons who took flight accompanied by a roar of thunder.

Drukpa Kunle (1455-1529). Also known as the Divine Madman. A respected lama from a collateral line of the Drukpa (Gya) hereditary lineage, famous for his unorthodox methods of teaching Buddhism. Grandfather of Tshewang Tenzin of Tango Monastery.

Genyen Jakpa Melen. A local deity of Thimphu, based at Dechenphu Lhakhang. Originally a Bon deity, subdued by Guru Rinpoche in the eighth century. Pledged to serve the Dharma before Jamyang Kunga Senge of the Drukpa hereditary lineage (the seventh of the Nine Senges), then dissolved into a rock at Dechenphu. Served Zhabdrung from the time of his arrival in Bhutan.

Gokar Drolma (1603-1684). Second consort of Zhabdrung. Mother of Jampel Dorji, a Drukpa hereditary lineage successor who could not accede to the throne due to a debility.

Gonpo Chamdrelsum. Three tenth-bhumi spiritual guardians of Buddhism who share a deep connection to the Drukpa Kargyu lineage. These three spiritual guardians are

> *Yeshe Gonpo.* Also known as Mahakala in Sanskrit. One of the oldest and principal protectors of Buddhism, originally worshipped in the Bon tradition. He resides in the eastern Himalayas with origins in India. Converted to Buddhism by Buddha Kasapa, one of the 1,002 buddhas. Main protector of the Drukpa Kargyu teachings and Buddhism in general.
>
> *Palden Lhamo.* Also known as Sri Devi or Mahakali, she is depicted as a wrathful female tantric Buddhist deity. Her primary role is as a wisdom protector of Buddhism, particularly safeguarding the Dharma in the Himalayan region. Zhabdrung entrusted his monastic community, the Zhung Dratshang, to her care during his efforts to unify Bhutan.
>
> *Legon Jarog Dongchen.* Also known as Karma Mahakala, he is an emanation of Mahakala in the form of a raven. Referred to as the Lord of Action or the Raven-Faced Protector, Legon Jarog Dongchen serves as the attendant to

Mahakala and is revered as Bhutan's protective deity. Mahakala is said to have taken on the form of a raven to safely guide Zhabdrung from Tibet to Bhutan.

Guru Rinpoche. An eighth-century tantric Buddhist master from modern-day Pakistan. Known as the Second Buddha in the Himalayan region. Introduced Vajrayana Buddhism to Tibet and Bhutan. Renowned for subjugating demons and transforming them into protectors of the Dharma. His teachings include oral lineage transmissions and hidden treasure texts (*terma*). Visited Bhutan at least three times. Also known as Padmasambhava, Pema Jungney, and Ugyen Guru Rinpoche.

Gya Jampel Sangwa (eighth century). One of the sources of the ancient Gya hereditary lineage. Buddhist scholar and disciple of Guru Rinpoche. Descendant of Lhaga, an emanation of Chenrezig, who helped bring the statue of Jowo Shakyamuni to Lhasa in the seventh century. He prophesied eighty-four emanations of Chenrezig to appear in the Gya (Drukpa) hereditary lineage.

Gyalse Tenzin Rabgye (1638-1696). A son of Damcho Tenzin (Zhabdrung's first consort) and Tshewang Tenzin of Tango (distant nephew of Zhabdrung). Heir to Drukpa hereditary lineage from a collateral line, regarded as Zhabdrung's successor. The fourth Druk Desi, he advanced Zhabdrung's vision of a unified land and solidified its national identity.

Jampel Dorji (1631-1681). The son of Zhabdrung and his second consort, Gokar Drolma. Zhabdrung's only son. Drukpa hereditary lineage holder. Unable to oversee the nation due to a debility.

Jela Dzong. A fortress built by Zhabdrung's great-great-grandfather, Ngawang Chogyal. Located on a ridge above Paro Dzong where Zhabdrung retreated during the first conflict.

Jigme Namgyal (1825-1881). The father of the first king of Bhutan, His Majesty Ugyen Wangchuck. Key figure in Bhutanese history. Known for his roles as both the Trongsa Ponlop and Druk Desi.

Lama Khag Nga. A collective term for dissident followers of lamas within Bhutan, originating from five Buddhist sects: Lhapa, Nenyingpa, Barawa, Chagzampa, and Ganden Shingtapa. These sects trace their ancestry to Tibet from the twelfth to the fifteenth centuries.

Lama Namse. One of the three lamas tasked with bringing the east under Zhabdrung's rule. A scholar from Tshatsi in northern present-day Pemagatsel dzongkhag (district) and a relative of Zhabdrung's father, Tenpai Nyima.

Lhaga (seventh century). One of two men who brought a statue of Shakyamuni Buddha (Jowo Shakyamuni) to Tibet from China during the time of King

Songtsen Gampo. The source of the Gya hereditary lineage. Considered an emanation of Chenrezig.

Lhatsawa Ngawang Zangpo. A close associate of the Tsang Desi, Phuntsok Namgyal, and disciple of Pema Karpo. Played a major role in recognizing Pagsam Wangpo as the reincarnation of Pema Karpo.

Lhawang Lodro. One of Zhabdrung's tutors in Ralung and a close disciple of Pema Karpo. Esteemed Drukpa Kargyu master, adept in Buddhist astrology. Instrumental in establishing Cheri Monastery and advancing Drukpa Kargyu teachings in Bhutan. Described by Tsang Khenchen as a bodhisattva in human form.

Lhodruk. Southern Drukpa Kargyu branch established in Bhutan by Zhabdrung.

Lhomon (also **Lhorong** and **Lhomon Khazhi**). Ancient names for Bhutan. *Lho* denotes south, indicating Bhutan's location to the south of Tibet. *Mon* signifies darkness, reflecting the primitive nature of the people who historically lacked a spiritual belief system. *Rong* refers to deep valleys or ravines, while *khazhi* denotes four directions, representing the four main entry points to Bhutan: Dungsamkha in the east, Pagsamkha in the south, Dalingkha in the west, and Tagtsherkha in the north.

Longdel Monastery. A small Drukpa Kargyu monastery established circa 1193 by Tsangpa Gyare.

Minjur Tenpa. The first Trongsa Ponlop and later the third Druk Desi. One of the three lamas instrumental in bringing the eastern areas of Bhutan under Zhabdrung's rule.

Mipham Chogyal (1543-1604). The grandfather and teacher of Zhabdrung. The sixteenth hereditary throne holder of Ralung.

Mipham Wangpo (1641-1717). A reincarnation of Pagsam Wangpo.

Monarchs of Bhutan.
His Majesty Ugyen Wangchuck (r. 1907-1926)
His Majesty Jigme Wangchuck (r. 1926-1952)
His Majesty Jigme Dorji Wangchuck (r. 1952-1972)
His Majesty Jigme Singye Wangchuck (r. 1972-2006)
His Majesty Jigme Khesar Namgyel Wangchuck (r. 2006-present)

Nangso Ngedub. A senior army general from Tibet. Captured by the Bhutanese during the first Gelug-Mongol war. Upon his release two years later, the Ganden Phodrang government ordered him to seize the Drukpa monastic estates in the U-Tsang region.

Ngagi Wangchuk (1517-1554). The great-grandfather of Zhabdrung. Meditated at the site of Trongsa Dzong.

Ngawang Chogyal (1465-1540). The great-great-grandfather of Zhabdrung and second cousin to Drukpa Kunle. Nephew of Kunga Peljor (1428-1476). Built Druk Choding Lhakhang in the center of Paro town around 1525. Founded Druk Phodrangding Lhakhang at Pangri Zampa where Zhabdrung first sheltered on his arrival in Bhutan.

Ngawang Tenzin. A son of Drukpa Kunle, a Drukpa hereditary lineage holder from a collateral line. Father of Tshewang Tenzin of Tango.

Obtsho Dzong. The fortress of the Obtsho lineage founded by Drubthob Ter-khungpa in the early thirteenth century in the Gasa district, located just south of Gasa Dzong. It is now in ruins.

Obtsho Lama. A close patron of Zhabdrung. Known as the Lord of the Gon region in the Gasa district. His lineage can be traced back to Drubthob Ter-khungpa, a close disciple of Tsangpa Gyare. Instrumental in formally inviting Zhabdrung to Bhutan.

Pagsam Wangpo (1593-1641). A rival candidate for the reincarnation of Pema Karpo, alongside Zhabdrung.

Palden Drukpa. Literally "Glorious Native Person of the Land of the Thunder Dragon."

Palden Drukyul. Literally "Glorious Land of the Thunder Dragon."

Paro Dzong (Rinpung Dzong). Completed by Zhabdrung around 1645-1646, located in the Paro district. It served both administrative and spiritual purposes and played a fortifying role for Bhutan's western regions.

Pawo Tsugla Gyatsho (1568-1633). A senior lama from the Karma Kagyu order. His party was involved in the ferry-crossing saga with Zhabdrung's party at the Tsangpo River in Tibet.

Pekar Jungne. The first Je Khenpo of Bhutan.

Pekar Rabgye. The first governor of Punakha Dzong, known as the dzongpon.

Pekar Tashi. An attendant to Lhawang Lodro, Zhabdrung's teacher. Accompanied him on his perilous journey to Bhutan. Later assumed the role of cook, attendant, and disciple to Zhabdrung.

Pekar Wangpo. A reincarnation of Zhabdrung's great-grandfather, Ngagi Wang-chuk. One of Zhabdrung's main teachers. Zhabdrung received many important teachings and empowerments from him.

Pema Karpo (1527-1592). The fourth Palden Drukpa Rinpoche and third rein-carnation of the Drukpa Kargyu founder, Tsangpa Gyare. The conflict over the recognition of his reincarnation was the outer catalyst for Zhabdrung to come to Bhutan. The Lhodruk sect in Bhutan worships Zhabdrung as Pema Karpo.

Phajo Drukgom Zhigpo (?1184-?1251). A Buddhist master from the region of Kham in Tibet. Brought the Drukpa Kargyu lineage teachings to Bhutan in the thirteenth century as prophesied by Tsangpa Gyare. His descendants played a significant role in supporting Zhabdrung's unification efforts in Bhutan. The only known biography of him states that he was possibly from a collateral line of the famed Drukpa (Gya) hereditary lineage, though this is debatable given Kham's distance from Ralung.

Punakha Dzong (Pungthang Dewachenpoi Phodrang). The winter residence of the Central Monastic Body. Established in 1637 by Zhabdrung as the central seat of the Drukpa Kargyu order in Bhutan on the banks of the Mo and the Pho Rivers in the Punakha district.

Ralung Monastery. The principal seat of the Drukpa hereditary lineage and the Drukpa Kargyu order. Tsangpa Gyare met his teacher, Lingrepa, at this location around 1180. He later established Ralung Monastery (also known as Shedrub Chokhor Ling or Druk Ralung) at the meeting site around 1196.

Sakya Dagchen, Sonam Wangpo (1559-1621). One of the preeminent heads of the Sakya school at the time of Zhabdrung's enthronement, bestowed upon him the name Zhabdrung. His successor, Sakya Dagchen Thutob Wangpo Dragpa Gyaltshen Palzang (1588-1637), offered Zhabdrung the Sakya monasteries in Bhutan to manage during his visit in 1632. Subsequently Sakya Dagchen Ngawang Kunga Sonam acted as an intermediary during the peace negotiations between Zhabdrung and the Pagsam Wangpo side. The Drukpa Kargyu and Sakya orders of Tibetan Buddhism shared good historic relations.

Sangye Dorji. A close disciple of Pema Karpo.

Simtokha Dzong (Sangag Zabdoen Phodrang). The first dzong built by Zhabdrung in 1629. Strategically located in Thimphu at the crossroads of three footpaths connecting Thimphu, Paro, and Wangdue Phodrang.

Sonam Paldron. The consort of Phajo Drukgom Zhigpo.

Southern Land. A name for Bhutan used in Tsang Khenchen's biography of Zhabdrung.

Taktsang (Tigers Nest). The site where Guru Rinpoche meditated in the eighth century. Guru Rinpoche prophesied that Taktsang would be cared for by a vajra holder, a prophecy later fulfilled by Zhabdrung, who claimed authority over the site after a series of auspicious signs. Located over three thousand meters above sea level on the cliffs of Paro Valley in the Paro district. A monastery was built at this site around 1692 by Gyalse Tenzin Rabgye.

Tango Monastery. A well-known Buddhist monastery located in northern Thimphu. Site founded by Phajo Drukgom Zhigpo in the thirteenth century when he saw a horse's head in its cliff face. Built in its current form by Gyalse Tenzin Rabgye, the fourth Druk Desi of Bhutan.

Tara. A female bodhisattva worshipped mainly in Tibetan Buddhism. Embodies the divine feminine qualities of compassion, nurturing, and wisdom.

Tashicho Dzong. The summer residence of the Central Monastic Body. Established in 1641 by Zhabdrung. Located in the capital city of Thimphu.

Tenpai Nyima (1567-1619). The father and root guru of Zhabdrung Ngawang Namgyal. Did not formally hold the Ralung throne. Officiated until Zhabdrung's maturity, as no documented enthronement ceremony for him exists in reliable sources.

Tenzin Drukdra. The half brother to Zhabdrung. Held the post of Paro Ponlop and later the second Druk Desi.

Tenzin Drukgyal (1591-1656). The first Druk Desi and a key figure in Bhutan's unification. From the Obtsho lineage of Gasa district. Assisted Zhabdrung's journey to Bhutan in 1616. Trusted attendant, responsible for Zhabdrung's care during his retreat from 1651.

Tsang Desi (Karma) Phuntsok Namgyal (1586-1621). The ruler of the Tsang region from 1611 to 1621. Son of Karma Tensung Wangpo, preceding Tsang Desi who ruled from 1599 to 1611.

Tsang Desi (Karma) Tenchong Wangpo (1606-1642). The ruler of the Tsang region from 1619 to 1642. Son of Phuntsok Namgyal, the preceding Tsang Desi who died in 1619, though his death was concealed initially, leading to date discrepancies.

Tsang Khenchen Jamyang Palden Gyatsho (1610-1684). A renowned Buddhist scholar and master artist from the Tsang region who settled in Bhutan. Known for his contributions as Zhabdrung Ngawang Namgyal's biographer.

Tsangpa Gyare (1161-1211). A Drukpa (Gya) hereditary lineage holder and the founder of the Drukpa Kargyu order. From Tsanga Gyare's time, the Gya hereditary lineage became known as the Drukpa hereditary lineage. Twenty-one of his vertebrae contained images of deities. His most precious topmost vertebra, known as the Rangjung Kharsapani, featuring the standing form of Chenrezig, is held in Bhutan.

Tshewang Tenzin (1574-1644). The grandson of Drukpa Kunle, a Drukpa hereditary lineage holder from a collateral line. Reincarnation of Phajo Drukgom Zhigpo. Overseer of the Tango area at the time of Zhabdrung's arrival. Gifted the entire Tango area and precious items to Zhabdrung. Married Zhabdrung's first consort, Damcho Tenzin, and fathered the fourth Druk Desi, Gyalse Tenzin Rabgye.

Tulku Zing (seventeenth century). A renowned Tibetan Karma Kagyu artist and sculptor. Crafted sacred images for gonkhangs at Punakha Dzong and Druk Phodrangding Lhakhang in Thimphu. Believed to have sculpted the Zhabdrung Khamsum Zilnon statue.

Wangdue Phodrang Dzong. Established in 1638 by Zhabdrung. Served an administrative and spiritual purpose and fulfilled a fortifying role for Bhutan's southern regions. Located fifteen kilometers south of Punakha Dzong in the Wangdue Phodrang district.

Yeshe Tshogyal: The principal consort of Guru Rinpoche.

Zhabdrung Machen. The mummified body of Zhabdrung.

Zhelngo Sithar. A patron of Zhabdrung from the Gon region in the Gasa district. Visited Zhabdrung in Ralung and, upon hearing of his difficulties, suggested his move to Bhutan.

Zhung Dratshang. The Central Monastic Body of Bhutan comprising monks from the Lhodruk branch—the southern branch of the Drukpa Kargyu order. It is led by the Je Khenpo, currently His Holiness Tulku Jigme Choedra, the seventieth Je Khenpo, and administered by the five high lamas known as the Lopen Lhengyes, who hold a rank equivalent to government ministers under the Constitution. The Zhung Dratshang traces its origins to around 1621, when Zhabdrung Ngawang Namgyal enrolled thirty novice monks at the newly built Cheri Monastery.

Glossary of Terms

beyul. Hidden spiritual land that has been blessed by Guru Rinpoche. Bhutan is considered a beyul.

bhumi. In Buddhism, bhumis refer to the stages or levels a bodhisattva progresses through on their path to enlightenment. In Mahayana Buddhism, there are ten final bhumis that one must pass through before attaining buddhahood.

bodhicitta. On the relative level, it is the aspiration to become enlightened for the benefit of all sentient beings, not just for oneself. On the absolute level, it is the direct insight into the ultimate nature of reality known as the mind of enlightenment.

bodhisattva. Wisdom being. A being who possesses a deep and genuine desire to attain enlightenment for the benefit of all beings.

Bon. Animistic and shamanistic indigenous tradition originating in Tibet. Practiced throughout the Himalayan region as well as parts of China and central Asia. When Buddhism arrived in Tibet in the seventh century, certain Bon practices and beliefs were assimilated into Tibetan Buddhism.

buddha nature. Qualities of buddhahood that inherently exist within all sentient beings. The practice of Buddhism, particularly within the Mahayana and Vajrayana traditions, aims to reveal this innate buddha nature.

buddhahood. Another word for enlightenment.

Chabgon. Epithet bestowed upon the highest lamas, meaning "His Holiness." The literal translation is "source of refuge" (*chab*) and "protection" (*gon*).

Chayig Chenmo. Literally "Great Code of Law." A legal framework closely connected to Buddhist canonical texts and implemented by Zhabdrung in the process of unifying the Southern Land.

chibdrel. Ceremonial procession of welcome for an honored guest, typically held at the outset of an important event to invoke auspiciousness and create favorable conditions.

Chokey. Writing system used for classical Tibetan, particularly for prayers and religious texts. Widely utilized in Bhutan's monastic institutions.

chosi nyiden. Dual system of governance dividing powers between a religious leader (chief abbot, Je Khenpo) and a civil leader (previously Druk Desi, now prime minister) and overseen by a supreme leader (previously Zhabdrung, now His Majesty Jigme Khesar Namgyel Wangchuck). Zhabdrung introduced this unique form of governance to Bhutan.

circumambulation. The act of walking clockwise around a holy object or being, symbolizing reverence and devotion in religious practice.

conch shell. One of the eight auspicious symbols in Tibetan Buddhism. Used ritually, it symbolizes the dissemination of Dharma, wisdom, purification, and the auspiciousness of Buddha's teachings.

constitutional monarchy. System featuring a hereditary symbolic head of state, like a king or queen, who performs representative duties without policy-making power. Governed by a constitution, legislative authority rests with an elected parliament, thereby limiting the monarch's role to largely ceremonial and leadership functions. In Bhutan, the monarch retains the royal prerogative to advise on matters of national importance.

dakini. A female celestial being embodying varying degrees of spiritual power. Symbolizes the nondual female principle, representing enlightened feminine energy. While a dakini is commonly perceived as an exceptional female practitioner with profound wisdom transcending intellect, dakini qualities extend beyond gender, emphasizing deep spiritual insight, fearlessness, and radical wisdom. In Vajrayana meditation, a dakini is seen as the essence of wisdom.

deity. A divine or spiritual being, often worshipped or revered, that exists in a spiritual realm or has influence over spiritual matters. In Buddhism, this can refer to a buddha, bodhisattva, or other spiritual entity that embodies enlightened qualities or powers.

Desi. Secular ruler.

Dhag Nang Ma. *Dhag* meaning "pure"; *nang* meaning "vision." Practice or teaching transmitted through pure vision from a master or deity residing in the spiritual realm.

Dharma. In Buddhism, the teachings of Buddha.

dharmapala. Protector of the Dharma.

dorji (Skt. *vajra*). Meaning "diamond" or "thunderbolt." A ritual object with a double-ended scepter and a central sphere. Extensively used in Tibetan Buddhist ceremonies, particularly within the Vajrayana tradition. Symbolizing the indestructible wisdom nature of the awakened mind, the dorji aids in cutting through defilements to reveal one's innate wisdom.

Driglam Namzhag. Code of etiquette; way of behaving in Bhutanese society.

dromcho. Sacred Vajrayana practice involving prayers, rituals, visualizations, and artistic expressions of dance and music to awaken pure perception of reality and receive blessings. A traditional festive meditation practice to dispel negativity and promote peace and harmony.

drubthob. (Skt. *siddha*). An advanced meditation practitioner.

Druk Desi. The head of the secular arm of government in Bhutan from Zhabdrung's time until the establishment of the monarchy in 1907. Responsible for day-to-day governance and administration. Abolished in 1907 during Bhutan's transition to a hereditary monarchy. The role of Druk Desi within the dual system of governance is now akin to the position of prime minister in the modern democratic constitutional monarchy.

Druk Gyalpo. Dragon King.

Drukpa. People of the Land of the Thunder Dragon. Refers to the people of Bhutan.

Drukpa Kargyu. The Tibetan Buddhist order founded by Tsangpa Gyare around the turn of the thirteenth century. One of the well-known branches of the Kagyu school of Tibetan Buddhism. *Druk* means "thunder dragon" in Tibetan, alluding to Tsangpa Gyare's mystical vision of dragons; *kar* refers to the white robes worn by his disciples, outwardly, and signifies the pure and unbroken oral teaching lineage, inwardly.

Drukyul. Land of the Thunder Dragon; also Land of the Drukpas. Refers to Bhutan.

dzong. Literally "fortress." The seat of religious and civil administration.

Dzongkha. The national language of Bhutan.

dzongpon. Governor of a dzong.

Ganden Phodrang. The government of Tibet established by the Fifth Dalai Lama (Ngawang Lobsang Gyatsho) in 1642 with support from the Mongol leader Gushri Khan. The Fifth Dalai Lama was the first Dalai Lama to become both the spiritual and political leader of Tibet.

Genja. A contractual document in the Dzongkha language.

genyen vows (Skt. *upasaka*). Lay Buddhist vows for dedicated practitioners, bestowed upon individuals seeking spiritual commitment. Genyen Jakpa Melen, a spiritual guardian, received these vows from Guru Rinpoche after being subdued, thus earning this epithet.

geshe. A title awarded to those who have completed advanced scholastic training in the Gelug tradition, equivalent to a doctorate in Buddhist philosophy, requiring years of study, debate, and examinations.

gho. The national dress of Bhutanese men. A knee-length robe tied at the waist by a traditional belt (*kera*), forming a large pouch at the front.

gonkhang. A sacred chapel in a Buddhist temple housing protective deities believed to be tenth-bhumi bodhisattvas. Equipped with essential sacred items for worship such as swords, armor, and cymbals. Praying to these deities aids in achieving enlightenment and overcoming adversity.

Gya hereditary lineage. Ancient family Buddhist lineage dating back to the seventh century, tracing its origin to Lhaga, believed to be an emanation of Chenrezig. Lhaga was granted an estate in the Ralung area by King Songtsen Gampo for his role in transporting the Jowo Shakyamuni statue from China to Tibet. His descendant, Gya Jampel Sangwa, a disciple of Guru Rinpoche, significantly contributed to establishing this lineage. Renowned Buddhist masters emerged from this lineage, leading to its recognition as the Gya hereditary lineage. During Tsangpa Gyare's time, its name changed to the Drukpa hereditary lineage.

Gyalwa. Means "victorious." Honorific title given to a highly realized Buddhist master.

Je Khenpo. Known as the chief abbot of the monastic body in Bhutan. The highest-ranking elected religious figure in Bhutan and the head of the Lhodruk (southern) branch of the Drukpa Kargyu order (the main religion of Bhutan). To this day, the Je Khenpo holds significant influence in religious matters and plays a vital role in upholding and preserving the spiritual and cultural heritage of Bhutan.

Kalachakra teachings. A complex system of Vajrayana Buddhist doctrine and practice, covering a wide range of topics including cosmology, astrology, philosophy, meditation, and ritual practice.

Kangyur. A collection of Buddhist scriptures regarded as the spoken words of the Buddha, translated into Tibetan. It includes sutras, tantras, and vinaya texts, forming the core of the Tibetan Buddhist canon.

karma. Sanskrit word for "action." The universal law of cause and effect, concerned with how intentional actions, both negative and positive, shape future experiences.

khenpo. A highly learned lama in the Kagyu, Nyingma, and Sakya traditions.

kira. The national dress of Bhutanese women. An ankle-length woven cloth wrapped around either the whole body (full kira), or the waist (half kira), and secured with a belt (*kera*). The full kira is fastened at the shoulders with brooches (*koma*).

kudung. The sacred corpse of a revered Buddhist master.

kudung chorten. Literally "body stupa," a structure containing the cremated remains of a highly realized Buddhist master.

lama. A title for a Tibetan Buddhist teacher.

lhakhang. Temple in Tibetan Buddhism. A place of worship displaying sacred Buddhist statues, murals, and relics.

machen. Sacred mummified body.

machen zimpon. A monk tasked with the oversight of the Zhabdrung Machen (the mummified body of Zhabdrung Ngawang Namgyal).

mahasiddha Great *drubthob*, or *siddha*. One who has achieved a high level of realization and miraculous powers through meditation and renunciation.

Mahayana. Literally "Great Vehicle," or "Universal Vehicle," encompassing various schools and traditions. Vajrayana practice is a subset of Mahayana Buddhism. At the heart of the Mahayana teachings is the aspiration to achieve enlightenment, or buddhahood, to free sentient beings from suffering (known as bodhicitta).

mandala. Elaborate geometric pattern, typically circular, symbolizing the cosmos or universe. Employed as a visual aid for meditation and spiritual practice, representing the journey toward enlightenment.

mantra. Series of words or syllables repeated as part of spiritual practice.

monastery. A residential institution where monks or nuns live, study, and practice.

Nga Chudrugma (known as the Sixteen *I*'s). Sixteen-line victory declaration composed by Zhabdrung during his retreat in Tango. Revealed Zhabdrung's intent to govern Bhutan and establish a formal code of law. The emblem, featuring sixteen spokes, was adopted as Bhutan's unification seal.

nirvana. Refers to the state of ultimate liberation and freedom from suffering, desire, and the cycle of birth and rebirth (*samsara*). A being who attains nirvana while still alive, like the Buddha did under the bodhi tree, continues to exist in the world but is free from suffering and karma.

oral transmission. Tradition in Tibetan Buddhism of transmitting teachings, scriptures, and practices verbally from teacher to student. This transmission occurs directly and often maintains an unbroken lineage.

parinirvana. The final passing away of a Buddha or an enlightened being. It is the end of their physical existence and complete release from the cycle of birth and rebirth. This moment marks not only the end of their earthly life but also the fulfillment of their spiritual path to total enlightenment.

ponlop. A feudal governor of a region.

puja. A devotional offering ceremony.

Rangjung Kharsapani. The uppermost vertebra of Tsangpa Gyare, the founder of the Drukpa Kargyu order, containing the standing image of Chenrezig. This vertebra relic is highly revered as the most precious object within the Drukpa Kargyu order in Bhutan and is reputed to possess predictive abilities. *Rangjung* means "self-arisen," and *Kharsapani* refers to the standing form of Chenrezig.

ringsel. Sacred objects found among the cremated remains of an enlightened master. Considered immensely precious and symbolically significant, they embody the spiritual wisdom and realization of the master, serving as tangible evidence of their elevated spiritual status. They may manifest in various forms, including pearl-like relics, crystallized body parts such as a tongue or eyeball, and even vertebrae, such as the Rangjung Kharsapani.

Rinpoche. Literally "precious one." An honorific title bestowed upon learned masters or reincarnate lamas.

root guru. A practitioner's primary spiritual teacher in Tibetan Buddhism. Regarded as the one who reveals the nature of one's own mind and to whom one holds deep devotion.

sadhana. A spiritual practice involving the recitation of a ritual text or prayer while visualizing a master or deity. Its purpose is to enhance devotion to the master or deity and attain spiritual accomplishment.

samsara. The cycle of birth, suffering, death, and rebirth that characterizes existence in the realms of cyclic existence.

sentient beings. Living beings with consciousness, capable of experiencing sensations, emotions, and varying degrees of awareness. They are subject to the cycle of birth, death, and rebirth (*samsara*), and include humans, animals, spirits, and other beings able to experience pleasure, pain, and mental states.

stupa. Literally "heap," in Tibetan *chorten*. A sacred mound-like structure that represents the enlightened mind of the Buddha and contains sacred relics. A stupa can be made from brick, stone, or concrete. Building or sponsoring stupas is a powerful way to accumulate merit and purify negative karma.

sutra. The body of Buddhist literature taught by the Buddha. Mahayana sutras are a collection of Buddhist scriptures that form the foundation of Mahayana Buddhism. These texts, written mainly in Sanskrit (and later translated into Tibetan and other languages), introduce key Mahayana concepts such as bodhisattva, bodhicitta, emptiness (*shunyata*), and buddha nature, as well as Buddhist cosmology.

tantra. Esoteric spiritual teachings. Vajrayana practices are considered forms of tantric teachings.

terma. Spiritual treasures, texts, and mind teachings believed to be hidden by Padmasambhava, also known as Guru Rinpoche, to be discovered at future times when specifically needed.

terton. Treasure discoverer. One who discovers terma (spiritual treasures).

thri. A religious throne in Tibetan Buddhism, symbolizing spiritual authority, where esteemed sect leaders sit. It differs from a political throne, as it is not associated with political rule over a region or nation.

Thrimzhung Chenmo. Literally "Great Government Law." Formulated and implemented during the reign of the third king of Bhutan. It signaled a broader shift in the state's focus from religious to secular concerns.

thukdam. A post-death meditative state entered into by highly advanced Buddhist masters following clinical death, during which their minds merge with the Buddha mind and they enter a state of luminosity.

Tibetan Buddhist traditions. The four main Tibetan Buddhist traditions are as follows:

1. The Kagyu tradition: Formally founded in the eleventh century by Marpa, Milarepa, and Gampopa. It traces its origins to the oral transmission of teachings from Naropa, Tilopa, and Vajradhara Buddha. Often called the oral transmission school, it emphasizes intensive meditation, guru yoga, devotion, and direct master-to-disciple transmission to realize the mind's true nature. The Kagyu tradition gave rise to numerous sub-schools, including the Drukpa Kargyu order.

2. The Nyingma tradition: Established in the eighth century by Guru Rinpoche, who introduced Vajrayana Buddhism to Tibet. The Nyingma school emphasizes Dzogchen (Great Perfection), a direct path to recognizing the mind's true nature. It also has a strong tradition of visionary revelations known as terma (hidden treasures), which Guru Rinpoche is believed to have concealed for future discovery by tertons (treasure revealers).

3. The Sakya tradition: Founded in the eleventh century by Khon Konchog Gyalpo (1034-1102) from the ancestral Khon hereditary lineage, which

remains unbroken to this day. This tradition emphasizes the integration of wisdom and compassion through meditation, tantric practices, deity visualization, and guru guidance.

4. The Gelug tradition: Established in the fourteenth century by Lama Tsongkhapa (1357–1419). It is based on the teachings of Atisha, an eleventh-century Indian Buddhist master who taught extensively in Tibet. The Gelug tradition emphasizes moral discipline, scholarship, debate, and devotion to bodhicitta. It became the dominant Tibetan Buddhist school in Tibet in the seventeenth century and is headed by the Dalai Lamas.

torma. A Buddhist ritual sculpture traditionally made from barley flour and butter.

tsa tsa. Miniature molded stupas largely made from a mixture of clay and medicinal herbs and left to harden. Can also be made by mixing in the ashes of cremated remains. Placed at holy sites and places of worship to honor the deceased or gain merit.

tulku. A person who is a recognized reincarnation of a former spiritual master. The tulku system is a unique feature of Tibetan Buddhism.

umze. Lead chant master in a Tibetan Buddhist monastery.

vajra. See *dorji*.

Vajrayana Buddhism. Also known as Tantric Buddhism, or Mantrayana. A form of esoteric Buddhist practice that originated in India and spread to neighboring countries such as Tibet, Bhutan, Nepal, and Mongolia. Renowned for its advanced meditative and ritual practices, it is said to offer the swiftest path to enlightenment.

yogi. A male spiritual practitioner of meditation.

yogini. A female spiritual practitioner of meditation.

Notes

1. Pronounced Zhab-droong Nga-wang Nam-gal.
2. A title given to a spiritual teacher in Tibetan Buddhism.
3. The concept of devotion in Tibetan Buddhism is a core element in the relationship between student and teacher. As opposed to blind faith, devotion is based on clear judgment that leads to a deep respect for the teacher and, in turn, a strong desire to emulate their spiritual qualities.
4. A practice where the Tibetan Buddhist practitioner enters a lifelong period of secluded meditation.
5. The biography of a religious saint is technically known as a hagiography (Tib. *namthar*). For simplicity, the general term "biography" is used throughout this book when referring to Zhabdrung's biography and those of other spiritual masters.
6. Additional details about Tsang Khenchen's life and his connection to Zhabdrung Ngawang Namgyal are provided in the appendix.
7. See the glossary of terms.
8. Outer accomplishments include, for example, the establishment of monastic institutions, the unification of a nation, and the preservation of a lineage. Inner (or secret) accomplishments refer to qualities developed through spiritual practice, such as spiritual attainment, compassion, and wisdom. Additionally, the inner realm includes deeply personal experiences leading to significant spiritual outcomes.
9. See the glossary of terms.
10. Vajrayana is a form of Tibetan Buddhism that emphasizes esoteric teachings, rituals, and meditation techniques to swiftly attain enlightenment. All four schools of Tibetan Buddhism incorporate Vajrayana principles and techniques into their spiritual path.
11. Also known as the state of Palden Drukpa, the "State of the Glorious Drukpas."
12. *Thukdam* refers to the state experienced by a highly realized Buddhist master after clinical death has occurred. During this time, the practitioner's

mind merges with the enlightened state, often described as buddha nature. It is a post-death meditative practice observed by accomplished Tibetan Buddhist masters and is seen as an auspicious occurrence in Tibetan Buddhism. Thukdam is considered a sure sign of the advanced level of the practitioner's spiritual achievement.

13. In Tibetan Buddhism, the concept of a throne, known as *thri*, signifies spiritual authority, not governing authority over a region, as per the standard definition.

14. The Ralung religious aristocracy largely adhered to a father-son succession system and, at times, an uncle-nephew succession (*khu on*) to maintain their lineage.

15. This book interprets the story of Zhabdrung from the latter approach by remaining as accurate as possible to the information gleaned from the descriptive language found in the ancient biographies about Zhabdrung.

16. "Lha" here refers to the gods.

17. An udumbara flower (here written as *udambara*) is a sacred white flower that blooms once every 3,000 years.

18. "Perfect freedom" here refers to enlightenment.

19. *Dorji Rig gi Nyenpar Jepai Ngodrub.*

20. The Four Noble Truths teach that suffering exists, is caused by desire and ignorance, can be overcome, and the way to end it is through following the path set down by the Buddha.

21. Lama Khag Nga is a collective term for dissident followers of lamas within Bhutan, originating from five Buddhist sects: Lhapa, Nenyingpa, Barawa, Chagzampa, and Ganden Shingtapa. These sects trace their ancestry to Tibet from the twelfth to the fifteenth centuries. Some accounts include the Kathogpas, affiliated with the Nyingma school of Buddhism, as part of this group. Origins of each school are as follows:

   1. The Lhapa sect is a branch of the Kagyu school of Buddhism founded by Lhanangpa Zijid Palbar, one of the three principal disciples of Drikung Jigten Gonpo Rinchen Pal. Lhanangpa established monasteries in Bhutan in the late twelfth century including the Do Ngon Dzong, which was later converted to Tashicho Dzong by Zhabdrung.

   2. The Nenyingpa sect is believed to have originated from Nenying, near Gyantse in Tibet, as an offshoot of the Drukpa Kargyu order. It traces its roots to Gya Jampel Sangwa of the Gya clan and later to Gotsangpa. The sect established numerous temples in western Bhutan, including Dzongdrakha Lhakhang in the Paro valley.

   3. The Barawa sect was founded by Barawa Gyaltshen Palzang, a disciple of Rinchen Palzang who was the reincarnation of Gyalwa Yangonpa from the Drukpa Kargyu order. He established Drangyekha Monastery

in Paro as the main seat along with minor seats in the Gon Tshephu area of Punakha and at Do Chorten in Paro.

4. The Chagzampa sect originated with Thangtong Gyalpo, renowned as the Iron-Bridge Builder, who constructed numerous temples and eight iron bridges in Bhutan. The lineage descending from his son, Dewa Zangpo, carried on the Chagzam tradition, which was later absorbed into other schools.

5. The Ganden Shingtapa sect was initiated by Palden Dorji of Phanyul, a disciple of Lama Tsongkhapa, the founder of the Gelug tradition of Tibetan Buddhism. Phanyul Palden Dorji received teachings from Guru Rinpoche via pure vision and established a monastery in the Gasa district. He dedicated numerous years to meditation in the Jomolhari region of Bhutan.

6. The Kathogpa sect is a branch of the Nyingma tradition. The Kathogpas are believed to have established temples in Bhutan in the fifteenth century, including a presence at Taktsang hermitage in Paro.

22. In Tibetan Buddhism, skillful means refers to the methods employed by enlightened beings to teach and guide others on the path to enlightenment. It acknowledges that a single approach may not be effective for everyone and emphasizes that the teacher should skillfully adapt their guidance to suit each individual.

23. In chapter 4, we learn that Zhabdrung was an incarnation of Naropa.

24. Zhabdrung was an emanation of Guru Rinpoche who was known as the Lotus King.

25. Referring to Bhutan.

26. A ritual object used in Tibetan Buddhist ceremonies.

27. See map at the front of the book for the location of Ngari, U, and Tsang.

28. Mon signifies darkness, reflecting the primitive nature of the people who historically lacked a spiritual belief system. Before Zhabdrung's arrival, Bhutan was known as Lhomon—the primitive south.

29. See the appendix for information on Phajo and the Drukpa Kargyu masters who assisted Zhabdrung in his unification efforts.

30. In some parts of Asia, a person is considered one year old at birth, with age increasing each lunar new year, unlike the Western system, which begins at zero at birth.

31. Pema Karpo's writings on the history of Buddhism in Tibet mention that nine dragons soared into the sky accompanied by a loud roar of thunder. The biographies of Zhabdrung by Tsang Khenchen and Je Geduen Rinchen mention thirteen dragons.

32. Tsangpa Gyare himself, the nine Senges (lions) and the three bodhisattva emanations—Manjushri, Vajrapani, and Chenrezig (Rigsum Namtrul). See the list of throne holders in the appendix.

33. *Druk* means "thunder dragon" in Tibetan, alluding to his mystical experience, while *kar* outwardly refers to the white robes worn by his disciples but inwardly signifies the pure and unbroken oral teaching lineage.

34. A close disciple of Buddha who was reborn as Tsangpa Gyare as stated by Tsang Khenchen.

35. The Land of Snows refers to Tibet.

36. As stated in Tsang Khenchen's biography of Zhabdrung. The biography also states that the *Manjushri Mula Tantra* predicted the birth of Tsangpa Gyare.

37. Both the third and fourth Palden Drukpa Rinpoches, Jamyang Chokyi Dragpa and Pema Karpo, belonged to the reincarnation lineage but not the Drukpa hereditary lineage. Consequently, the Drukpa family did not acknowledge them as throne holders (see p. 25).

38. If Tenpai Nyima, as an officiating throne holder of Ralung is counted, then Zhabdrung would be the eighteenth throne holder of Ralung.

39. This is the name for Bhutan used in Tsang Khenchen's biography of Zhabdrung.

40. The controversy over Pema Karpo's reincarnation should be viewed in the context of its time—an era marked by frequent power struggles, conflicts over seemingly minor matters, and strict adherence to protocol. However, the followers of each side were adamant that only their own candidate—either Zhabdrung or Pagsam Wangpo—could rightfully claim to be the true reincarnation of Pema Karpo.

41. The biography of Lhatsawa Ngawang Zangpo, compiled by Rinpung Dazang and Sangye Dorji (a disciple of Pema Karpo), describes these events, including Pagsam Wangpo's refusal to accept the white cotton cloth of a yogi that was offered to him.

42. Reliable sources, including oral accounts, suggest that this was likely the route Zhabdrung followed.

43. Known as Dorden in some texts.

44. (1) The descendants of Phajo ruled in the western regions of Paro, Thimphu, Punakha, and Wangdue Phodrang. The Phajo lineage of the Hungral clan ruled in Paro, Dodena in northern Thimphu, and Changangkha in central Thimphu. The Phajo lineage of the Gon Sangme clan ruled in the Punakha district, and the Phajo lineage of the Wachen clan ruled in Wangdue Phodrang district. (2) The Obtsho family were prominent in the Gasa district, (3) the Zarchen family, also descendants of Phajo, in the Paro district, (4) Drukpa Kunle's descendants in the Thimphu district (Tango), and (5) the Tshamdrag family in the Chukha district.

45. See p. 62.

46. Also called Tandin Nye.

47. A gesture of devotion to a religious figure or an object of worship, where an individual kneels or lies face down on the ground, with five points: the forehead, palms of the hand, and knees touching the ground.

48. The Gelug school of Tibetan Buddhism forged a powerful alliance with the Mongol Khans in the seventeenth century. This partnership played a pivotal role in establishing the Gelug school as the dominant Buddhist tradition in both Tibet and Mongolia.

49. *Jaro* refers to the raven-faced spiritual guardian, Legon Jarog Dongchen, and *gang* means "hill" or "mountain" in the local language.

50. A portable structure with many doors, commonly found in Bhutan.

51. The widely accepted view is that the names Drukpa and Drukyul emerged during the unification process while Zhabdrung was still alive—a logical assumption given his determination to establish a nation-state under the Drukpa Kargyu tradition.

52. John Ardussi, in Richard Whitecross, "Like a Pot without a Handle: Law, Meaning and Practice in Medieval Bhutan," *Cahiers d'Extreme-Asie* 26 (2017): 87-104.

53. Historical texts mention Zhabdrung's concerted efforts to distinguish his newly formed state in various aspects, including Buddhist ceremonies, ceremonial implements, and codes of conduct.

54. *Zhug*, "seat"; *drel*, "row"; *phunsum tshogpa*, the triple qualities of prosperity, perfection, and auspiciousness; *tendrel*, a "good omen."

55. This quote is often attributed to the novelist Robert Louis Stevenson.

56. Ugyen Wangchuck (b. 1862-d. 1926), like his father Jigme Namgyal (b. 1825-d. 1881), held the position of Trongsa Ponlop.

57. Full prayer in the appendix.

58. Within the Drukpa Kargyu order, most are only followers and do not possess a lineage through either blood or reincarnation.

59. The fourth Senge, Senge Sherab, though a member of the Drukpa family clan, did not assume the throne of Ralung.

60. The names in bold in this diagram are reincarnations of Tsangpa Gyare.

61. Tenpai Nyima (1567-1619), the father of Zhabdrung Ngawang Namgyal and the son of Mipham Chogyal, was an officiating throne holder but never formally acceded to the throne.

62. The main Drukpa hereditary lineage line of Ralung effectively ended with the announcement of the death of Zhabdrung's son, Jampel Dorji, in 1681, as he was unable to produce a viable male heir.

63. Two of the four reincarnations of Tsangpa Gyare—Jamyang Chokyi Dragpa and Pema Karpo—were born outside the Drukpa bloodline lineage.

64. I have placed the names in inverted commas to emphasize the predestined nature of their meeting. This aligns with Tsangpa Gyare's prophecy, made

centuries earlier, about meeting Phajo again at a later date (see prophecy on p. 62). It seems this prophecy was fulfilled in the meeting between "Zhabdrung" (reincarnation of "Tsangpa Gyare") and "Tshewang Tenzin" (reincarnation of "Phajo").

Bibliography

Sources in English

Ardussi, John. "Bhutan as Recognised by History." *Druk Journal* 1, no. 1 (Spring 2015): 50-65.

——. "Formation of the State of Bhutan ('Brug gzhung) in the 17th Century and Its Tibetan Antecedents." *Journal of Bhutan Studies* 11 (Winter 2004): 10-32.

——. "The gDung Lineages of Central and Eastern Bhutan: A Reappraisal of Their Origin, Based on Literary Sources." In *The Spider and the Piglet: Proceedings of the First Seminar on Bhutan Studies*, edited by Karma Ura and Sonam Kinga, 60-72. Thimphu, Bhutan: Centre for Bhutan Studies, 2004.

——. "The Rapprochement Between Bhutan and Tibet Under the Enlightened Rule of Sde-srid XIII Shes-rab-dbang-phyug (r. 1744-63)." *Journal of Bhutan Studies* 1, no. 1 (1999): 64-83.

——. "The Traditional Institutions of Governance in Bhutan Before 1907 and Their Modification with the Coming Monarchy." *Druk Journal*, Winter 2015.

Aris, Michael, and Ardussi, John. *Sources for the History of Bhutan*. Delhi: Motilal Banarsidass, 2009.

Baillie, Luiza Maria. "Father Estevao Cacella's Report on Bhutan in 1627." *Journal of Bhutan Studies* 1, no. 1 (1999): 1-35.

Bartholomew, Terese, and John Johnston, eds. *The Dragon's Gift: The Sacred Arts of Bhutan*. Chicago: Serindia, 2008.

Blancke, Kristin. "Gampopa Sonam Rinchen Meets Jetsun Mila." Unpublished manuscript, 2021.

Blavatsky, Helena Petrovna. *Collected Writings*. Vol. 6. Wheaton, IL: Theosophical Publishing House, 1975.

——. *Collected Writings*. Vol. 14. Wheaton, IL: Theosophical Publishing House, 1975.

Choegyal, Panchen Tenzin. *The History of the South: Garland of Gentle Voice's Aspiration*. Thimphu, Bhutan: KMT Publishing House, 2004.

Dargye, Yonten, and Per K. Sørensen. *The Biography of Pha 'Brug-Sgom Zhig-Po*

Called the Current of Compassion. Thimphu, Bhutan: National Library of Bhutan, 2001.

Dargye, Yonten, Per K. Sørensen, and Gyonpo Tshering. *Play of the Omniscient One: Life and Works of Jamgön Ngawang Gyaltshen, an Eminent 17th-18th Century Drukpa Master.* Thimphu, Bhutan: National Library and Archives of Bhutan, 2008.

Deleplanque, Jetsun. "From Tibet to Bhutan: The Life and Legacy of Tsang Khenchen Jamyang Palden Gyatso." In *Reasons and Lives in Buddhist Traditions: Studies in Honor of Matthew Kapstein,* edited by Dan Arnold, Cécile Ducher, and Pierre-Julien Harter, 149-61. Somerville, MA: Wisdom, 2019.

Dorji, Gembo. "The Lho-Druk Tradition of Bhutan." In *Without Borders: Proceedings of the International Conference on Globalized Buddhism, Bumthang, Bhutan, May 21-23, 2012,* edited by Karma Ura and Dendup Chophel, 185-90. Thimphu, Bhutan: Centre for Bhutan Studies, 2012.

Dorji, Samten. *The Dharma King: A Tribute to His Majesty Jigme Singye Wangchuck: The Fourth King of Bhutan.* Thimphu, Bhutan: Dratshang Lhentshog, 2014.

Dorji, Sangye. *The Biography of Zhabdrung Ngawang Namgyal: Pal Drukpa Rinpoche.* Translated by Sonam Kinga. Edited by Pema Wangdi and Christopher Fynn. Thimphu, Bhutan: KMT Publishing House, 2008.

———. "A Brief Account of Hungrel Drung Drung." In *The Spider and the Piglet: Proceedings of the First Seminar on Bhutan Studies,* edited by Karma Ura and Sonam Kinga, 21-50. Thimphu, Bhutan: Centre for Bhutan Studies, 2004.

Dorji, Sherub. "Gelephu Mindfulness City Unveils Its Vision for a Greener and Cleaner Future." Bhutan Broadcasting Service. Accessed September 13, 2024. https://www.bbs.bt/news/?p=208589.

Gampopa. *The Jewel Ornament of Liberation: The Wish-Fulfilling Gem of the Noble Teachings.* Translated by Khenpo Konchog Gyaltsen Rinpoche. Edited by Ani K. Trinlay Chödron. Ithaca, NY: Snow Lion, 1998.

Gelephu Mindfulness City. "About Us." Accessed September 13, 2024. https://gmc.bt.

Givel, Michael, and Laura Figueroa. "Early Happiness Policy as a Government Mission of Bhutan: A Survey of the Bhutanese Unwritten Constitution from 1619 to 1729." *Journal of Bhutan Studies* 31 (Winter 2014): 1-21.

Guenther, Herbert V. *The Life and Teaching of Naropa.* Boulder: Shambhala, 1995.

Gyalwang Drukpa. "'Oceans of Methods' Teaching and Empowerment." January 2013. Accessed March 23, 2022. https://www.dnaindia.com/press-releases/press-release-oceans-of-methods-teaching-and-empowerment-conducted-by-the-gyalwang-drukpa-1793968.

Haas, Michaela. *Dakini Power: Twelve Extraordinary Women Shaping the Transmission of Tibetan Buddhism in the West.* Ithaca, NY: Snow Lion, 2013.

Imaeda, Yoshiro. *The Successors of Zhabdrung Ngawang Namgyel: Hereditary Heirs and Reincarnations.* Thimphu, Bhutan: Riyang Books, 2013.

Khandu, Khenchen Sangye. *Sixteen Wondrous Biography: Dharmaraja—A Reminiscence.* Thimphu, Bhutan: Institute of Science of Mind, 2021.

Kragh, Ulrich T. "Culture and Subculture: A Study of the Mahamudra Teachings of Sgam po pa." Master's thesis, Department of Asian Studies, University of Copenhagen, June 1998.

Maitreya, Arya, and Jamgon Kongtrul Lodro Thaye, eds. *Buddha Nature: The Mahayana Uttaratantra Shastra with Commentary.* Translated by Rosemarie Fuchs. Commentary by Khenpo Tsultrim Gyamtso Rinpoche. Ithaca, NY: Snow Lion, 2013.

Maki, Ariana. "Tracing the Legacy of Tsang Khenchen Penden Gyatso (1610-84) in Bhutanese Art." *Orientations* 48, no. 3 (2017):108-17.

———. "A Zhabdrung Phuensum Tshogpa (Zhabs drung phun sum tshogs pa) Thangka." *Journal of Bhutan Studies* 25 (Winter 2011): 1-49.

National Library of Bhutan. *Driglam Namzhag: A Manual.* Thimphu, Bhutan: National Library of Bhutan, 1999.

Nyinjadh, Jigme Pema. "The Founder of the Drukpa Lineage." Gyalwa Dokham pa. Accessed January 2023. https://khamtrul.org/about/the-founder-of-the-drukpa-lineage.

Oro Bank. "Gelephu Mindfulness City: A Vision of Harmonious Living." Accessed December 13, 2024. https://www.oro.bank/gelephu-mindfulness-city/.

Penjore, Dorji. "Rows of Auspicious Seats: The Role of 'Bzugs Gral Phun Sum Tshogs Pa'i Rten 'Brel' Ritual in the Founding of the First Bhutanese State in the 17th Century." *Journal of Bhutan Studies* 24, no. 1 (Summer 2011): 1-41.

Phuntsho, Karma. *The History of Bhutan.* Gurgaon: Random House India, 2015.

Royal Textile Academy. *Zhabdrung Ngawang Namgyel: The Founding Father.* Thimphu, Bhutan: Royal Textile Museum, 2016.

Sangpo, Gelong Lodro, and Bhikkhu K. L. Dhammajoti. *Adhidharmakosa-Bhasya of Vasubandhu.* Vol. 2. Translated by Gelong Lodro Sangpo. Delhi: Motilal Banarsidass, 2012.

Shar, Nima. *Bhutanese Encourage Honest.* Thimphu, Bhutan: Tago Dorden Tashithang Buddhist University, 2018.

Tashi, Khenpo Phuntsok, ed. "Fortress of the Dragon: The Proceedings of the Fourth Colloquium." Paro, Bhutan: National Museum of Bhutan, 2009.

———. "The Soul and Substance of Bhutan's Cultural Heritage: The Proceedings of the Fifth Colloquium." Paro, Bhutan: National Museum of Bhutan, 2009.

Tashi, Tshering. "The Dharma Wheel Statue of Zhabdrung Ngawang Namgyel." *Kuensel Online.* Accessed July 2022. https://kuenselonline.com/news/the-dharma-wheel-statue-of-zhabdrung-ngawang-namgyel.

Thinley, Kunzang. "Guru Rinpoche's Exclusive Sacred Places in Bhutan." Translated by Phuntsho Gyaltshen. *Journal of Bhutan Studies* 34 (Summer 2016): 57-79.

Trungpa, Chögyam. *Cutting Through Spiritual Materialism*. Boulder: Shambhala, 2012.

Tsang Khenchen Jamyang Palden Jamtsho. *The Melody of the Great Dharma Cloud: The Extended Biography of Pal Drukpa Rinpoche Ngawang Tenzin Namgyal* [Zhabdrung Rinpoche]. Translated by the Research Division of Tago Institute for Advanced Vajrayana Studies in collaboration with Tago Dorden Tashithang Buddhist University. Thimphu, Bhutan: Zhung Dratshang, 2022.

Tshering, Khenpo. *The Smiling Moon: A Biography of the 69th Je Khenpo, His Holiness Gedun Rinchen*. Translated by Kencho Tobgyel. New Delhi,India: Self-published, 2020.

Ura, Karma. "The Advent of Zhabdrung Rinpoche." *Kuensel Online*. Accessed May 2021. https://kuenselonline.com/the-advent-of-zhabdrung-rinpoche/.

Wangchuk, Kezang. "A Hobbesian Look into the Genja Contract of 1907." 2015. https://www.academia.edu/12895932/A_Hobbesian_Look_into_the_Genja_Contract_of_1907/.

Wangchuk, Phende Legshe. "The History of Taktsang Monastery." In *The Soul and Substance of Bhutan's Cultural Heritage: The Proceedings of the Fifth Colloquium*. Vol. 1. 2nd ed. 183-205. Paro: National Museum of Bhutan, 2009.

Wangchuk, T. Sangay. *Seeing with the Third Eye: Growing Up with Angay in Rural Bhutan*. Illustrated by Rinchen Wangdi. Edited by Felicity Shaw. Self-published, 2006.

Whitecross, Richard. "Law, 'Tradition' and Legitimacy: Contesting Driglam Namzha." In *Development Challenges in Bhutan*, edited by Johannes Dragsbaek Schmidt, 115-34. Cham, Switzerland: Springer, 2017.

———. "Like a Pot without a Handle: Law, Meaning and Practice in Medieval Bhutan." *Cahiers d'Extrême-Asie* 26, no. 1 (2017): 87-103.

Yezer, Jigme, and Sangay Dorji. *Zhabdrung Ngawang Namgyel: A Biography through Kuthangs*. Thimphu, Bhutan: Royal Textile Academy, 2016.

Sources in Tibetan

Dorji, Ngawang Losel Jangchub. *Grub chen bya btang pad dkar bkra shis kyi rnam thar* [The biography of Drubchen Jatang Pekar Tashi]. Thimphu, Bhutan: KMT Publishing House, 2012.

Gyaltshen, Jamyang. *Rje btsun dam pa ngag dbang kun dga' rgya mtsho'i rtogs pa brjod pa mchog gi dang po'i rba rlabs* [The waves of foremost excellence: A biography of the supreme master Ngawang Kuenga Gyamtsho]. In *Sku bzhi'i dbang phyug ngag dbang yon tan mtha' yas kyi bka' 'bum rnam thar dang bcas pa* [The collected works of Ngawang Yonten Thaye, lord of the four kayas, with a biography], 216-315. Thimphu, Bhutan: Gzhung grva tshang gsung rab par khang, 2022.

Karpo, Pema. *Chos 'byung bstan pa'i pad+ma rgyas pa'i nyin byed* [The sun that opens the lotus of buddhadharma]. Sarnath, India: Central Institute of Higher Tibetan Studies, 2004.

Rinchen, Je Gedun. *Dpal ldan 'brug pa'i gdul zhing lho phyogs nags mo'i ljong kyi chos 'byung blo gsar rna ba'i rgyan* [The ear ornament of fresh intelligence: The religious history of the Southern Land of forest, the field of subjugation of Palden Drukpa]. In *Dpal ldan 'brug pa'i skyabs rje khri rabs 69 pa mkhas grub chen po dge d'dun rin chen dpal bzang po'i bka' 'bum* [The collected works of Gedun Rinchen, the sixty-ninth Je Khenpo of Bhutan], vol. 11, 11-285. Thimphu, Bhutan: Dge rin bu slob bkod tshogs, 2022.

———. *Dpal 'brug pa rin po che mthu chen chos kyi rgyal po ngag dbang rnam rgyal gyi rnam thar rgya mtsho'i snying po* [Essence of the ocean: The biography of Palden Drukpa Rinpoche Thuchen Choki Gyalpo Ngawang Namgyal]. In *Dpal ldan 'brug pa'i skyabs rje khri rabs 69 pa mkhas grub chen po dge d'dun rin chen dpal bzang po'i bka' 'bum* [The collected works of Gedun Rinchen, the sixty-ninth Je Khenpo of Bhutan], vol. 9, 341-491. Thimphu, Bhutan: Dge rin bu slob bkod tshogs, 2022.

In Memoriam

Throughout the inconceivable length of kalpas—eons so vast they encompass countless world systems and innumerable sentient beings—great beings like Zhabdrung Ngawang Namgyal occasionally appear in service to all. It is when we can look beyond merely our survival and our self to seek a higher purpose and meaning of existence that buddhas and bodhisattvas appear to demonstrate the path to enlightenment. We have, however, few opportunities to unlock the boundless potential of human consciousness—being born human and being shown the way to break the cycle of suffering and light the way to liberation for others does not come easily.

The birth of a being such as Zhabdrung Ngawang Namgyal, who dedicated his life to the establishment of a culturally unique state known as Bhutan and who consolidated and advanced the teachings of the Drukpa Kargyu order to light the path to liberation, is a feat that we should all rejoice in. By doing so, it evokes within us a deeper appreciation of his unconditional service to, most particularly, the nation of Bhutan. The visible and invisible legacy left in the wake of his death serves to create a solid connection with this legendary figure and not so legendary present. Knowing that the potential threats and challenges for Buddhism, Buddhists, and Bhutan that would arise in the future would require solutions that would be as relevant now as it was then, he laid out a thoughtfully crafted plan, dovetailing the domains of culture and governance with the spiritual. For this, I think it is fair to say that without his foresight, wisdom, and great compassion, we would not be reaping the benefits that are enjoyed within Bhutan today.

With this incomparable and indelible legacy, Zhabdrung Ngawang Namgyal will forever be known as a man of great insight, compassion, and deep conviction for the upholding of what is precious and important. May his memory be a blessing, and may his legacy not make us proud, as pride divides, but make us live with humility and gratitude for his very existence and all that he has achieved for the benefit of sentient beings.

Index

Sasha Wakefield (Photo © 2024 Elena Neri)

About the Author

Sasha Wakefield is the daughter of Czech and Japanese migrants and grew up in Sydney, Australia. Raised outside organized religion, she formed a world-view distinct from her peers. Excelling at school, she looks back with deep gratitude on an idyllic childhood by the local beach—aware it was a privilege not afforded to everyone.

After earning bachelor's and master's degrees in finance, economics, and international development, she began a career as an investment banker and worked at several leading firms for over a decade. With the support of her husband and children, she later chose to shift her focus toward more spiritual pursuits.

From a young age, she harbored a keen interest in the spiritual path, exploring various esoteric sciences and philosophies. At just ten years old, she expressed an urgent desire to visit Bhutan in search of her teacher, despite not knowing if such a place even existed. Decades later, in 2006, she finally set foot in this mystical land and was struck by a peculiar sense of déjà vu. There, she met her teacher—a humble and wise man with whom she shared a powerful karmic connection, leading her to study, practice, serve, and write about spiritual subjects.

Sasha has completed the Ngondro, the foundational set of practices on the Vajrayana path, and authored a book offering practical guidance drawn from her teacher's instructions. In partnership with Rotary Australia, she established a social investment to preserve a historically significant Drukpa Kargyu monastery in Bhutan, ensuring sustainable financial support for the education and basic needs of its young monks. Sasha also taught for many years at Dorden Tashithang Buddhist University in Thimphu. Deeply connected to Bhutan on a spiritual level, she is extremely grateful for the opportunity to live in and serve the country, where she has spent the past nineteen years contributing to education and the preservation of its spiritual heritage. Learn more about Sasha Wakefield at www .sasha-wakefield.com.

2 04
J